Prosperity Gospel Latinos and Their American Dream

WHERE RELIGION LIVES

Kristy Nabhan-Warren, editor

Where Religion Lives publishes ethnographies of religious life. The series features the methods of religious studies along with anthropological approaches to lived religion. The religious studies perspective encompasses attention to historical contingency, theory, religious doctrine and texts, and religious practitioners' intimate, personal narratives. The series also highlights the critical realities of migration and transnationalism.

Prosperity Gospel Latinos and Their American Dream

Tony Tian-Ren Lin

The University of North Carolina Press CHAPEL HILL

Set in Merope Basic by Westchester Publishing Services
Manufactured in the United States of America

The University of North Carolina Press has been a member of the
Green Press Initiative since 2003.

Library of Congress Cataloging-in-Publication Data
Names: Lin, Tony Tian-Ren, author.
Title: Prosperity Gospel Latinos and their American dream / Tony Tian-Ren Lin.
Other titles: Where religion lives.
Description: Chapel Hill : The University of North Carolina Press, 2020. |
Series: Where religion lives | Includes bibliographical references and index.
Identifiers: LCCN 2019046686 | ISBN 9781469658940 (cloth) |
ISBN 9781469658957 (paperback) | ISBN 9781469658964 (ebook)
Subjects: LCSH: Latin Americans—Cultural assimilation—United States—
Religious aspects. | Faith movement (Hagin)—United States. | Pentecostalism—
United States. | Pentecostalism—Latin America. | Hispanic Americans—
Religion. | Latin Americans—United States—Religion.
Classification: LCC BR1644.5.U6 L56 2020 | DDC 277.308/208968—dc23
LC record available at https://lccn.loc.gov/2019046686

Cover illustration: Front view of Walking Liberty coin © iStock.com/desertsolitaire.

Para Bee-Ca Lin

Contents

Acknowledgments ix

Introduction 1
The Gospel of the American Dream

CHAPTER ONE
Communities of Dreamers 30

CHAPTER TWO
The Prescription for the Dream 66

CHAPTER THREE
Changed by the Dream 98

CHAPTER FOUR
Dreaming of Prosperity at Home 121

Conclusion 149
The Dream of Meritocracy

Notes 171
Bibliography 181
Index 191

Acknowledgments

This book spotlights the power of the American dream as it plays out at the intersection of two changes transforming America in the twenty-first century: the rapid and continuous growth of the Latinx population, and the increasing influence of Prosperity Gospel Pentecostalism in American culture. The two central claims in this book could be considered controversial. First, I argue that spiritual maturity in Prosperity Gospel Pentecostalism is synonymous with achieving the American dream. Therefore, the pursuit of Prosperity Gospel holiness is equivalent to the pursuit of the American dream. Second, I claim that unbeknownst to them, these immigrants are being assimilated and integrated into American culture through Prosperity Gospel Pentecostalism.

As the economic challenges of the twenty-first century threaten the very idea of the American dream, modern American Christianity—as embodied in Prosperity Gospel Pentecostalism—has risen to rescue it. The practices and doctrines of this faith are the spiritualized version of the ideology that built America. Prosperity Gospel preachers keep that dream alive regardless of economic realities or the possibility of upward mobility. This book follows first-generation Latinx immigrants who have converted to this faith in order to understand the ways that Prosperity Gospel Pentecostalism is shaping this subset of new Americans.

I am aware that this work will affect the way some people view, for better or for worse, this form of Christianity as well as the Latinx immigrant community. I have attempted to show the sophistication of these immigrants as they adopt and adapt this faith to make it their own while simultaneously being shaped by this inherently American form of Christianity and shaping America as well. I only hope that I have achieved this goal.

Like every academic, I am indebted to a multitude of colleagues, friends, and family for their scholarly advice and moral support. I am most grateful to James Davison Hunter, whose mentorship through the years has shaped my intellectual curiosity and helped me understand the deeper structures of culture that animate contemporary life. James read every page of this manuscript multiple times at different stages of its development, always offering helpful comments. He is a gracious scholar who supported me in every way, not least through the Institute for Advanced Studies in Culture at the University of Virginia, which, in addition to the financial support to expand the project and complete this manuscript, offered a community of scholars who helped me bring this book to completion, including Joe Davis, Josh Yates, Jennifer Geddes, Charles Mathewes, and the many faculty fellows who graced the institute over the years. I am also indebted to W. Bradford Wilcox for his feedback and encouragement in this project. The opportunity to work with him in the Religion and Relationships in Urban America project was critical for this research. I am also grateful to my current intellectual family, the New York Theological Seminary whose diverse intellectual community has energized my own scholarship. Most importantly, this project would not be possible without the three communities featured in this book and all the people who opened their lives to me.

I am grateful for the help of the following individuals who gave of their time and energy in providing feedback and advice, often asking hard questions to make this book better. I welcomed Milton Vickerman's expertise on race and immigration. I received help and advice over many years from Maurice Wallace, Larycia Hawkins, Garnette Cadogan, Johann Neem, Rachel Wahl, Jeffrey Guhin, Jonathan Calvillo, Emily Hunt-Hinojosa, Nathan Walton, John Inazu, Kate Bowler, Nancy Ammerman, Michael O. Emerson, Margaret Poloma, Sharon Hays, Sarah Corse, Jeffrey Dill, Young-Il Kim, Matthew S. Hedstrom, Jacob A. Sargent, Alana Bibeau, Evren Savci, Mary Caler, Tatiana Tatarchevskiy, Christopher Einolf, and Sema Akboga. I benefited from the editorial assistance of Betsy Wells Stokes and Emily O. Gravett. I thank Hanna Rosin who read earlier parts of this manuscript and asked probing questions that made this a better book. To Junot Diaz and his constant encouragement: gracias 'mano! I am grateful to the members of Providence Presbyterian Church in Gum Spring, Virginia, whose support for my family was invaluable in the completion of this book. During my formative years at Princeton, I benefited greatly from my interactions with Mark C. Lee, Ron Choong, Joanne Rodriguez, David Ramos, Joseph Han, Luis Rivera-Pagan, Scott Hendrix, the PTS Sushi Club—Revs. William Buie, John Bradley, and Fernando Otero—and my mentor the late reverend Jack Chiang.

I also thank Kristy Nabhan-Warren, the series creator and editor of Where Religion Lives, and Elaine Maisner, the executive editor at the University of North Carolina Press. Kristy saw the potential of my manuscript early on and has been a constant source of encouragement. Elaine and her colleagues at the University of North Carolina Press are the dream team of academic publishing. They were always efficient, timely, and gracious in doing the invisible yet critical work of bringing ideas into reality. I am indebted to them for this book.

I am most profoundly indebted to my family. My parents, Eng-Zyh Lin and Shou-Yoen Wu, and my sister, Lih-Wen Lin, and her family—Samson, Selina, and Brianna Chu—offered steadfast encouragement and support (both tangible and intangible). I also thank my friends and family around the world. Their support from a distance was vital. I especially thank my Tío Ramon Lin, Alejandro Canton, la familia Bianchetti, Alicia Gonzalez, and 'La Pandilla' del San Pedro. I would not be the person I am today without them.

I am grateful to my children, Claudia, Calvin, and Clara, whose love and affection carried me through the completion of this project. Finally, I must thank my wife, Bee-Ca, whose sacrifice through the years has been immeasurable. She spent many evenings and weekends as the proverbial "academic widow" while I conducted my research and wrote. Her dedication and love for our family made it possible for me to pursue this work. She made the most important contribution to this book, and for that reason, this is dedicated to her. *Cada día te quiero más.*

Prosperity Gospel Latinos and Their American Dream

Introduction
The Gospel of the American Dream

God-Given Prosperity

On a chilly fall evening, Gustavo ran into the storefront church, apologizing for his tardiness. He scrambled with the calendar on his electronic device, which he is never without, as he took one last look before letting his body sink into a chair in front of me. Though he was visibly tired, his bright dark eyes beamed with satisfaction and pride. Letting out a deep breath, he explained that he was a half hour late to our meeting because he was building a deck on his new house and wanted to finish a section before wrapping up for the night. He had just purchased the home a month before, and he joked about the ever-growing to-do list his wife had put together for him: updating the kitchen cabinets, painting the house, installing newer appliances, and building a larger deck with a roof so they could spend more time outside. He had a lot going on, but as he picked off dried paint from the back of his hands, he smiled with pleasure because the house was his.

When not working on his new house, Gustavo owns and runs a painting company, managing over thirty men and four vans on multiple job sites in Charlottesville, Virginia. He knows many of the city's builders and is responsible for painting many of the luxury subdivisions cropping up on the outskirts of the city. He is fast and reliable and has an impeccable reputation. Lately Gustavo has been very busy. Beyond his responsibility at work and at home, Gustavo leads a Bible study at his church and is one of the most active members. He is often one of the first to show up on Sunday mornings, opening all the doors, checking the thermostats, and making sure there's toilet paper in the bathrooms. Sometimes he goes to the convenience store across the street to get supplies before congregants arrive. He often assists the pastor during the worship service. His participation in the life of the church gives him joy, but it also accomplishes something that has far-reaching effects in his life and the community that is forming around this church: it motivates him to work hard at his job and serve others.

Though in many ways he lives the life of an average blue-collar, church-going American, Gustavo is neither average nor technically an American. He is one of roughly eleven million undocumented immigrants living in the

United States. His socioeconomic rise would be considered impressive, even for a U.S. citizen. But Gustavo can barely speak English. He was born in the state of Tabasco, Mexico, in a village near Chiapas, one of the poorest states in the country. He was the youngest of six children, with an alcoholic father who was rarely home; when he was, he often brought girlfriends with him. His mother was forced to work multiple jobs to support the family. They lived in a mud-and-brick structure, with a makeshift roof made out of metal sheets weighted down with discarded tires. He joked that the only running water in their house came from the leaky roof during rainstorms. Their source of electricity was an extension cord slipped through a crack in this leaky roof, often dangerously plugged into a lamp, the only source of light at night. When it rained, he remembers, water dripped off the light bulb. He never realized there was any danger until many years later. At some point, they got a TV and had to choose between light or television. The children sometimes collected wood and trash for their mother to fuel an open fire in the corner of their home, occasionally used for cooking. They got water from a nearby hand-pumped well.

Gustavo never liked school, and he walked away from all formal education at the age of fourteen, the end of compulsory education in Mexico. He has foggy memories of his time at school, alternating between being mischievous and being constantly disciplined. "No aprendí nada" (I didn't learn anything) he says of his time at school. The absence of adult supervision, combined with the social pressures of his village, led him to try drugs and alcohol during his preteen years. Looking back as an adult, he is thankful that alcohol was easier to obtain than drugs. He spent most of his time on the streets or at his friends' houses, sometimes not seeing his mother for weeks. At the age of nineteen, Gustavo ran into some friends who were heading north. On the spur of the moment, without telling anyone, he joined them, and a week later crossed the border into California. He now lives in a nice town and is married and drug- and alcohol-free, manages a successful business, operates a six-figure business account, and recently moved into his own home. Even after the economic crisis of 2008 and the collapse of the housing industry, Gustavo prospered because of his faultless reputation. His entrepreneurial mind and the trust he built in this community kept him gainfully employed through the darkest economic times.

How had this twenty-nine-year-old gone from a small village in Mexico to the American suburban dream, all in less than ten years? How did he do this without a firm command of English or any formal training? Was it luck? Was it grit and hard work? Was it charity? When I ask him, Gustavo proclaims animatedly: "Mi fé en Dios, hermano! Mi fé en Dios! Dios me ha dado la prosperidad!" (My faith in God, brother! My faith in God! God has given me prosperity!)

Gustavo embodies the classic story of a young immigrant whose hard work and determination is rewarded with the American dream. He firmly believes that dedication and perseverance contributed to his success. But for Gustavo, there is another element to his commendable achievement—an indispensable element—his *fé* (faith). Gustavo is part of an increasing number of Latinx immigrants who embrace Prosperity Gospel Pentecostalism, the belief that God will grant true believers wealth and health if they have enough faith to claim their prize. The story of Gustavo is the story of two phenomena that are transforming America in the twenty-first century: the rapid and continuous growth of the Latinx population, and the increasing influence of Prosperity Gospel in American culture. This book tells the stories of Latinos who are learning to be "Americans" through the theology and practices of an inherently American religion.

Latinx Immigrants

Americans of Latin American descent have had a complicated history in the United States because of their racial ambiguity. They do not fit easily into the black and white racial dichotomy that defines racial relations in this country. Many are not even immigrants, since their homelands became part of the United States. As some residents of the American Southwest claim, they did not cross the border, but the border crossed them.[1] These Latinos can trace their ancestry to the time when the American Southwest belonged to Mexico.

Among those who immigrated, many trace their roots back to Spain and Portugal, making them Americans of European descent. But the complexion of their skin, their Catholic faith, and the distinctiveness of Latinx cultures make them too different for acceptance as "Americans," traditionally defined as white Anglo-Saxon Protestant. As a group, the plurality of Latinx cultures and ethnicities have often been ignored and stereotyped into a homogeneous collective. They did not have an official racial or ethnic categorization until 1970, when the Nixon administration baptized them as "Hispanics" for census purposes.[2] Until then, the only option for Hispanics was "white." Today, Americans labeled as "Hispanic" account for more than half of U.S. population growth since 2000. In the first decade of the twenty-first century, there was an increase of over fifteen million Hispanics.

Gustavo is one of over fifty-six million Hispanics living in the United States (of which only roughly nineteen million are foreign born). Hispanics are already the largest ethnic group in America, and their total number is expected to rise to 120 million by 2060.[3] While the percentage of immigrants from Latin America entering the United States has declined since 2010, the Hispanic population continues to grow. Hispanics are disproportionately young compared to U.S. population as a whole, with over half of all Hispanics being under the age of eighteen. Three-quarters of U.S.-born Hispanics are under the age of thirty-three.[4] The sheer number of young Hispanics and their historically higher fertility rates fuel their continuous demographic growth.[5]

Hispanics have risen not just in numbers but also in power and influence. Economically, Latinos were estimated to have $686 billion in buying power in 2004, and that number grew to $992 billion in 2009. By 2015, Latinx buying power was estimated at $1.5 trillion.[6] Latinx celebrities have secured a place in American popular culture playing leading roles in mainstream entertainment and prime-time television shows. It is hard to imagine that George Lopez's sitcom, simply named *George Lopez*, was considered revolutionary in 2002 because it was named after a Mexican American and was led by a Latinx cast. While nonwhite representation continues to lag in all forms of media, it is no longer rare to see Latinos represented in American popular culture.

Politically, Latinos have held prominent political positions in every branch of government and on both sides of the political divide. Judge Sonia Sotomayor, the daughter of Puerto Rican immigrants, was appointed to the Supreme Court in 2009, becoming the first Latina to serve in the highest court of the land. Alberto Gonzales, of Mexican descent, became the highest-ranking Latino to serve in the executive branch when he was appointed attorney general of the United States (2005–2007) under President George W. Bush. And while there are numerous governors, senators, and representatives, Cuban American senators Marco Rubio and Ted Cruz made history in 2016 when they ran for the Republican presidential nomination, with Cruz making it the furthest. The booming Latinx population in swing states has made Latinos an increasingly important voting bloc. The role of Latinos was central in the 2016 presidential election. The anti-immigrant and anti-Mexican rhetoric of Donald Trump's campaign contributed to his election victory. That strategy has further alienated some Latinos, leading many of them to declare themselves independents.[7] Until the 2016 presidential election, the two major political parties consistently broke records in Spanish-language ads.[8] This trend is expected to grow, as Hispanics are the youngest ethnic group in America, with a larger percentage of them becoming eligible to vote yearly.[9]

Whether it is arts, politics, economy, food, or media, it is impossible to understand modern America without seriously considering the role Latinos played in building this nation and shaping its future.

The Genesis of Pentecostalism

In 1906, a one-eyed black preacher from Louisiana named William Joseph Seymour arrived in Los Angeles. He was the son of former slaves and grew up in poverty at a time when Louisiana had the highest rates of lynching in the nation. Despite the challenges of growing up black and poor, Seymour was determined to improve his lot. With little formal education, he learned to read the Bible, moved out of the South, and became a respected preacher, even among white Christians. In Los Angeles, his ministry had a rocky start. He was kicked out of his own church because of theological disagreements, but he soon began leading prayer meetings that often lasted all night. On April 9, 1906, a participant at his prayer meeting shook uncontrollably and uttered indiscernible sounds. None of those in attendance could decipher what was being said (some believed it was Chinese), but there was a general consensus that this phenomenon was the visible sign of the presence of the Holy Spirit. These utterances were interpreted as evidence that God had taken over a person. This was not a belief invented in Los Angeles. It originates in Acts 2. According to that biblical account, when the Holy Spirit descended on the disciples on the day of Pentecost, they were miraculously able to speak in languages they had never learned. This practice is known as glossolalia, or speaking in tongues, and it became the physical confirmation that someone had received the Holy Spirit. Word spread quickly about the events that took place during that prayer meeting, and crowds began to gather. Some were curious onlookers, but many were genuinely seeking for an encounter with the divine. Seymour had to move his meetings from a house to a larger space on Azusa Street.[10] Seymour's prayer meetings became known as the Azusa Street Revival.

The Azusa Street Revival included many Latinos, particularly of Mexican descent, who converted to Protestantism during the revival in large numbers.[11] As a result, Pentecostalism immediately spread to Latin America. Multiple factors led to the division of the original movement, which scattered adherents to establish similar churches elsewhere. Latinx Pentecostals were active from the beginning, and they were instrumental in spreading the faith to Spanish-speaking communities in the United States and beyond.[12] Today, Pentecostalism is the fastest-growing form of Christianity in the world. This version of Christianity offers individuals a deeply personal and powerful encounter with God, as evidenced through physical manifestations. Since early followers were members of the lower socioeconomic classes, the movement was largely regarded as a religious trend of the uneducated and the outcast. Adherents were ridiculed for their highly expressive and emotional practices, which made little sense to outside observers. This originally disenfranchised movement, however, has influenced every form of Christianity in the world. In 1995, Harvard Divinity School professor Harvey Cox estimated that the total number of Pentecostals in the world was about 450 million. By 2001, it was estimated to have grown to 500 million. In 2010, the World Christian Database estimated that the total number of Pentecostals had exceeded 640 million adherents worldwide.[13] This means that presently, about one in every four Christians in the world is a spiritual descendant of this movement. This growth rate, which took place in less than a century, is simply unprecedented in the history of religions in general and Christian sects specifically.[14]

Despite starting the most widely practiced form of Christianity in the world, Seymour is rarely recognized as a significant figure in Christian history. The racism of early twentieth-century America and internal strife within the church barred him from the movement he started. By the time of his death at the age of fifty-two, the church was a shadow of what it had been when he started it. Yet the practices and style of worship continued through splinter movements. It evolved and spread around the world as it was adapted into existing Christian denominations. The events and manifestations taking place in Seymour's first prayer meetings are still trademarks for Pentecostals around the world.

The emphasis on visible and concrete displays of God's intervention in this world and in individuals' lives made this an extremely attractive religion. The message was simple: in Pentecostalism, one could see God at work and experience it personally. The incomprehensible utterances during Pentecostal meetings are only one such display. Early Pentecostalism emphasized God's ability to perform miracles in the everyday lives of the faithful. They were encouraged to look for signs of God's work in routine activities, but they were especially encouraged to seek God in times of trial. Physical healing was always part of the movement, but the emphasis on material blessings, emphasized in Prosperity Gospel today, was not present in the early days. Many of the early Pentecostal preachers emphasized a life of simplicity, rejecting the comforts of the material world as evil.

Pentecostals today are still known as those who believe in the baptism of the Holy Spirit, as evidenced by speaking in tongues and the exercise of spiritual miracles—such as healing and prophecy—in the daily lives of believers. Pentecostals are also more likely to believe in the existence of spiritual beings, both good and evil, which battle daily in the world around them. There are black and Latinx Pentecostal churches that preach liberation theology, which emphasizes the injustice perpetrated toward the poor by the rich, and criticizes capitalist materialism as a form of slavery. But liberation theology churches are increasingly the exception in Latinx communities, since they often hold liberal views of family and moral behaviors. Black and Latinx Christians have historically been more resistant to liberal moral norms. While a majority of Latinos favor gay marriage, only 25 percent of Latinx evangelicals and 46 percent of Latinx mainline Christians support it.[15] Black Protestants are the least likely group to support gay marriage after white evangelical Christians.[16] Black and Latinx Christians are also less likely to support abortion than whites.[17] There is a well-known phrase in Latin American church history: "Liberation theology chose the poor, but the poor chose Pentecostalism." They did not choose just any form of Pentecostalism—they chose the type that promised to get them out of poverty.

Modern Pentecostalism, often referred to as neo-Pentecostalism, adheres to a profoundly optimistic set of beliefs; few Pentecostal churches today would advocate as strongly against material wealth as did some of their predecessors, which opposed anything "from the world." Neo-Pentecostalism has crossed denominational lines; it has taken the core Pentecostal principles and popularized them for a general audience. While healing, glossolalia, and prophecy are still part of Pentecostals' beliefs, they are not central to their practice. Neo-Pentecostal beliefs can be found among both Protestants and Catholics.[18] Catholic churches with large Latinx memberships often have charismatic prayer services that are indistinguishable from those at Pentecostal churches. They sing the same songs and preach the same message by male and female members alike even though women are not permitted to be priests in the Catholic church. Today, neo-Pentecostalism is playing a central role in shaping American culture. Its practitioners hold prominent positions in all walks of life, and its preachers' books appear on *New York Times* bestseller lists.[19] No longer relegated to worshipping in back-alley warehouses (though some still do), neo-Pentecostal churches own some of the most desired real estate in America. These churches are powerful institutions with significant economic and political influence in the towns and cities they call home. Neo-Pentecostals are represented in the fields of sports, entertainment, business, and politics. It is no longer rare to see modern Pentecostals holding or aspiring to political office. Like Latinos, Pentecostals are represented across the American political spectrum, both conservative and liberal. Sarah Palin and Al Sharpton, for example, are both from the Pentecostal tradition. While there are important distinctions between traditional Pentecostalism and neo-Pentecostalism, I refer to the churches in this book as Pentecostal because some of their practices lean further in the traditional camp, meaning they have not yet adopted the "softer" Pentecostalism practiced by neo-Pentecostals. It is important to clarify that not all Pentecostals believe in the Prosperity Gospel and not all Prosperity Gospel Christians are Pentecostal.

Prosperity Gospel Pentecostalism

The idea that religious devotion can bring financial wealth is not exclusive to Christianity, and neither is the idea that Christian practices can lead to financial rewards.[20] Christianity as self-help and self-improvement has existed for a long time. Turn-of-the-century revival preachers such as D. L. Moody and Billy Sunday taught a utilitarian form of Christianity whereby believers could improve every aspect of their lives if they believed in Jesus. Christian businessmen groups rose to prominence in the early 1900s with the promise of helping men be better and more profitable in their work.[21]

The precise origin of the Prosperity Gospel movement is uncertain, but most historians point to two ministers for popularizing the form of Prosperity Gospel that exists around the world today: Kenneth Erwin Hagin (1917–2003) and Oral Roberts (1918–2009). Hagin experienced what he considered a miraculous healing from a heart defect in his late teens, which led him to establish the Word of Faith movement. Hagin asserted that individual believers had the creative power of God to verbally speak things into reality. Taking most of his theological foundations from New Thought metaphysics, a philosophy popular in New England at the time, Hagin taught that positive thinking, which he spiritualized by calling it "faithful speaking," had the power to influence the material world. Hagin's efforts led to an international radio show; *Word of Faith* magazine; the Rhema (meaning "spoken word" in Greek) Bible Training Center in Tulsa, Oklahoma; and more than one hundred books. For over half a century, Hagin's availability and mass appeal made him the most notable champion of Word of Faith teachings. Hagin planted the seeds from which the doctrinal roots of the Prosperity Gospel branch of Pentecostalism would grow. Today, many of these churches are known as Word of Faith churches or simply Faith Churches.

In 1947, Oral Roberts, a minister's son and traveling faith healer, credited God's hand with directing him to 3 John 1:2: "Beloved, I wish above all things that thou mayest prosper and be in health, even as thy soul prospereth" (King James Version). Against traditional interpretations of that passage,[22] Roberts began teaching that God desired financial prosperity and health for his "beloved." He preached this message with reference to new cars, houses, and his worldwide ministry. Roberts spoke publicly about God's desire for him to expand his ministry and worldwide outreach. In 1954, he invented the "blessing pact" system, which promised financial blessings to those who gave $100 or more to his ministry. This idea gave way to the broader "seed faith" concept: believers could "sow" (contribute) money into the work of a preacher with the promise that God would return the favor in the form of a prosperous financial "harvest." Roberts's influence through his teachings and through Oral Roberts University in Tulsa, Oklahoma, is significant to this day. While many Prosperity Gospel preachers have their own schools or training centers, few can rival the reputation and influence of Oral Roberts University, which has trained some of the most prominent Prosperity Gospel preachers in the world.[23] At the heart of their teaching was the idea that faith could move the hands of God to provide for the faithful.

The idea that Christians could manipulate their reality though their faith was taken to the mainstream by Norman Vincent Peale (1898–1993). Peale was the pastor of Marble Collegiate Church in Manhattan and the most prominent self-help guru of his time. His cheery demeanor and relatable anecdotal sermons made his preaching more acceptable than the more expressive Pentecostalism of Roberts and Hagin. Plus, New York City gave Peale a level of legitimacy that his more rural counterparts did not have. Peale infused American Christianity with psychological language, which was gaining prominence in the 1950s. He offered a therapeutic faith that promised happiness and success. Peale is not considered a founder of Prosperity Gospel because he did not preach wealth and health specifically. His church was made up largely of the already wealthy. But the logic of Peale's theology was the same. While Hagin and Roberts told their followers that they could speak and claim things into reality, Peale taught his parishioners to think their way out of problems and into success.[24] The evidence of the blending of positive thinking and Prosperity Gospel is embodied in President Donald Trump, who claims Norman Vincent Peale as his pastor and mentor.[25] His spiritual advisers are made up almost completely of Prosperity Gospel preachers. While President Donald Trump is not a representative of Prosperity Gospel, New Thought metaphysics, or any form of Pentecostalism, he has surrounded himself with leaders of that tradition.

Today, Prosperity Gospel has emerged from the shadows of Pentecostalism and, along with neo-Pentecostalism, has established itself as one of the most visible forms of American Christianity.[26] Whereas the original version of Pentecostalism focused on otherworldly rewards, Prosperity Gospel Pentecostalism confidently and unashamedly promises financial prosperity in the here and now for all those who have enough faith in God. Pentecostals in the Prosperity Gospel camp are arguably practicing the most common form of Pentecostalism around the world. In addition to the conventional Pentecostal doctrines and practices mentioned earlier, there are two unique assertions that distinguish Prosperity Gospel Pentecostalism from traditional Pentecostalism:

- All believers are entitled to prosperity and health because it is God's will for them.
- Positive confession and acts of faith are required on behalf of the believers to materialize this health and prosperity into their lives.

Like other Christians, they believe that God *can* heal them and help them financially. What is unique about Prosperity Gospel Pentecostals is that they believe they are *entitled* to those palpable signs of God's love. In Prosperity Gospel Pentecostalism, every believer has the God-given authority to claim and demand from God his or her blessings. These claims are asserted through positive confessions: verbalizing something that one desires (whether physical healing, a good marriage, or a new car, for example) and steadfastly believing that God will deliver. Any doubts or fears, viewed as negative thoughts, are signs of unfaithfulness that will sabotage one's demand. Sinful or immoral actions similarly short-circuit the process. In order for believers to obtain their desired prosperity, they must claim it from God and faithfully believe that their wishes will materialize. It is a guaranteed transaction provided that the believers hold up their end of the bargain. The second assertion leads to what I call *miraculous meritocracy*. While they believe they are entitled to blessings, they also believe that they must *do* something to open the gates of heaven. That action must be significant enough to get God's attention. This logic leads Prosperity Gospel Pentecostals to work hard and take risks, which are seen as "steps of faith," so that they can be blessed. Prosperity Gospel Pentecostals do not wait around idly for miraculous wealth.

They search for jobs, start businesses, and actively seek opportunities for advancement because all that hard work will move the hand of God to grant them prosperity. Prosperity Gospel Pentecostalism is a thoroughly meritocratic religion. The faithful who work the hardest and make the greatest investments and sacrifices are the ones who are rewarded with a miracle—in the form of a payoff for all their hard work.

Miraculous meritocracy leads them to work hard for their miracle, but it also traps them in what I call the paradox of Prosperity Gospel Pentecostalism. This paradox provides an interpretive lens through which Prosperity Gospel logic can be understood. It is paradoxical in two ways. First, it is the *paradox of the means as the ends*. In order to apply the Prosperity Gospel formula, one must have complete faith that it is true and never doubt. If one is at all uncertain of the efficacy of the formula, it is immediately invalidated. Believing in the Prosperity Gospel formula is the point of the religion. But this practice also leads to the *paradox of the means derailing the ends*. As I will explain in this book, this is the more problematic challenge. Miraculous meritocracy requires believers to perform spiritual work *and* real paid work in order to get their blessing. Spiritual work includes prayer, fasting, giving money, evangelistic trips, and other services to the church, which demand a lot of time. In fact, many believers are in church three or four nights a week, plus all weekends. This time spent in spiritual work sometimes conflicts with their ability to perform paid work. Thus, the more they apply the formula for prosperity, the fewer chances they have to work for money. This paradox is at the center of the Prosperity Gospel worldview.

The emphasis on this form of material fortune has led many in the movement to disown this label even if they continue to preach its doctrines. The rejection of the label is reflected in recent surveys in which many Christians refuse to identify as Prosperity Gospel because of its negative connotations. This is especially true of the modern neo-Pentecostals, who want to shake off their stereotypical origins. Prominent preachers such as T. D. Jakes and Joel Osteen have publicly rejected the accusation that they are Prosperity Gospel preachers even though their message bares evidence to the contrary.[27] Modern Prosperity Gospel preachers have shunned the more extreme forms of material wealth while choosing to teach a "softer" form of prosperity that focuses on psychological well-being and self-actualization. Today, those who were derogatorily labeled "health-and-wealth" or "name-it-and-claim-it" preachers have entered and blended into mainstream Christianity and even mainstream American culture.[28] Though their prevalence in both membership and number of churches might not exceed that of other Christian traditions, their visibility is disproportionately higher through their aggressive marketing efforts via television, radio, and print media. Prosperity Gospel is the most widely available source of religious media in America and the world. In addition, the media's fascination with their over-the-top leaders often places them in the national spotlight. Celebrity pastors are often invited for interviews and television specials because of their charismatic personalities and the controversial things they say. Celebrity Prosperity Gospel Pentecostal preachers are relentlessly self-promoting and often pompous, to the point of having their own reality television shows.[29] Three of the largest churches in the United States belong to the Prosperity Gospel tradition: Joel Osteen's Lakewood Church in Houston, T. D. Jakes's Potter's House in Dallas, and Creflo Dollar's World Changers Church International in Atlanta. It is no coincidence that all three of these pastors can be viewed weekly on televisions across America, some even around the world, and often more than once a week. Prosperity Gospel preachers are friends with cultural icons such as Oprah Winfrey and are given a stage to introduce their teachings to a larger non-Christian audience. To those unfamiliar with Christianity, they are promoted as "motivational speakers," "life coaches," or "spiritual mentors," which allows a wider audience to more readily accept their authority and their teachings. To a secular audience, belief in God is often replaced with belief in self, but the logic for success and the outcomes are the same: if you believe it, you will obtain it. Prosperity Gospel leaders have even graced the cover of national magazines and have access to the White House. No longer segregated in rural revival camps, they now stand with presidents; run for political office; influence mainstream Christian circles; and produce music, movies, and television shows, all while promoting the principles of Prosperity Gospel Pentecostalism.

Scholarly interest in the Prosperity Gospel movement is relatively new, since this modern version did not start until the prosperous years following World War II, and it had only limited reach until the 1960s.[30] It began as a regional movement in southern states, often advocated through tent revivals, though there were also some notable Prosperity Gospel preachers in New York and Boston. As a movement, it gained national attention in the 1980s, as televangelists and their scandalous downfalls became national news. Since the late 1990s, just as some Pentecostal preachers softened their language to appeal to a larger audience, a new generation of Prosperity Gospel preachers moderated their prosperity message by placing a greater emphasis on positive thinking and self-esteem.[31] In Prosperity Gospel, the means by which one reaches prosperity is always more important than the prosperity itself.

That is, the positive attitude and relentless optimism that adherents are required to maintain is one of the main reasons this movement has grown so rapidly on a global scale. Most believers are attracted to Prosperity Gospel because its doctrines inspire them to pursue their dreams and offer them hope in the face of hopelessness. In Prosperity Gospel Pentecostalism, regardless of the outcome, the process is its own reward.

Latin American Prosperity Gospel Pentecostalism

The Prosperity Gospel Pentecostal movement is having a greater impact on Latinos than on any other immigrant group. While only one in five non–Latin American Protestants and only one in ten non-Latinx Catholics would classify themselves as Pentecostal, more than half of all Latinx Christians—Catholic or Protestant—identify as Pentecostal or charismatic.[32] Even if they do not claim any affiliation with the Prosperity Gospel movement, the majority (73 percent) of all Latinx Christians believe that faith can lead to prosperity, including about 65 percent of Christian Latinos who are not affiliated with any Pentecostal or charismatic denominations. The impact of Prosperity Gospel is evidenced by the fact that even Christians who are not affiliated with traditional Pentecostal denominations are shaped by their theology and practice. It is not uncommon to find weekly charismatic meetings in Catholic churches with large Latinx memberships. These charismatic Catholic meetings are almost identical to a Prosperity Gospel Pentecostal service. There is singing, healing, and speaking in tongues, and lay leaders of both genders lead the meetings. This unprecedented reach of Prosperity Gospel theology makes it unusually dominant in Latinx Christianity and American Christianity in general.

The actual percentage of Latinos who are affiliated with Pentecostal churches might be small, but 70 percent of these churches report that they try to win new converts to the faith weekly. While every form of Christianity has an imperative to evangelize, no other branch of Christianity comes close to the Pentecostals' campaign to recruit new members. Their missionary strategies are not just an individual effort to win souls, as they have local, national, and international institutions that support this effort. These churches organize regular evangelistic outings, during which they knock on doors, hand out flyers, and offer to pray with individuals. They host spiritual revivals, holiday celebrations, free clinics with local organizations, educational workshops, concerts, and programs for preschoolers through teenagers. These events are sometimes cosponsored by other national or international ministries. This imperative to share their faith at all times and by any means necessary leads them to build partnerships with all forms of media, making them appear larger than life. Two of the three churches profiled in this book air their services over their local community television station. Latinos who tune in to Spanish-language channels like Telemundo and Univision inevitably bring Pentecostal preachers into their homes in some way, as they fill much of the airtime of the channels' local affiliates. In addition, Trinity Broadcasting Network, the largest Prosperity Gospel broadcaster in the world, has a Spanish-language channel called Enlace, which streams Prosperity Gospel preachers into viewers' homes twenty-four hours a day. Regardless of the number of actual conversions, this relentless evangelistic zeal is bound to have powerful effects on the evangelists and their targets. This practice reaffirms the beliefs of the faithful because they have to constantly defend their faith as they present it to skeptics. At the same time, a lot more people are likely to hear the therapeutic and optimistic message of Prosperity Gospel Pentecostalism through these interactions. In a world filled with pessimism, an optimistic message can go a long way. This continuous effort to share their faith is not in vain. The number of converts in these churches is growing faster than that in churches of other traditions. Over half of all Latinx Evangelical Protestants are converts; of those, 43 percent converted from Catholicism.[33] Because recent converts are tasked with the responsibility of recruiting new members, the growth of Latin American Prosperity Gospel Pentecostals could be exponential.

The Paradox of Assimilation

While religion can be a powerful force in the lives of all individuals, it has special significance for uprooted and transplanted people. Sociologists have long emphasized the power of religion to create group cohesiveness. In the early twentieth century, Émile Durkheim described the ways that religion provides rituals and beliefs for individuals experiencing a sense of isolation and aimlessness.[34] As individuals suffer social isolation and uncertainty of cultural norms, they often turn to religion for guidance and direction. Religion serves as the compass by which people navigate their social worlds. Immigrants are more drawn to religion, not only for social identity and cohesion but because they are in need of guidance to help them make sense of their new world.

Classical assimilation theory can be simply understood as the process of upward mobility for immigrants and their offspring. In other words, as time goes by, each generation of immigrant achieves higher social and economic status as the result of becoming more culturally and linguistically similar to mainstream middle-class Americans.[35] Assimilation theory typically embraces native whites as the reference group to which immigrants' adaptation is compared.[36] In 1964, Milton Gordon argued that immigrants used religion to assimilate into the American mainstream through a series of stages, shedding their ethnic identities and becoming more like white middle-class Protestant Americans.[37] But the definition of an American has been contested from the beginning, and the process of becoming an American is equally problematic. Linear assimilation theory may apply to white immigrants, but it has never worked for nonwhites. From its inception, America defined its citizens as free whites.[38] Nonwhites could not be legal Americans no matter what beliefs or practices they adopted. Though no longer the legal definition of a U.S. citizen, racial identity continues to mar the definition of an American today.

Chinese immigrants, for example, have been observed to have a higher rate of conversion to Christianity because they wish to adopt the practices of America.[39] But while Fenggang Yang found that assimilation was part of the motivation for Chinese conversions, these immigrants were not seeking to assimilate wholesale. Yang describes the process of "adhesive integration," in which these immigrants combine multiple identities while resisting the urge to lose any particular one. The process is difficult and leaves converts alienated and confused, yet they still manage to adopt an ideology that helps them make sense of their world. Sociologist Alejandro Portes and Min Zhou point to what they call "selective assimilation" as part of their segmented assimilation theory, in which immigrants adopt certain practices of the dominant culture while rejecting others.[40] Segmented assimilation theory recognizes the plurality of cultures in American society. It argues that new immigrants may assimilate into different subgroups of Americans and may take divergent paths, including the conventional upward, or "straight-line," assimilation; "downward assimilation"; or "selective assimilation."

But that does not explain the high rate of Latinx conversion to Pentecostal and charismatic faiths. Socially, most immigrant churches serve as cultural centers that help immigrants preserve and transfer their traditions to the next generation. The Catholic Church has long served as the organizing force for Latinos. The growth of Pentecostalism among Latinos is puzzling on many levels because the choice seems to go against their self-interest. Latinx Pentecostal churches are usually smaller, providing fewer resources and opportunities to network. More importantly, they are volunteering to be part of a marginalized religious group. Spanish-speaking Catholic Churches are often linked to English-speaking congregations that meet in the same building; they are further tied to the resources from the diocese and the national church. Pentecostal churches, like the ones in this book, are independent, with loose connections to larger networks. While Prosperity Gospel Pentecostalism might be widely popular in America, Spanish-speaking Pentecostal churches remain at the fringe of American society. In addition, while Latin America remains largely Catholic, Pentecostal churches are not rare. It would be wrong to assume that these immigrants "discovered" Pentecostalism for the first time in America. The great majority were exposed to *Evagélicos, Cristianos,* or *Pentecostales* in their native countries.

The conversion of Latinx immigrants to Prosperity Gospel Pentecostalism is one manifestation of the failure of the secularization theory. It is perplexing that individuals who leave their homeland in search of the comforts of modernity would convert into what Durkheim would classify as a "primitive religion," filled with spirits and magical thinking.[41] They readily adopt aspects of modern America—such as the use of technology, late-capitalist economic systems, and the pursuit of higher education—yet they immerse themselves in a worldview sustained by supernatural beliefs. Gustavo and his fellow worshippers are representative of this trend. Prosperity Gospel Pentecostalism is not primitive at all but inherently modern in its ideals, logics, and goals.

Gustavo did not embrace this faith because he is simplistic; rather, what seems on the surface to be a primitive religion is genuinely sophisticated. Prosperity Gospel Pentecostalism is a product of the twentieth century, with modern and even late modern logic that helps believers navigate contemporary America. It relies on a scientific-like formula for obtaining blessings from God. No religion is ever adopted wholesale, and this is especially true of Prosperity Gospel Pentecostalism. Immigrant adherents adjust these teachings in ingenious ways to make meaning of their lives in this new land. This is critical, since the American dream that Prosperity Gospel Pentecostalism sells is also a modern invention. Unlike the American dream of previous centuries, today's Prosperity Gospel Pentecostals dream a very specifically post–World War II American dream—one filled with the hope of self-actualization and material goods. This faith tradition, firmly grounded in individualism and materialism, shows immigrants how they may thrive in a late-capitalist society.

The beliefs and practices of Prosperity Gospel Pentecostalism embodies today's middle-class white American ideals so closely that to be a good

Prosperity Gospel Pentecostal leads them to adopt middle-class white American norms. Yet unlike European immigrants, most of these Latinos never reach that ideal because of the color of their skin. For the immigrants I encountered in this project, not reaching the white Anglo-Saxon Protestant definition of an American is not a problem because it is not their goal. They do not wish to be Americans in the traditional racial sense; they are living a new form of assimilation.

Instead of being assimilated into a generic white America or even a segment of America, Prosperity Gospel Pentecostal theology is giving them the tools necessary to hold dual, sometimes even multiple, contradictory identities. The paradoxical logic of this faith allows them to create a fluid identity that simultaneously validates their presence in America and accounts for why they do not belong. Prosperity Gospel offers them a reason to persevere and a way to appreciate the challenges they face in this country. It weaves their trials into a larger story that guarantees a happy ending. It keeps the American dream alive, even when everything around them feels like an American myth or even a nightmare. There is a strong correlation between the intensity with which Prosperity Gospel Pentecostal Latinos practice their faith and their integration into modern America. Their faithfulness leads them to buy homes, invest in and start businesses, learn English, and engage with their communities. Prosperity Gospel Pentecostalism is the gospel of the American dream. This book is the story of how Latinos use a religion to become part of America on their own terms.

The Scope of This Book

This book is an attempt to understand the fusion of two monumental trends shaping modern America: the rise of the largest ethnic group in the United States, and the fastest growing Christian movement in the world. More than one out of every two Latinx Christians believe in some form of Prosperity Gospel.[42] The focus of this book is an attempt to understand why many first-generation Latin American immigrants adhere to Prosperity Gospel Pentecostalism. What is it about this form of Christianity that attracts them? This book joins other important works of scholarship in shedding light on the ways that Pentecostalism shapes the identity of Latinx immigrants.[43]

As with all religious movements, Prosperity Gospel Pentecostalism not only shapes individuals but also reorganizes and creates a community and social life that calls for greater understanding. This is especially pertinent as more and more Americans adopt this worldview. By focusing on Latinx immigrants, we can learn how new immigrants use these beliefs and practices. At the heart of the immigration challenge is the question of pluralism and integration. How will new immigrants become part of their new country? Immigrants are, by definition, individuals who desire change, often both internal and external. They employ different tools to negotiate this difficult balance of shedding the old and adopting the new. As increasing segments of Americans are informed and influenced by the doctrines of Prosperity Gospel Pentecostalism, we understand this movement because it has already had significant economic, cultural, and political consequences in America.

The goal of this book is to introduce readers to a strange yet familiar world. It will be strange for some in that the supernatural coexists with the natural; God is ever present and ever active in this world. Yet it will be familiar because it's the story of departures and arrivals. It is the story of pilgrims who left their native lands in the hope of making a new and better life for themselves and their children. It is the story of the American dreamers who work hard to write their own rags-to-riches stories. Their doctrines and practices might be new to some readers, but the struggles and hopes of these Prosperity Gospel Pentecostals are universal. Life, liberty, and the pursuit of happiness are central to why they came to America and the reason why they believe in Prosperity Gospel. The desire for material riches is only a small part of their story. Like Gustavo, some succeed, or at least get richer than they were before. Most importantly, however, they receive nonmaterial benefits.[44]

This book begins with a description of the three churches that will serve as guides through this world. They will be the windows through which readers can peek into the Latinx immigrant Prosperity Gospel Pentecostal world. I explain the way Prosperity Gospel doctrines shape their thinking, transform their families, and ultimately help them become something different from what they were before arriving to America. These three churches are located in different parts of the country and are made up of Hispanic immigrant communities at different stages of immigration. They represent those who recently arrived, those who have been here for some time, and those who have been here for many decades. I include a brief discussion of Prosperity Gospel Pentecostalism and describe how its practices shape church members' cosmology. For these immigrants, their everyday world is literally foreign to them and often hostile; thus, the activities they engage in and the relationships they form in the churches have special significance. These churches help them make sense of their lives. It is in these churches that they find shelter and the strength to face a foreign country. It is the place where believers are given the tools needed to craft new identities and build new lives. Members also take on the foremost responsibility of every Pentecostal: to share their faith with others and to do their part in making this world a holier place.

Having come to understand the people in the churches, I explain the uniqueness of Prosperity Gospel Pentecostal beliefs and practices. Devotion to Prosperity Gospel Pentecostalism is not just about personal spiritual growth; it helps these immigrants pursue the American dream and gives them a new perspective in life. I pay special attention to the paradox of Prosperity Gospel Pentecostalism. Their claims and their reality are often at odds, yet Prosperity Gospel believers can hold them in harmony. The contradiction can be puzzling to the outside observer: Why is it that people who are promised wealth but never receive it become more ardent believers instead of turning away from this faith? How is it that members of a conservative church with high moral values can live as undocumented aliens? How does this faith help them flourish in America? The answers to these questions are discovered through the relativism of their reasoning; they justify and legitimize their lives through the paradox of Prosperity Gospel Pentecostalism. I show how this faith validates, empowers, and encourages these immigrants by providing a therapeutic ethos that appeases the worries of an uncertain life. After all, not everybody gets rich, but everyone feels better.

Once readers understand these churches and their teachings, I describe how these doctrines and practices affect the daily lives and perspectives of Prosperity Gospel Pentecostals. Immigrant Latinx life in modern America as interpreted through Prosperity Gospel ideals is different than that for nonimmigrants. I explore the specific ways they negotiate the demands of Prosperity Gospel Pentecostalism as first-generation immigrants trying to carve out a space in America. What does it mean to become "American"? I show how the paradox of Prosperity Gospel Pentecostalism helps them make sense of their lives in this country while allowing them to see themselves as foreigners. As they seek faithfulness through Prosperity Gospel Pentecostalism, they adopt certain practices and perform specific tasks that integrate them into America. But unlike past immigrants, the threat of deportation is ever present. Even while they are rooting themselves in this country, they are very aware that they could be ripped away at any moment. For that reason, there is little desire to be "Americans." This is not a simple story of assimilation; rather, it is a story of survival and adaptability.

I then focus on one aspect of their lives that shows how they negotiate the paradox of Prosperity Gospel Pentecostalism: family life. In Christianity, the traditional family is a small-scale replica of the church. There is a father who serves as the priest, a mother who is his assistant, and children and sometimes extended family who make up the congregation and need instruction and guidance. While families try to live up to those traditional standards, their reality is much more complicated. Financial pressures make it impossible for wives to stay home and be the ideal homemaker. Marital challenges are aggravated by the perils of immigration, which intensify conflicts between spouses, often leading to separation and divorce. In this, they also have a logic of their own to make sense of the disparities between their reality and their ideals. Families are caught in the paradox of Prosperity Gospel. For them, the family has a reciprocal relationship with the father's religious status. A successful (nuclear) family gives the parents (mainly the father) greater status in church life. But problems at home are also attributed to a lack of spiritual maturity in the parents. Viewing the average parishioner's family life reveals the private day-to-day negotiations Prosperity Gospel Pentecostals make in order to make sense of their lives.

Finally, I conclude with a discussion of the impact of these churchgoers' beliefs in their own lives, their communities, and America as a whole. Belief in meritocracy thrives at the extremes of the socioeconomic ladder. It justifies the wealth of the rich and vindicates their financial possessions in the face of the poverty of others. At the other extreme, it gives hope to the poor and pacifies the oppressed into the very system that subdues them. The conclusion explores questions of alienation and power, limitations and potentials, their past and what we can assess about their future. Meritocracy reproduces the inequalities in society and erases any evidence that contradicts its virtues. As a result, the paradox of Prosperity Gospel is the paradox of meritocracy. It is a paradox that explains modern life. I also look at the global implications of what is happening in the microcosms of these Prosperity Gospel Pentecostal churches. After all, if Prosperity Gospel Pentecostalism is helping Latinx immigrants become their own versions of modern Americans, what influence is it having in other parts of the world? Inasmuch as Prosperity Gospel is an American invention born out of American cultural ideals, communities around the world must sacrifice their native cultural norms in order to adopt this form of individualistic, materialistic, and therapeutic Christianity. The value of such incorporation must be understood in the context of each of those cultures. Though these sorts of issue are beyond the scope of this book—a study focusing on immigrants to America—I do reflect on the implications and the need for further research.

Studying Pentecostals

In *The Sacred Canopy: Elements of a Sociological Theory of Religion*, originally published in 1967, Peter Berger argued that a system of religious belief can be understood as a dialectic between the ordering of the world the religion creates and the everyday social interaction of the people who inhabit that world. Because people create religious ideas while simultaneously being shaped by those beliefs, there is a reciprocal relationship between every religion and its adherents: each one informs and shapes the other. In order to fully understand a religious community, a researcher must explore the community's ideas—expounded on by its doctrines—and examine both the sacred and the everyday habits that exemplify and sometimes modify these ideas. One must be embedded in that dialectical interaction in order to understand it. It is not enough to simply observe those experiencing their religion—it is necessary to experience it with them. Demographic measures and survey data provide insight for a macro-level analysis, but they are insufficient sources for revealing the inner workings of religious groups. Thoughtful observation is required, and this observation can come only through personal encounters and embedded experiences. For this research, I embedded myself in these communities to learn how Prosperity Gospel Pentecostalism was subjectively experienced by Latinx immigrants.

This book is the product of extended periods of sharing life with three groups of Prosperity Gospel Pentecostal communities: Iglesia Cristiana del Padre in Charlottesville, Virginia, a city with a growing Latinx population; Iglesia del Dios Victorioso in Oceanside, California, a city north of San Diego with a substantial and historically long presence of Latinos but with many recent and transient immigrants due to its relative proximity to the border; and Iglesia Pentecostal del Rey Divino in New York City, where Latinos have lived for many generations. These three churches represent three cities and three communities in different stages of their faith. Iglesia Cristiana del Padre is made up largely of immigrants who have been in the United States for over ten years. The majority of the members at Iglesia del Dios Victorioso have been in the country for less than five years. And those at Iglesia Pentecostal del Rey Divino are mostly senior citizens who have been Pentecostals for decades. Despite their very different geographic locations, selecting churches with identical theologies and practices helped to minimize variables other than religion. In this way, I could discover outcomes that were truly distinctive to Prosperity Gospel doctrine and not mere effects of other social factors.

Selecting the three churches also allowed me to examine different stages in the institutional life cycle of immigrant Prosperity Gospel Pentecostal churches. The church in Virginia is relatively new, with an active congregation and fewer than one hundred members. In California, the church is well established, with over three hundred members, mostly new converts and very few long-time attendees. In New York City, the church (and its membership of about thirty) is in its twilight years. These three churches are a small sampling of the many Spanish-speaking Pentecostal churches across the United States.

My primary method of research was participant observation; I immersed myself in these churches, participating as thoroughly as possible in the members' lives and pursuing relationships with them. Most of the events described in this work took place between 2005 and 2007, with several others occurring during follow-up visits to the communities between 2008 and 2014. All the events recounted in this book were witnessed firsthand by me. A digital recorder captured all the quotations, and I translated everything from Spanish. Additional printed and prerecorded information (such as sermons) was obtained directly from the churches. The names of churches, pastors, and parishioners have been changed to protect their privacy.

I did not hide my intentions to record and analyze all that I was experiencing—church members knew I was a researcher from the University of Virginia who was interested in their lives. I made every effort to get as close as possible to them in order to observe them practicing their faith, both in public and private. I attended all Sunday worship services, prayer meetings, and Bible studies, and helped with their many church activities. I focused on their congregational gatherings in order to understand what an average person experiences when walking into a Prosperity Gospel Pentecostal church for the first time. Congregations are institutionally embedded with the logic and norms of a community.[45] These are explicitly and implicitly transferred onto church members in order to socialize them to the standards of the group. Participant observation revealed the transformative experiences that result from frequent gatherings with fellow believers. Congregations are especially important in providing support for immigrants.[46] They are the place where new immigrants learn how their compatriots negotiate the demands of this nation and are socialized into their new country. Research shows that immersion in Pentecostal churches is more significant to Latin American Protestants than to white Protestants or even to Latin American Catholics.[47] Inside the walls of their churches, I saw them learn the nuanced logic of Prosperity Gospel Pentecostalism and freely express their faith in the safety of numbers. Prosperity Gospel Pentecostal churches replicate the findings of congregational studies but also complicate them by their emphasis on the charismatic leaders. In Pentecostalism, the pastor and his family are the ideal type, role models, for the congregation. Instead of seeing fellow church members as their models, members are taught that the pastor represents success and holiness. Church members push themselves to replicate the perfection of their pastors. Prosperity Gospel Pentecostals learn to imitate their charismatic pastors by watching other members.

Since religion lives in a much larger and more pervasive space than congregations alone, I also spent time with them outside church. I was invited to their homes, picnics, and celebrations. I visited the sick in the hospital, and assisted with their translation needs in schools, banks, and workplaces. I helped children with their homework and, when appropriate, spent time with church members at their places of work. Through these interactions, I was able to observe how their faith was practiced at home and beyond the gaze of fellow church members. It also gave me the opportunity to see how they represented their faith when interacting with non–Prosperity Gospel Pentecostals.

Secondary to participant observation, I conducted interviews with all the leaders and some of the members of each congregation. While ethnographic research allowed me to see the dialectical interactions between their doctrines, skills, and symbols as they performed their faith, I could not read their minds. Interviews gave me the opportunity to gain further insight into the people's lives and clarify things I'd heard, especially during "testimony times" in worship services. Through interviews, I heard accounts of conversion; life stories; and views on families, jobs, immigration, the state of the world, and the importance of their faith. In Virginia and California, I was able to hire female interviewers to assist me in interviewing the women in these churches, thereby minimizing interviewer effect due to gender differences. All the interviews were face to face except those in New York, where many of the church members lived and worked far from the church. I traveled to visit Staten Island parishioners numerous times, but for those who lived in the outer boroughs and in New Jersey, it was much more practical to conduct telephone interviews—especially considering the members' work schedules.

I found my participant observation decidedly more useful than the interviews. To put into words one's most intimate spiritual experiences is difficult for even the most eloquent speakers. This was even harder for many of the subjects of this study, who are not used to thinking in abstract concepts, much less verbalizing them. They can tell someone what happened, but they cannot accurately explain it, certainly not to a social scientist. Unlike fundamentalists, whose identities are formed in opposition to the mainstream, these believers are not perpetually prepared to give a verbal defense of their faith.[48] Their goal is not to convince others of the truthfulness of Prosperity Gospel Pentecostalism; their goal is to help people experience it for themselves. Many of the members of these churches are also recent converts and do not yet have the vocabulary to fully express or explain supernatural experiences. What's more, Pentecostalism is characterized by emotional outbursts and expressive actions. Interviews and surveys, which necessarily require a distanced reinterpretation of past events, do not (and cannot) fully capture the richness of the Pentecostal experience. To put it plainly, with a Pentecostal worship service, you just had to *be* there.

Perhaps most importantly, a major research question of mine involved something that I believed was happening inadvertently: the utilization, by immigrant church members, of Prosperity Gospel practices and doctrines to more effectively integrate into their new country. I do not believe that assimilation was the reason for their conversion. For the most part, assimilation is something that happens unintentionally. There are some concrete things that all immigrants do to fit into the dominant culture. They may adopt new names, learn the language, celebrate local holidays, and join local institutions. But internal assimilation often happens inadvertently. The acquisition of new tastes, habits, and certain beliefs is gradual. If this transformation was an unintentional consequence of their faith, I did not expect to learn about it through interviews. It was only through living with them that I could see it play out. Through this faith, these immigrants were shaped into traditional middle-class families with the privilege of middle-class whites. While American culture tends to normalize white Anglo-Saxon Protestant culture, these immigrants' desire for the white middle-class life is a hegemonic idea that most of them brought from their homelands. The idea that America is better—and, more specifically, the coveted white middle-class American—is one that has dominated the imagination of those living in the global South. Like most hegemonic ideas, its power lies in the fact that it is taken for granted.

Becoming One of Them

I'm often asked how it was that I was able to gain access to these churches. Earning the trust necessary for useful participant-observation research can be difficult with any group. Religious organizations are more complicated because they have such clear symbolic boundaries for insiders and outsiders. Pentecostals, especially those inclined to Prosperity Gospel, have suffered ridicule from the media. Colleagues warned me that Pentecostal churches are sometimes hostile to researchers. A journalist told me he was escorted off the premises of a Prosperity Gospel Pentecostal church in Queens, New York, because he introduced himself as a reporter. Some of the larger churches have ushers who act more like guards than attendants. However, I was a cultural insider and had several advantages in my efforts. First, I identify as Latino. I am ethnically Asian but a native of Argentina. I speak Spanish fluently with an Argentinean accent (which all the church members recognized). My not "looking" Latino was not an issue for them because being Latino has more to do with cultural ties than with one's race. All the church members were used to seeing fellow Latinos who look very different from themselves. This was true in all the churches in this study but particularly true in New York City, where church members came in every shade of skin and hair color. From the blonde Puerto Rican to the pastor who could have been the twin of former television talk-show host Montel Williams, who is black. Plus, Chinese people have been part of many Latin American countries for centuries. As a fellow South American immigrant, I understood the struggles of displacement and resettlement. Our stories were different yet very similar.

Another advantage was that one of the best-known Pentecostal preachers in the Spanish-speaking world is from Buenos Aires, Argentina. The Reverend Claudio Freidzon is the pastor credited with the start of the famous Toronto Blessing, a revival that began in 1994 and became internationally known for its eccentric displays of faith, including uncontrollable laughing and the mimicking of animal sounds.[49] The pastors of both Iglesia Christiana del Padre and Iglesia del Dios Victorioso described their admiration for him and asked me if I knew Rev. Freidzon (I answered in the negative; though I had casually met him at his church in Buenos Aires, it would have been inaccurate to imply that I knew him personally) or if I had attended his church in Argentina (I visited but was never part of the congregation). In New York, Pastor Ramirez asked with similar hopefulness if I knew Pastor Dante Gebel. Pastor Gebel is a young, dynamic Argentine revival preacher and disciple of Claudio Freidzon, who in 2010 became the pastor of Hispanic ministries in Orange County's famous Crystal Cathedral. His ministry was extremely successful, and in early 2012 Gebel left the bankrupted Crystal Cathedral to start Favor-Day Church at the Anaheim Convention Center, later renamed River Church. To Pastor Ramirez's disappointment, I have never met Dante Gebel.

Although accepted as a cultural insider, I was able to maintain a level of social distance from them because I was partially a cultural outsider. Each country in Latin America is culturally unique, and the differences are stark for those of us who are often grouped together. More significantly, my socioeconomic background and immigration trajectory are very different from those of the people in these churches. While I was a fellow immigrant, I did not share their experiences of terror. I did not have to live with the threat of deportation that haunted them daily.

Religiously, I was also both an insider and an outsider. On my first Sunday at these churches, I introduced myself to the pastors. In all three cases, I was immediately asked if I was a Christian. Though I am not a Pentecostal, I could answer in the positive and was an ordained Presbyterian minister. Not being a Pentecostal was not problematic because in Latin America, denominational lines are less divisive than they are in the United States. All Protestants, regardless of denomination, are referred to as *Cristianos* or *Evangélicos* in Latin America. *Evangélico* does not carry the political implications it does in the United States. If there is a distinction, Latin American Christians divide themselves among *Cristianos* and *Católicos* but not between different forms of Protestants. My status as clergy did not create the barrier it might have in more hierarchical religious structures. Pentecostal churches are more generous with their ecclesiastical titles than traditional American churches. Receiving the title of pastor is a much easier process in Pentecostalism. In fact, many of these titles are self-imposed. At one point, the pastor of one of these churches changed his title from "pastor" to "apostle" on his own. Because I am a Christian and because I could speak their language, quote their Bible, and relate to their practices, I was quickly accepted into their communities. As far as I can tell, most of the public events I attended went undisturbed by my presence; I conformed to their norms, following their dress code and manners. Weeks into my research, most members treated me as just another churchgoer.

All three of the pastors endorsed my research openly, encouraging church members to speak with me. In California, the pastor helped me identify prospective church members to interview in order to help me get a representative sample of the age groups and family structures in his church. In one church, the pastor gave me full access to church records, often leaving me alone in the office to browse through the files, including financials, only reminding me to lock the door behind me when I was finished. I was invited on pastoral calls and to share some private thoughts, often being told, "I can tell you because you are a pastor, too." In this regard, my ecclesiastical role served to gain me valuable insight into the churches. None of these private thoughts, however, appear in this book, as it would not have been appropriate or necessary to incorporate them in this study.

Despite being a Christian, I was a religious outsider because I was not a Pentecostal and had never experienced charismatic Christianity. I am a lifelong "frozen chosen" Presbyterian. My tradition is viewed as the antithesis of Pentecostalism, both in theology and practice. While I grew up in a conservative Taiwanese household, I did not grow up around conservative Christianity. Plus, I was never part of a Spanish-speaking church. What I experienced in these communities was new to me. I never took part in the Pentecostal practices of speaking in tongues, engaging in excessive emotional outbursts, or falling to the ground during worship because I thought it would be disrespectful to those who believe in the divinity of such practices. But I did not stand out by not participating, as some of the leaders and other church members did not take part either.

Through my time in the field, and especially during the data analysis stage, I was intentionally self-reflective about my role. In a context where prosperity is critical, they were eager to accept a person who shared their background and showed the signs of success. Though some of them were better off financially than I was, I appeared wealthier than most of the members in these churches. I was an immigrant who spoke English as well as Spanish, and I was educated; I was married to a woman, and we had children; and I did not live in fear of deportation or of a foreign world. I enjoyed many of the benefits that could not be purchased. The reality is that most believers who are faithful to the prosperity formula do not miraculously get wealthy. The poor stay poor, and the already wealthy stay that way. Exceptions to that rule can be found, but they are rare. Tangible evidence in support of the Prosperity Gospel formula is sparse. Although no one ever said it, some in these churches probably saw me as evidence of a faithful Christian who was rewarded with success and prosperity. Even though I never practiced any of their beliefs nor hinted that I applied the Prosperity Gospel formula for prosperity, it is easy to imagine how my life could be rationalized to justify their beliefs.

While I am fairly confident that most of the members of these churches remained unchanged as a result of their encounter with me, I cannot say the same for me. Sharing life with people who had experienced many hardships and who continued to face them daily transforms one's perspective on life. The courage, optimism, and faith these immigrants maintained under the harshest challenges is truly admirable. When non-Pentecostal Christians, both liberals and conservatives, learn about the subject of my study, they are quick to ask for anecdotes to confirm their stereotypes of this faith. They inquire about stories of financial abuse and demand gossip about the moral lives of these Christians. Many urge me to fuel the heretical flames with insights of heterodox teaching. I would not share such stories out of respect for the people who welcomed me into their lives, but I also do not have such stories to share. The pastors of these churches genuinely cared for their congregants. There was no financial abuse or moral impropriety in any of the churches profiled in this book. The scandals of prime-time television shows were absent. These Christians are smarter than they are given credit for, and they are not passive recipients of the faith. Their faith gives them agency in their lives, and they apply it to actively interpreting the faith for themselves and for their benefit. I often tell skeptics about the hope and confidence these people gain in these churches. I tell them the stories of the immigrants in this book, the many lives that were saved and changed for the better, and the stories of immigrants whose only source of encouragement and hope comes from Prosperity Gospel Pentecostalism. I sometimes wonder what the critics have to offer these immigrants. Can their versions of Christianity give hope to the hopeless the way that Prosperity Gospel Pentecostalism does?

Looking Ahead

Since the day I started this project, many of my own assumptions have been radically challenged. I originally felt like a social and spiritual outsider to Prosperity Gospel Pentecostalism, but the years I spent with these churches have made me feel like I am one of them without being one of them. As a student of a religion filled with contradictions, this feeling makes sense. My participant observation helped me better understand the attraction of subjective late-modern religions, in which individual interpretations supersede traditional teachings, and facts are less important than feelings. The members of these churches taught me that religion is not only a matter of the mind or the heart, as most traditional Christian denominations would emphasize; rather, they showed me that one could worship with the mind *and* the body. Though I still hold personal differences with some of their beliefs, their faith has pushed me to think beyond stereotypes, especially those of conservative religions. The leaders of these churches were more generous than I expected and gave sacrificially to the people they were called to lead. The faithful parishioners in pursuit of prosperity were outstanding humanitarians, holding the highest esteem for all people—even those outside their church. Seeing them give financially and personally, even when they had little, was moving. Most of all, the testimonies from the lives that were transformed were truly impressive. While none of the interviewees' personal histories have been verified, I have presented their first-person accounts as factual because of the power they ascribe to their experience. I can testify to the ways that they work hard, treat their families, and serve in their churches and communities. I observed Prosperity Gospel Pentecostals living the life they claim came as a result of traumatic past experiences. Their background stories hold the same place as their God and the power of their faith. They cannot be established as truth, but they are certainly shaping the way these immigrants are living their lives today.

Throughout this book I have sought to avoid the trap of cynicism and theological critiques, which is not the role of a social scientist. At the same time, I have steered clear from being an apologist for Prosperity Gospel Pentecostalism, because while I *felt* like one of them at times, I am *not* one of them in reality and am unqualified to defend their faith. This is a religion in which experience is more important than knowledge. I possess the latter as a scholar, but I do not have the former. Instead, my goal in this book has been to climb inside their world, understand them, and thereby help readers understand the world of the average Latin American Prosperity Gospel Pentecostal immigrant; once this world is understood, readers are free to decide the benefit or harm derived from such practices. My hope is that readers will learn something from these churches and their adherents and in turn understand this community better. I also hope that this book will help every American understand themselves better, especially in light of the paradoxes in American ideology and the American dream. Former president Bill Clinton summarized it best in a 1993 speech to the Democratic Leadership Council: "The American Dream that we were all raised on is a simple but powerful one—if you work hard and play by the rules you should be given a chance to go as far as your God-given ability will take you."[50] In the following chapters, you will meet immigrants hoping to go as far as their "God-given abilities" will take them, relying just as much on God as they do on the abilities given to them by this God. In the midst of it all, they believe in the "good news" preached by this nation from its inception: the gospel of the American dream.

CHAPTER ONE

Communities of Dreamers

The Floodgates of Heaven

On a sunny Sunday morning in April, a group of about fifty Latinos gathered in the former warehouse of a printing press in Charlottesville, Virginia—a small but growing town with a steady stream of immigrants from Latin America since 2000. There were exactly one hundred chairs neatly lined up, auditorium style, in the windowless yet newly carpeted and brightly lit room. The distinctive smell of fresh paint lingered in the air, and the walls were lined with the colorful flags of Colombia, El Salvador, the Dominican Republic, Mexico, Honduras, Guatemala, Panama, Venezuela, and the United States. The flag of the State of Israel hung in the very front, behind the speaking podium and the band.[1]

Everyone sat, attentively listening to a middle-aged man in a black, double-breasted suit, an oversized diamond ring on his right hand and a diamond-encrusted wedding ring on his left. In a deep voice and using charismatic hand gestures, he made those gathered before him a very tempting offer: anyone who placed $100 in a small white envelope and put it in his hand would receive a return of one hundred times that amount before the end of the year. He guaranteed that a $100 investment today would yield a $10,000 return within eight months. Eleven poor, working-class immigrants—most of them undocumented—approached and handed this man the requested amount. He pleaded with those who did not come forward to seize the moment, for this offer would expire. The tone of desperation was clear in his voice. He begged the congregants not to miss this opportunity. Four more people went up and placed an envelope in his hand. He gave one final call: "This is your last chance to receive $10,000 by the end of the year." A woman got up from her seat, quickly went to see her sister, who was in the next room with her children, and returned within moments with a check in her hand. Two young men who had run across the street to the ATM machine in the convenience store returned with their "investments." The man in the black suit lifted the envelopes high in the air in his right hand. Holding the microphone with his left, he proclaimed: "I will now ask God to grant each one of you $10,000 before the end of this year, because this is not my promise. It is God's promise, and he will make it happen!"

Turning to the congregation, he yelled, "Know your God and see that He is faithful! Have faith! He will do it!" The congregation responded with cheers and applause. "Lift your hands and pray with me. Agree with me as we pray! Ask God to multiply these gifts! Multiplica! Multiplica! Multiplicalo Señor!" The congregation raised their hands in unison, praying, praising, and repeating the chant. The band started a song, and the crowd began to dance and celebrate. One woman fell to her knees with her hands lifted high, sobbing in joy as if she had already received her $10,000.

The man in the suit was Pastor Federico Gielis. Originally from Colombia, he is a mortgage loan officer by day and pastor of the Iglesia Cristiana del Padre (Christian Church of the Father) on nights and weekends. This church gathers every Sunday for a charismatic worship service filled with music, shouting, tongue speaking, and spiritual healing. The worship service at this church is similar to that of many Pentecostal churches; what is distinctive is its teaching on prosperity.

Iglesia Cristiana del Padre is one of a growing number of neo-Pentecostal churches, a new rendition of Pentecostal Christianity. They are part of the Prosperity Gospel movement—or, as some have called it, "Word of Faith," "name-it-and-claim-it," or "the health-and-wealth gospel."[2] Prosperity Gospel Pentecostalism has historically been most popular among the poor, but this type of Christianity is both creating a culture that is unique to itself and crossing over denominational lines to influence other forms of Christianity.[3] Prosperity Gospel Pentecostals adapt and translate psychological language and rationale into Christianity and offer a worldview that focuses on the instrumental outcomes of faith. Christian groups that are influenced by Prosperity Gospel Pentecostalism might not be as blatant in their promise of wealth, but they teach the same logic and use the same language because their belief is the core of every religion: good behavior on the part of the believer should lead to a reward from the deity. For Prosperity Gospel Pentecostalism, its promises and formulas for attaining wealth and health have drawn criticism from established Pentecostal denominations, such as the Assemblies of God, which passed a resolution in 2000 prohibiting the use of divine rewards as a fund-raising strategy. Yet the growth and visibility of this belief is increasing rapidly; 46 percent of all Americans completely or mostly agree that God will grant prosperity to all believers who have enough faith. For Pentecostals, two-thirds believe this. In Latin America, Africa, and Asia, the percentage of Pentecostals who believe in Prosperity Gospel is even higher than those in America.[4]

A Logic of Their Own

The idea that people can do earthly things to influence heavenly outcomes is not new to Christianity. Money and salvation have been at the center of Christian conflict from its early days. The monastic movement in the fourth century was born as a rejection of the material benefits Christians received from the Roman Empire. During the sixteenth century, certificates were sold to guarantee salvation for those who could afford it. The practice was common even though it was never officially sanctioned by the Roman Catholic Church. Religious people of all faiths have long sought to influence their gods by their earthly actions. Prosperity Gospel Pentecostals are no different. Their methods are more modern than those of previous Christians, but their goal is the same.

The biblical, theological, and historical lessons woven into weekly sermons are designed to speak to, and hopefully move, the heart. These lessons are impressively bold; the personal experience and interpretation of the preacher and the parishioners supersede any other authority—including that of ancient Christian traditions, established doctrines, and even the Bible itself. Leaders are free to "quote" from the Bible, regardless of precision, sometimes even paraphrasing scripture to the point of biblical inaccuracy. The charismatic authority of the pastors gives them authority to interpret the Bible as they see fit. They have no need to seek validation from other sources. The preachers have the power to completely dismiss long-held beliefs of the Christian faith as misinterpretations or errors in belief. As the parishioners learn in these churches, they do not just absorb the pastor's interpretation of Christian lessons; rather, they learn the logic behind these sermons and eventually learn to reinterpret things for themselves. While the pastors explain biblical passages to their liking, the parishioners are also reinterpreting the lessons to suit their needs.

The preachers spend great amounts of time every week creating a biblical connect-the-dots trail that leads to their predetermined conclusions. During the weekly sermons, they lead their parishioners in a biblical, cultural, and historical scavenger hunt for the treasured message of comfort, prosperity, and abundance. Most church members, regardless of educational background, can follow the clues. I made it a routine to ask church members about the sermons of the previous Sunday during casual conversation at the beginning of every interview, and found that the majority could successfully connect the dots, probably because the conclusion was always the same. Individuals walk away comforted and confident; they then use this logic to derive meaning from their own life conditions. It is common to hear church members quote the pastor or use the logic of his sermons in explaining their daily decisions.

The critical lessons they learn from their pastor are not only the message of prosperity and hope; they also learn to think through a logic of their own. Prosperity Gospel is about self-empowerment. The average church members learn that they have the power to reject or ignore the details that do not contribute to their desired outcome. They learn to interpret and rationalize their reality in a way that benefits them. They face the world with confidence, convinced that God has a plan for them and that He will cause them to prosper, no matter how many obstacles are against them. This confidence coats their worldview and reassures them of the way things are and the way things will be. That is, Prosperity Gospel Pentecostals know exactly how things will work out. No matter what challenges they encounter, they are certain that God will give them victory. Where the average person sees only failure, Prosperity Gospel Pentecostals are assured of success because they have faithfully followed the formula that guarantees it. The nature of this faith empowers believers to make sense of their own lives and create narratives for their daily challenges. The church is where these teachings take place and where they see their fellow believers live out and proclaim such faith.

The Churches

The churches selected in this study were intentionally chosen to represent different stages of immigrant life in America. Iglesia Cristiana del Padre is a small church (under one hundred members) located in Charlottesville, Virginia, a small city where Latinx immigrants began arriving in larger numbers beginning in 2000. This city is unique because while there are different areas where Latinos gather, residents of Charlottesville are hard-pressed to find Latinos in their daily lives. Latinos in this city feel the very real challenges of being a minority group. Iglesia del Dios Victorioso is a large church (over three hundred members) in Oceanside, California, a city north of San Diego where the majority of immigrants arrived before 2000, though the members of the church are more recent immigrants, due to its proximity to the southern border. Latinos have a large and visible presence in Oceanside, as many of them moved there to escape the high cost of living in San Diego.

The third church, Iglesia Pentecostal del Rey Divino in New York City, was once one of the largest Latin American Pentecostal churches in Manhattan, but it has dwindled to about thirty active members, most of them elderly.

Though these three churches are located in very different places and hold different denominational affiliations, their doctrines and practices are identical. Their Sunday services are indistinguishable, and they sing the same songs, sell the same books and music in their stores, and follow the same general worship order. All three of the pastors are financially wealthier than their congregation, and they exemplify the lifestyle and mentality of prosperity. Most importantly, the membership of all three churches is composed entirely of first-generation Latin American immigrants and their families. The adherents profiled in this study are all immigrants who had to navigate the challenges of integrating into a new country, and they were guided through that transition by the teachings and practices of Prosperity Gospel Pentecostalism. One constant theme in all three churches, which is present in all Latin American Prosperity Gospel churches, is the intentional use of the language of migration and displacement in their symbols and rituals. From the decoration of the church to the preaching, testimonies, prayers, Bible readings, and songs, everything reminds members that they have a native home, a new opportunity in their current country, and a hope at the promise of Heaven, which they hope will be realized on earth. There is a deliberate focus on the struggles that displaced people face and the hope needed to overcome those challenges.

I describe Iglesia Cristiana del Padre (in Virginia) in the most detail because it is the most representative of an average Prosperity Gospel Pentecostal church: it is small, is housed in a storefront, and was founded by the current pastor. The U.S. Latinx community is not uniform but rich and diverse, composed of numerous Spanish-speaking nationalities, each with a distinctive tradition and culture. Latin American immigrants in large cities tend to self-segregate on Sundays, worshipping with those from their countries of origin. That is, Mexicans will gather at the majority Mexican Pentecostal church, while Salvadorans will gather with their compatriots at their own Pentecostal church, even if both churches are small in size and close in location.[5] Iglesia Cristiana del Padre, however, is located in a town where the numbers of Latinx immigrants are not large enough to segregate by nationality. Hence, at this church, they worship together by a common language, not a common national identity. There is no distinguishable national majority in the congregation; worshippers represent many Central and South American countries. It is, in this way, a microcosm of what is happening in the greater Latinx community and of the influence of Latin American Prosperity Gospel Pentecostalism in American culture. In this book, I generalize my findings to the entire Latinx community but acknowledge that each nationality has a unique path to assimilation. That is, Mexican Americans will adapt the teachings of Prosperity Gospel Pentecostalism to their process of integration differently than will Dominicans or Cubans. This process is further complicated by the complexion of each person's skin.

Iglesia Cristiana del Padre in Charlottesville, Virginia

Pastor Federico Gielis and his wife Veronica had been living in Charlottesville for about two years when they agreed that God wanted them to start a church for Spanish speakers. They had both been involved in church ministry before moving to Virginia and felt the need to offer God's word to the growing Latinx population in their community. There were only two Spanish-speaking churches in Charlottesville then, both of them Pentecostal but not Prosperity Gospel. In addition, one of the local Catholic churches held an afternoon Spanish-language Mass. In 2001, Pastor Gielis and his wife started the church in their house—specifically, in their basement. At first, the Sunday service involved the pastor, his wife, his in-laws, and a family friend named Lorena. Ironically, every original member of this Spanish-speaking church was fluent in English, yet they intentionally conducted every aspect of their worship in Spanish. They worshipped in the basement for a year, welcoming visitors who became frequent attendees. The basement served as the place for revivals, worship services, and even a wedding. As their attendance grew to about twenty people, they rented a small space in an office park and began worshipping wholeheartedly with the help of a CD player and a single-speaker sound system. Not long after, a small publishing company decided to vacate its space near the downtown area. The space seemed perfect for the now-growing church: it had parking for twenty cars, a large open warehouse for worship service, and seven offices that could serve as classrooms.

The owner was asking $3,000 a month in rent, which was fair market value but unrealistic for the small church. Yet in typical Prosperity Gospel fashion, Pastor Gielis was undaunted. He explained:

> I went to see el señor. And before I went, I prayed, and I claimed the building in Christ's name. I said, "Christ Jesus, you know this is the best place for us, but we don't have the money yet. So let this señor

rent it to us for $1,000 a month." I went to meet him, Mr. Steven, very nice man. And I explained to him what God had told me about planting a church and told him what we did and the ministry we were doing. Then I looked at him in the eyes, and I said, "I'll sign a lease right now for $1,000 a month for one year, my friend!" He looked at me, and he said, "OK." I said, "Hallelujah! God is good to us."

Two years later, the church paid more than $1,000 a month for the space, though still not its full market value.

The Meeting Place

The church is conveniently located in a residential part of town frequented by Latinos; immediately across the street is a Latinx grocery store. There are a few other Latinx-owned stores within walking distance, but it would be a stretch to describe the area as a Latinx neighborhood. Latinos and Latinx-owned stores do not have a significant presence in that city.

The church's name is prominently displayed at the front of the building. The name of the pastor and the times of its activities, however, are surprisingly absent from the sign. This information appears on most church signs, but it is especially important for Pentecostal churches, as they are personality driven.[6] In many cases, the pastor of a Prosperity Gospel Pentecostalism church *is* the church. Yet Iglesia Cristiana del Padre had omitted this information from its sign because the person who volunteered to make it was a new convert and did not know the proper protocol. Pastor Gielis refused to change it because he was "believing" in a membership growth that would require them to go to a new and bigger space. Two years after my time at Iglesia Cristiana del Padre concluded, the congregation was able to purchase its own building—a former warehouse in the industrial area just outside the city, on which the pastor's name is prominently displayed.

The church has a phone line, but there is no voice mail or full-time office assistant. Unless one calls during meeting times, there is no one to answer the phone. The church has no web presence or any form of social media. Yet despite its lackluster marketing, the church continues to grow by word of mouth (thanks in part to the Latinx store owner across the street, who informs inquirers of the church's worship times). The power of networks within immigrant communities is real. Even without the aid of social media, church events are well attended, and the church's reputation is widespread throughout the community.

The interior layout of the church displays its cultural hierarchy. The design sheds much light into the theology and power structures of the community.[7] Every church discussed in this book has a store in which they sell Christian music, Prosperity Gospel books, inspirational decorations, snacks, and even children's toys. Each store is a small version of a combination dollar store, Christian bookstore, and convenience store. The toys and snacks are for parents who need something to entertain their children with during long meetings. Only Prosperity Gospel authors (such as Joyce Meyer, T. D. Jakes, and Morris Cerullo) are represented in the bookstores, and everything is in Spanish. A number of Kenneth Hagin booklets are available for free, with titles such as *Seven Hindrances to Healing, Is Your Miracle Passing You By? Don't Blame God!*, and *You Can Have What You Say!* While Latin American Prosperity Gospel preachers have been extremely prolific, every author in these bookstores is from the United States. The sources of authority in these churches are distinctively American, not the indigenized versions of Prosperity Gospel that can be found abroad, where native teachers have taken the teachings of American preachers and adapted them to their own context. Also for sale are video recordings of the pastor's sermons, though these are often given out for free. Next to the tabletop bookstore is a small refrigerator out of which the teenagers sell snacks and drinks after worship for $1 as a way to raise money for their activities.

To the right of the main door of Iglesia Cristiana del Padre are eighty neatly arranged chairs, lined up with an open center aisle about five feet wide. Because the building is L shaped, there are an additional twenty chairs around the corner. A large stage, about twenty feet by ten feet, which rises about five inches off the floor, sits against the corner. The stage holds a cross-encrusted crystal podium, a drum set, two guitars, a keyboard, two microphones on stands, other assorted instruments, and two tall speakers on either side. Even with so many things on it, the stage looks neat and organized. The flag of the State of Israel hangs on the wall directly behind the podium. Like most traditional conservative churches, they are Christian Zionist.[8] They believe that the reestablishment of the State of Israel was a fulfillment of God's prophecy and a sign of the imminent Second Coming of Jesus. The display of the flag of Israel is a reminder that God still establishes his kingdom on earth.

In front of the stage is a large open space, roughly twenty by thirty-five feet, where the pastor can walk around as he preaches. This is the space where the most important practice of Prosperity Gospel Pentecostalism takes place: the healing and anointing of the people. It is the epicenter of

Pentecostal faith experience—the space where one's faith is displayed and received, the space where miracles are most likely to happen, the space where believers are most likely to encounter divine intervention. The only items invading the hallowed space are a large leather chair and an end table. Even the uninitiated can tell that this chair is a sacred throne. It is where the pastor sits every Sunday before he goes up on the stage to preach. The table is also important. Every week, the pastor places his car key on that table—a large black electronic key with the Mercedes-Benz insignia shining brightly for all to see. The table also holds bottles of anointing oil and a box of tissues.

The Members

Since the church holds no records of membership or attendance in any systematic way, the exact demographics of membership are hard to establish. This was true for all churches in this book, as none of them had a formal process for joining. The list of members that I was given at Iglesia Cristiana del Padre included only those who had responsibilities at the church. The (very few) regular church members who did not have responsibilities were not included. By the time I asked for that list, a few months after my ethnographic research, I was also listed, even though they knew I was a researcher doing a study of their church. The church also had a mailing list different from the "membership list," which included individuals and institutions outside the United States who received updates from the church. Many of these were the pastor's personal friends, churches, and other religious organizations. There are no rituals or confessional requirements in place to mark someone being classified as a member except perhaps for one: a few months after I started attending, the pastor handed me a key to the church, because "every member needs to have one." (In reality, I think he gave me the key because I always arrived early and he wanted me to open the doors for everyone else. I came to this conclusion because I found out later that every "member" did not have a key to the church, especially the women.) This tenuous definition of membership is understandable, given the transient nature of the church's demographic. There are new visitors each week who come for different reasons. Some come seeking a miracle, others are invited by friends, and still others are just curious. There are also many seasonal workers, who eventually move on. Few of the visitors stay for long. Those who become regulars tend to have previous relationships with existing active members.

Soon after I started my research at Iglesia Cristiana del Padre, Pastor Gielis distributed a survey on my behalf that asked for basic demographical information. Most of the church members were happy to return the completed survey. The information presented here on church members' age, education, income, and marital status come from this informal survey as well as the background information form they filled out before interviews. Average weekly attendance hovers at around fifty adult congregants, low attendance being around twenty and high around eighty. Special events sometimes draw over one hundred adults, but never significantly more (their meeting space can hold only about 120 people without anyone standing in the sacred space in front of the stage). The average age in the church is in the mid-twenties, which is not far from the overall U.S. Latinx population (median age 27.4 years).[9] At least fifteen children attend on any given Sunday, and they range from newborn to teenagers. The oldest attendee is a very active seventy-one-year-old man (the next oldest is twelve years his junior, and the oldest after that is in her late forties). This seventy-one-year-old gentleman still works a full-time job at Sam's Club, and I was surprised when I learned his age due to his youthful appearance.

Data about income was difficult to obtain, as few people relish revealing their financial situation. In this case, however, it was even harder, as the majority of church members are typically paid in cash for irregular work. Thus, their yearly estimates are unreliable. According to the information I was able to gather, the average income of regular church attendees (not including the clergy) is slightly under $17,000 a year. This is also representative of the overall Latinx population, as 43 percent of all Latinos had a household income of less than $30,000 at the time of the study.[10] Among the men of the church, I met blue-collar workers representative of most Latino men in America: painters, construction workers, restaurant workers, mechanics, and an Army private. The women also work in traditional gendered professions: four clean houses for a living, one is a hair stylist, one is a preschool teacher, two provide childcare in their homes, and two sell beauty products (Mary Kay and Avon) part time. The educational level of the members of Iglesia Cristiana del Padre is consistent with the national trend. Most of the lay church members, like 47 percent of Latinos in the United States at that time, have a high school diploma.[11] None of the church members had completed four-year college degrees.

Like most Christian organizations, there are more women than men on any given Sunday,[12] though the difference rarely reaches double digits. Three single mothers bring their children every week; there are no single fathers, though sometimes a father will bring the children while the mother is at work. Juanita, a single mother in her mid-thirties, has three daughters: one in college, one in middle school, and one in kindergarten. Paulina, also a single mother, arrived in the United States with her eight-year-old daughter two weeks after I started attending the church. There is also an assortment of single women, widows, and married women whose husbands do not attend the church. About ten men attend alone, most of whom are single, though some have partners who are not in the country. Many of these "single" men have left their wives and children in their homeland. Mario has been in the United States for six years, working and sending money home to his wife and children in order to build a house in Mexico. Gerardo came ten years ago and has worked his way, state by state, from California to Virginia. Feliciano is a single young man who works as a cook at a Thai restaurant and wants to send money back to Mexico for his brother to start a "computer school." All these men are active members who help organize and run the events of the church.

Five married couples with children anchor the church. They are the church members who are there consistently every week, not just as active members but as visible symbols of what a family is supposed to look like. The pastor makes no small effort to highlight these nuclear families, which include Gustavo the painter and his wife, Mariela, who is a childcare provider; Alejandro the mechanic and his wife, Marta, a hairstylist, and their three girls: twelve-year-old twins and a toddler; and Sandro and his wife, Yolanda, who have two preteen children. These busy working parents all hold some type of leadership role in the church.

The Leaders

A clear social and economic divide exists between the church leaders holding official ecclesiastical titles—pastor, evangelist, apostle—and the lay church members (who still serve in leadership roles, perhaps as an usher or the coordinator of a specific ministry).

Pastor Federico Gielis was born in Colombia, but his family moved to New York City when he was a child. His family was involved in the illegal drug trade, and following their example, he began abusing substances at the age of thirteen, heavily using both alcohol and crack cocaine. He was part of the drug scene in New York back in the 1980s. To help him escape some legal problems, his family sent him to Florida as a teenager, but little changed. By his mid-twenties, he had been diagnosed with cirrhosis of the liver and told that he would not live much longer. Soon after, however, he found God at a church revival meeting, and God completely healed him. He left the life of drugs and alcohol and met his future wife, Veronica, and the two soon got married. He got a steady job selling flowers on the streets and to businesses. Later, he worked as an office clerk. After moving to Virginia, he worked for social services with at-risk youth because of his experience working with youth in his old church. By the time I met him, he had been working as a loan officer at a bank. His personal experience was evidence that God could heal and restore all people, and his financial prosperity confirmed that faith could surely bring wealth and success. He began to pastor for the first time when he started Iglesia Cristiana del Padre.

Pastor Gielis holds an associate degree from a two-year Bible college as well as multiple certifications for workshops and special training courses he attended as a loan officer and at Christian training conferences. All these certificates are framed in his office. His most prized certificate is from Morris Cerullo World Evangelism Institute in San Diego, California. Morris Cerullo is a semiretired Prosperity Gospel preacher who traveled extensively throughout Latin America. Pastor Gielis, who has served as Cerullo's translator in many revivals throughout Latin America, considers Cerullo to be his mentor.

Veronica Gielis is the child of a Puerto Rican mother and an Argentinean father who met and settled in Florida. The family was middle class and did not go to church. When she was seventeen, she attended a revival service and became a Christian. From that time on, she felt called to ministry and was a youth evangelist at her church. She takes credit for her parents' faith. Her mother was an active member, but her father never attended the church while I was there, and no explanation was ever given for his absence, though Pastor Gielis spoke positively of his father-in-law numerous times during his sermons. Veronica met Pastor Gielis at their church in Florida, where Pastor Gielis first became a Christian. They have worked together ever since.

Lorena (mentioned earlier as a founding member) is the church's evangelist. She moved to central Virginia with her Dominican parents and siblings. She grew up in a stable, two-parent household and is still close to her parents and siblings, though they do not attend church with her. She is a licensed real-estate agent and often "testifies" during worship services about the commissions she earns. There is no specific job description for her role as evangelist, but she occasionally preaches on Sundays and often teaches Bible study. A confident woman in her thirties, she is the only woman in this church with no children or romantic partner. This is culturally unusual for Latinos—especially in conservative Christian churches.

All the church leaders are fluent in English, and all are U.S. citizens. This gives them a very important economic and cultural advantage over the rest of the congregation. Both the pastor and his wife grew up speaking primarily in English. During their personal conversations, they often speak to each other and their children in English and are not shy about asking the congregation for help with Spanish terms and idioms. The average income among the church leaders is over $120,000 a year. Pastor Gielis alone claims to make over $300,000 a year as a mortgage loan officer (which, during the housing bubble of the mid-2000s, was not an implausible claim). Lorena, as a real-estate agent in the rapidly growing city, also makes an above-average salary. These Prosperity Gospel preachers do not build their wealth on the back of their church members. Rather, it is their documented status, fluency in English, and cultural knowledge that leads to higher paying jobs.

Sunday Worship

For the more involved members, Iglesia Cristiana del Padre dominates their lives. Their days and weeks are largely, and sometimes completely, determined by church events, including their work schedules. It is normal for church members to turn down jobs or overtime if it conflicts with their worship schedule. Sunday worship is the highlight of the week, but there are also Monday night miracle services, Wednesday night Bible studies, and Friday night prayer meetings, in addition to special planning meetings and leadership gatherings. There are also special events for the youth group, the men's group, and the women's group. Highly active members, including the pastor and his wife, are often at the church every night of the week.

For members, this system of social involvement ameliorates their immigration experience, which might otherwise feel very chaotic and lonely. At church, they wear their best clothes, socialize with people they consider family, and worship together through hopeful songs and uplifting sermons. After worship, many eat lunch together and visit at one another's homes. In the summertime, families picnic together at nearby parks, where the children can play together.[13]

Sunday visitors will notice that Iglesia Cristiana del Padre sounds and feels like an average small church. They are greeted by ushers, usually with a hug, and led to a seat. There are no orders of worship to hand out in this church, as one never knows how the Spirit will lead the service. The Sunday morning service averages just under two hours, though it has taken as long as three. Mario, a man in his early forties, is the music leader, and he takes the stage before the pastor arrives. A number of men and women—and often children—join him in singing and playing the instruments onstage (the makeup varies from week to week). Mario selects the songs and directs the musicians who will participate as the congregation comes and goes from their seats. The quality of the music is impressive given the short time they have to practice and the fact that none of the musicians have formal training.

The worship time officially begins when the pastor arrives and sits on his leather "throne." People, without rushing, naturally finish their conversations and move to their seats. The music then continues for about forty-five minutes (but sometimes as long as seventy-five minutes), interrupted by spontaneous prayers and testimonies. Mario acts as the guide for the congregation during the time of praise, telling them when to pray, what to say, and how to feel. Prerecorded music might also be used, or the congregation sings along to a CD. Whatever the method, the music is always much louder than necessary for the space in an effort to encourage singing from the congregation. Even if they are out of tune, the music coming from the speakers drowns out every voice.

After the singing is finished, there is a brief time for announcements. Since all the announcements are made verbally only on Sundays, those who miss a service are left to hear of the events by word of mouth—an approach that was very effective. Announcements usually involve upcoming midweek activities, including the topics of the Bible studies and any special guests. The pastor and his wife may also introduce new visitors and explain why they are visiting. After announcements, there is a time of greeting, where members hug and kiss one another.

La Oportunidad de Prosperar *(The Opportunity to Prosper)*

Up to this point, most of their service falls within the norms of traditional Pentecostal churches. What distinguishes Prosperity Gospel Pentecostal churches like this one from other churches is their offering time. Every single week, worshippers at these churches are given "the opportunity to prosper."

Following the announcements, a qualified person is asked to collect the offering. Collectors have been screened by the pastor to ensure that they fully subscribe to and will promote the Prosperity Gospel message (men and women are equally selected). The pastor or his wife collects the offering only when there is no one else available. This is the only ministry, aside from preaching, where the pastor himself thoroughly screens the participant.

There is no passing of the plate in this church. The person in charge of collecting the offering will often begin with a pep rally, asking the congregation: "Are you ready to give? Are you ready to prosper?" The person will repeatedly emphasize the difference between a tithe and a regular offering. While the offering is a gift of an indiscriminate amount, the tithe is a religious practice whereby believers are required to bring 10 percent of their earnings before God.[14] The teaching of tithing is common among many Christian traditions (though research shows that it is rarely practiced).[15] What makes Prosperity Gospel distinctive is the *motivation* for giving. Every person who stands before the congregation to receive the tithes and offering offers a testimony, personal or otherwise, of a person who "offered up" money in faith and was richly rewarded by God. Once Sandro shared a story he heard while watching Robert Tilton's *Success-N-Life* late at night when he was younger. (Tilton is a notorious televangelist who has been exposed numerous times for his fund-raising scandals.) Sandro was moved by that story of prosperity and has followed that example for many years in hopes of his own prosperity. Nearly every week, the person receiving the offering quotes Malachi 3:10: "'Bring the whole tithe into the storehouse, that there may be food in my house. Test me in this,' says the Lord Almighty, 'and see if I will not throw open the floodgates of heaven and pour out so much blessing that you will not have room enough for it.'"[16] The offering collector emphasizes the "testing" part of this passage (the pastor does the same during his sermon). To "test God," according to Prosperity Gospel doctrine, is to give your tithe to the church to see if God truly follows through on the promise of wealth. It is not the percentage that is important in a tithe. The tithe is a "seed" that believers are required to plant in order to reap a prosperous harvest, and the leader often calls for a greater amount than 10 percent. Whatever the percentage, the amount must be sacrificial—an amount greater than what one is comfortable giving—for God to reward the giver. The point is to "suffer" with their giving because only sacrificial offerings will get God's attention. During my conversations with members of Iglesia Cristiana del Padre, I found that most church members do not know the technical definition of the Spanish word "*diezmo*" or "tithe." They just understand it as a special, sacrificial offering, not one ruled by a percentage.

Bible stories of God's miraculous provisions for those who gave beyond their means are often presented during offering times. A recurrent story told in this church is found in 1 Kings 17, in which a poor widow and her son give their last meal to the prophet Elijah and are miraculously provided with food for the remainder of a terrible drought. Once, while collecting the offering, Alejandro said, "We must give like the widow":

> She gave to the prophet of God first. She gave to God first, even out of her need. She gave what she needed for her and her family, but God gave her more. And that's what we are doing this morning when we bring our offerings before God. We are bringing our gifts in faith. Amen? We bring them in faith, not focusing on what we need at home, not focusing on the rent, not focusing on the electric bills, not focusing on how you will buy food or what you will do next month. Because God will provide. We must have faith, because the Word says that God will provide. God provides for us now! How many can testify that God provides right now?

The congregation broke out in applause and cheers. Alejandro continued: "Praise God! All of you can. Do you believe this? Do you believe it? Bring your offerings, then!"

The ushers usually hand out small white envelopes specifically designed for money and checks as music plays. One by one, church members conspicuously approach the pulpit, in the center of the stage, to place their envelope at its base. Once the entire offering has been collected, a prayer is offered by the collector. The first part of the prayer is thanksgiving for God's miracle in providing for church members. The second and longer part of the prayer is a request for God to miraculously provide financially for the good of those who gave an offering. The prayer will often ask for a doubling or some other multiplication of the given amount. Sometimes the prayers demand a specific amount of money as a harvest (as in the case described at the beginning of this chapter).

La Predicacíon *(The Preaching)*

Following the offering is the longest part of the service, the preaching. The sermon is the centerpiece of the worship experience—the time during which the authority of the pastor is on clear display. Pastor Gielis is the perfect embodiment of charisma and authority. Members of the church are devoted to him. He is regarded as a man of God with the power to perform miracles. They believe that his level of sanctity exceeds that of the average person. His heroic faith, and that of his family, is a point of pride for church members, not least because Pastor Gielis constantly reminds them of it. His personal character is also beyond reproach. He is the perfect blend of kind, generous, and charismatic, with a touch of narcissism. Pastor Gielis is the ideal Christian for the church, and his family is the ideal everyone in the church works toward. Most of the congregants are in this church because of him and his leadership over them. His care for them is genuine, and he takes the role of a shepherd seriously. He knows the details of each parishioner's troubles. He goes to their homes and sits with them in times of pain. Through the years, he has earned their trust to be their role model and sole source of authority. This authority has never been abused.

In the eyes of the congregation, Pastor Gielis's personal wealth and success confirm that he is a blessed man. During his sermons, he often refers to his house, his job, and his salary as signs of God's blessing, and he encourages believers to "take hold of their promise" like he did. Pastor Gielis often describes his ministry as "confirmed by signs, prophecies, and miracles, not only in the physical, emotional, and spiritual area, but also in the area of finances." His personal testimony of overcoming drug addiction and a childhood of neglect and poverty inspire the congregation to dream it for themselves. The single mothers of the church have not missed the significance of his example for their children. Ana, who raises a ten-year-old boy on her own, told me, "It's very important to me and my family to be under the leadership of a holy man, a man who is anointed by God and who can show my son what God does for people, what God can do for everyone." Justina, a single mother with three daughters, sees her pastor as the man who inspires her to stay faithful to God and to hope for success for herself and her children. The men in the church sometimes identify with Pastor Gielis's background of drugs and alcohol, and they are inspired to overcome these addictions as their pastor did. For those who have already overcome addictions, Pastor Gielis is a constant reminder of what is possible for former alcoholics and drug addicts.

At least one of every ten sermons at Iglesia Cristiana del Padre centers on some part of the pastor's personal testimony of transformation. The majority of the other sermons are similarly peppered with his personal experiences or other stories and anecdotes. Unlike other Christian churches, exegesis or expositions of the Bible are rare. Sermons may focus on specific passages of the Bible that motivate congregants. The Bible is quoted often throughout a sermon, though only to illustrate the pastor's point, not as the foundation of the sermon.

Sermon stories at Prosperity Gospel Pentecostal churches always involve a tragedy, an act of faith, and the success of those who believed. The sermons follow the formula for prosperity and the paradox of Prosperity Gospel described in chapter 2. Overall themes focus on comfort, empowerment, positive thinking, and the entitlement of all believers to demand and receive anything and everything they want from God. The moral boundaries for these requests are unclear, and parishioners seem to rely on intuition to decide what constitutes a permissible request. Requesting protection from police harassment while driving without a license is permissible, but wishing harm on those police officers is not allowed. God saves but does not attack. It is during these sermons that parishioners are taught and reminded of the logic of Prosperity Gospel Pentecostalism. During sermons, they learn strategies for coping with the challenges of immigrant life and hear testimonies of the ways it worked for those who have gone before them.

A number of parishioners pointed specifically to the pastor's "anointing" as the main reason they joined. By "anointing," church members refer to the Hebrew Bible's reference of pouring oil on God's chosen leaders, including kings and prophets. Claiming that someone is anointed confers a particular divine endorsement from God in the things that the person does or says. This is where the charisma of the pastor is unusually critical in the life of the congregation. Whereas fellow believers shape one another in other congregations, it is primarily the pastor who does so in Pentecostal churches. Gerardo, for example, credits the church as his main source of religious education and spiritual fulfillment: "The church is a school for me. The anointing of the pastor is very clear, and I get his anointing when I hear him. He shares his anointing fully, and it fills me. It's spectacular." Sandro commented, "The pastor has God's power in him. He is reaching the whole world. I want to be here to see how God is transforming the world through this man. It's amazing." When asked for the sources of his knowledge, Mario answered, "My pastor. The pastor is my only source. I read the Bible outside of the church when I have time, but I don't read or listen to anyone else. Not because I don't want to, but I don't have time, and I feel that I get everything I need from my pastor. The pastor has a powerful anointing."

La Oración y los Milagros *(The Prayer and the Miracles)*

Every Sunday after the sermon, the pastor invites anyone who wishes to come to the sacred space in the front for the traditional Pentecostal practice of prayer and healing.[17] On special occasions, this could last over an hour, but on most Sundays it was never longer than the sermon. Whereas many evangelical churches offer an "altar call," when worshippers are encouraged to step forward and make a profession of faith to accept Jesus Christ as their personal Lord and Savior, this rarely occurs at Iglesia Cristiana del Padre. Pastor Gielis only offered such an opportunity a handful of times during my time in the church. Two of those times were at specific requests by members of the congregation, who told the pastor they had brought a friend ready to be "saved." The opportunity to receive the Holy Spirit and to experience a miracle, however, is presented every week, because in a Pentecostal church, it is more important to experience God outwardly than to know Him inwardly. Pentecostalism is not overly concerned with doctrines and orthodox practices. The entire faith hinges on experiencing God with all the senses.

This process is surprisingly well organized for what seems like a spontaneous event. Those who wish to pray kneel before the stage on either side of the pulpit and are left alone to do so. Those who wish to receive prayer from the pastor go forward from the center aisle and stand in line, facing the front, waiting their turn. Ushers, usually two women and two men, stand behind those receiving prayer, and the musicians play background music. The other congregants are quiet and respectful of the gravity of the moment. All those who play a supporting role during this time know exactly what to do.

This is the highlight of the Pentecostal worship service. Whereas the sermon is the main source of teaching, prayer time is the highlight for church members. It is during this time that the congregation takes over the worship service. The focus is fully on those who go before the pastor to receive prayer. The pastor serves as a guide during prayer time, but the intensity of each parishioner's reaction to the prayer dictates the power of the presence of God and the duration of the prayer. There is no time limit for this part of the service; it will go as long as the parishioners want.

During prayer time, worshippers—often the same individuals week after week—gather to receive prayer for a variety of problems. The pastor often asks what they desire to receive from God. Problems range from difficulties at work to something as serious as the inability to conceive a child.[18] In every case, the pastor lays his hands on the individual's forehead and prays in a loud and dramatic style, often praying right into the microphone. At times, the pastor's wife always joins him, especially when he is praying for women. As the healing prayers start, those who had quietly knelt on the sides of the stage move away discreetly, either returning to their seats or joining those in line to create more space in the front.

The efficacy of the healing prayer is discerned immediately. Believers do not need to go home and wait to see if a prayer has been answered. A direct correlation is drawn between the efficacy of the prayer and the physical/affective state of the one receiving prayer. Believers receive confirmation that God's favor has been bestowed on them when they lose control of their bodies. Three main signs are used to confirm the prayer's potency. The first (in order of frequency) is suddenly falling backwards to the ground when the pastor touches a worshipper on the forehead. This practice has been called "slain in the spirit." The ushers catch the person and gently lay them down. (Cloths are used to cover the lower extremities of women wearing skirts in order to protect their modesty.) Pastor Gielis explained this phenomenon as follows:

> People fall because they are so overpowered by the Spirit that their bodies can't take it, and they fall. Sometimes people lose control of their emotions. Some people laugh; some people cry. But the Spirit is too much for us. Sometimes it's too much for me, too, and I'll fall, too, after feeling the Holy Spirit go through me.
>
> Question: "How about the people who don't fall?"
>
> Pastor Gielis: "Sometimes people are not open to receive the Spirit, so they fight it. But sometimes people are filled differently, in a softer way. The spirit falls on them softer (*les cae mas suave*). But many times, people will just not be open to receiving the Spirit."

The second sign of an effectual prayer is emotional outburst, the most typical being tears. The pastor often stops praying or draws his prayer to a close once a person has begun to cry. On one occasion, a man recently released from prison for hitting his wife was brought to the front for prayer. The men of the church circled around him and prayed for him as he stood quietly, displaying no emotion. The group prayed with great conviction that this man would be delivered from the spirit of violence and his marriage restored. As those who prayed for him dispersed, the pastor's mother-in-law gathered some women and said, "He is not finished yet. We need to work on him some more." To her, the previous prayer had not "worked" because the man did not show any emotion. As a result, the women re-created the men's circle and prayed for him. It was only when the man began to shed tears that the women, and then the men, burst forth in praise, claiming that the prayer had been effective. His emotions proved that he had repented and was now sanctified.

On a different occasion, Feliciano went up to receive prayer from a healer who was visiting the church by invitation of the pastor. As the healer touched him, he put his hands up in the air and started jumping up and down while screaming uncontrollably. This was the first time I had observed him doing that. The next day I asked him what he had experienced. "I was filled with the Spirit," he explained. "I felt this power coming inside of me. It was in my stomach, and I couldn't help but to release that power. I jumped and screamed to let the power out or I would have exploded." When I asked if this was how he knew that his prayer was answered, Feliciano replied, "Yes, I always feel it in me. Sometimes I pray when I'm too distracted, and nothing happens. But when I'm deep in prayer, I feel it inside me and I have to scream."

The third sign is the traditional Pentecostal indicator of the filling of the Holy Spirit: glossolalia, also known as speaking in tongues, when believers utter unintelligible syllables and sounds interpreted as the language of the angels, too advanced for humans. This practice is not specific to Prosperity Gospel but is common for all Pentecostals. During the times of prayer, the pastor often places his hand on people's stomachs and prays for God to "loosen" their tongue. He often screams at an individual, saying, "Let it go! Let it come out!" The individual might then begin to scream or speak in seemingly nonsensical utterances. The pastor sometimes joins the person in the tongue speaking and points out to the congregation, "There it is! There it is! The Spirit is on him! He received his healing. He got it." The first two signs were significantly more common than glossolalia; the pastor and his wife were the most frequent practitioners of it. The majority of the church members did not speak in tongues during public meetings.

¡Este Es Su Tiempo! *(This Is Your Time!)*

As the prayer time comes to a close, worshippers return to their seats, and the pastor resumes his place at the pulpit. He offers some words of praise for the miracles that took place in their midst. Then he calls the congregation to stand and join him in reciting in unison Isaiah 40:31: "But they that wait upon the Lord shall renew their strength; they shall mount up with wings as eagles; they shall run, and not be weary; and they shall walk and not faint" (King James Version).[19]

Pastor Gielis then continues to lead the congregation. "Repeat after me!" he shouts. "The blessings of God are upon me! We will not give up! God will bless us! We will be victorious!" The congregation shouts each phrase in turn with enthusiasm and energy. Then Pastor Gielis wraps up with his favorite phrase: "*¡Este es su tiempo!*" (This is your time!).

"This is your time" is the message of empowerment believers take away. What distinguishes these believers from the average Latin American Pentecostal is not demographics or socioeconomic status; it is the belief that because of their faith, this *is* their time. It is their time for victory, for prosperity, and for success. Their very worldview and expectations are shaped by this empowering message as they embrace their entitlement to the American dream.

As the Sunday program draws to a close, most everyone gathers in the aisles or in the back of the church. Even visitors stick around to chat. Some church members go across the street to the Hispanic grocery, get food, and come back to eat it at the church and continue their conversations, which generally revolve around work and family issues. Similar to most churches in the United States, friends catch up on what has happened since they last met and talk about their plans for the coming week.

Visitors, no matter what their opinion of the service, would find the pastor and members of Iglesia Cristiana del Padre normal in every way. They hold jobs similar to those of most Latin American immigrants, have a similar number of children, eat similar foods, hold the same traditions, enjoy playing and talking about soccer, and live in similar neighborhoods. They are socioeconomically no different from the average Hispanic. Yet they possess a psychological boost that might well be missing at non–Prosperity Gospel churches. They live their lives knowing that every moment is *their* time, their opportunity, and their right to claim a successful future of their own.

Iglesia del Dios Victorioso in Oceanside, California

In the decade between 1950 and 1960, the population of San Diego nearly doubled, from 550,000 to over 1,000,000. The majority of San Diego's present-day attractions were established during that decade. The National Football League inaugurated the Chargers and expanded its stadium; the Padres baseball team was promoted to the majors; large, modern shopping centers were built; the University of California school system opened its new campus in San Diego; and SeaWorld opened to great acclaim. These events helped establish San Diego as one of the most important cities in the state of California. Though the area always had a Latinx presence, the rapid growth of the 1960s brought an influx of immigrants for jobs and new opportunities.

It was during the growth of the 1960s that a small group of charismatic, Spanish-speaking Christians gathered together for worship and Bible study outside the city of San Diego, in the town of Oceanside. They settled about forty-five minutes north of San Diego because of the lower costs of living. The history of the church is not well known; none of the founding members were around by the time I arrived, and no written record had been kept.

A few of the older members were able to relate some of the history, but none could confirm the reliability. Even the original name of the church had been lost. Most remember it as an average "Christian church." Through the decades, it is believed that the group changed names several times, varying in size from fewer than ten people to over one hundred. By the mid-1990s, there was no pastor, and only about twenty people were gathering for prayer and occasional Bible study.

In 1999, the current pastors, Pedro and Cecilia Nolasco, began what became a highly successful renewal of the church. They had been church planters in Mexico and had established many churches among the indigenous people in its mountainous regions. Upon their arrival, the Nolascos renamed the church Iglesia del Dios Victorioso, the Church of the Victorious God. Even though church membership was low, the Nolascos believed that God had already given victory to this church, which meant numeric and financial growth. By the time of my visit years later, the victory they claimed appears to have been granted. Over three hundred people gathered for worship each Sunday, with additional people attending the evening prayer meetings and Bible studies during the week.

The worship services at Iglesia del Dios Victorioso are very similar to those at Iglesia Cristiana del Padre in Virginia, but Iglesia del Dios Victorioso does everything on a much larger scale. The praise team includes more instruments and more singers. The musicians are still volunteer amateurs, but they are more talented than those at Iglesia Cristiana del Padre. The overall programs at Iglesia del Dios Victorioso are much better organized than the storefront operation of Iglesia Cristiana del Padre. There are male and female ushers both inside and outside the church. Helpful parking-lot attendants wear orange vests and wield flashlights at night. The leadership structure is also a lot more complicated. There are specific church leaders for each age group: a youth pastor (*pastor de jóvenes*), many children's ministers of both genders (*maestros/as de niños*), and young-adult leaders (*directores del ministerio de jóvenes*). In addition, this church has a comprehensive video-recording program. During every public meeting, a team of five young men dressed in matching navy-blue shirts and equipped with earpieces, walkie-talkies, and professional recording equipment are stationed at different spots of the sanctuary to record the service from different angles, including the reactions of the congregation. These recordings are then edited on-site and offered for sale on the church's website and at the church store.

A Place of Victory

Iglesia del Dios Victorioso meets in a former supermarket that was built in the 1960s. When the church took over and renovated the space, a large rectangular space was created in the center for worship, and the surrounding space was divided up for offices and classrooms. From the top, the space is a big rectangle inside a bigger rectangle. Church members did the renovations themselves to save money, and many corners were cut. When one walks in, there is a distinctive 1960s feel to the place. The color of the walls, the style of the building, and the minor details of the worship area all relay a classic 1960s style.

Pastor Nolasco's office is on the right side of the front door, and the church store is on the left. Directly in front of the main entrance is a narrow hallway leading into the worship area. A long hallway on the left leads to the bathrooms and six classrooms. The doors to these classrooms are always open, even when class is in session. The rooms in the back have been designated for storage with the exception of a large video-editing room, professionally stocked with state-of-the-art equipment.

The setup of the worship area is almost identical to that of Iglesia Cristiana del Padre, but Iglesia del Dios Victorioso has over 450 seats, evenly divided on each side of the center aisle. The chairs are lined up very tightly, which makes the space feel smaller than it actually is. It is difficult for two individuals to walk down the aisle without rubbing elbows. As in the case of Iglesia Cristiana del Padre, and as is common for most Pentecostal churches, the large space between the stage and the first row of seats is designated for prayer and healing. There is also an open space in the last row, where parents can park their strollers and young children can stretch their legs during the long services.

The stage at Iglesia del Dios Victorioso is also much larger than the one at Iglesia Cristiana del Padre. It is elevated about three feet off the ground, with stairs at the front and back. High up on the right side of the stage is a baptismal pool, measuring roughly four feet wide, eight feet long, and only about four feet deep. There is a set of stairs on the side to allow the pastor to walk in, and a set of stairs in the front where ushers help those receiving baptism to enter the pool.

At the center of the stage stands a plain glass pulpit, with some silk shrubs and flowers placed at the base. There is a drum set on the left side of the stage, set up behind a wall of Plexiglas to control the volume. There is also a keyboard in the back, as well as multiple microphones throughout the stage for the praise band. Audio speakers stand on the stage in various places, and there are speakers along the walls in the sanctuary. At the beginning and end of every meeting, two large screens are electronically lowered from the ceiling to display announcements. The screens also display compelling images and song lyrics when appropriate. (The screens are retracted when not in use.) All told, the microphones (both wire and wireless), the projectors, the video-recording equipment, and the editing room are all state of the art. Even the sound equipment was clearly fitted for the space by a professional. Iglesia del Dios Victorioso may have skipped out on a designer and an interior decorator for the space, but it clearly did not spare anything in terms of electronic equipment.

Seekers of Victory

Attendance at Iglesia del Dios Victorioso hovers around three hundred people. The maximum-occupancy sign in the back of the church states that 485 people can safely be in that space. Large families who arrive late usually have to sit separately. During the weekday meetings, about half the room is filled. Members of Iglesia del Dios Victorioso are not very different from the members of Iglesia Cristiana del Padre. Though Iglesia del Dios Victorioso has more members who have been in the United States for over ten years, there are also a significant number of people who recently arrived. The proportion of transient members is also comparable. About 10 percent of those who attend the church in Virginia are seasonal workers who came and left based on their work. The percentage was similar in California but for different types of work. There were a lot more farmworkers in Oceanside, California.

I met Diego, a day laborer, and his wife, Cristina. This young couple in their early twenties converted at Iglesia del Dios Victorioso and were married there. They had a two-year-old and were expecting a baby within months. They attend because, through this church, God gave them victory over their troubled relationship (they lived together before they were married; they credit being "right before God" by getting married as the reason for staying together), and they believe God will give them victory through life. There is Francisco, a former gang member who came to this country with hopes of financial prosperity through the dealing of drugs and weapons. He walked over the Mexico-California border with the plan to bring drugs from Mexico, sell them in the United States, and return with American guns to sell in Mexico. Now a new convert, he is part of the audio-video crew and pursues prosperity through his service in the church and his faith in God. And there is Daniela, a hardworking young woman who believes that God has prepared a perfect husband for her; she just needs to remain faithful for that man to materialize. There are also many traditional nuclear families who worship weekly at the church. Each person has a unique story, yet all are unified in their belief in the Prosperity Gospel formula to bring about their success. Together they learn and earnestly apply the principles of miraculous meritocracy.

Leading in Victory

The leaders at Iglesia del Dios Victorioso are also socioeconomically similar to their counterparts at Iglesia Cristiana del Padre. Though they are not as fluent in English as the leaders of Iglesia Cristiana del Padre, they can all communicate comfortably. While Pastor Gielis grew up in New York City, Pastor Nolasco grew up in Mexico. However, they both share a background of drug dealing and abuse. Nolasco's family was deeply involved in drug trafficking. By the time he was a teenager, he was a heavy user and managed part of the drug operation for his family. This continued into his marriage. One day, when he was twenty-eight years old, he went to a secret airstrip in northwestern Mexico, where he was to pick up a large shipment of drugs. It was on that day that he had a supernatural encounter that led to his conversion.

"I was standing around with my men. I had the money, and we could hear the plane coming," Pastor Nolasco recounted to me.

> Then all of the sudden, everything went dark. I couldn't see anything. I thought I lost my sight, but I realized that my eyes were open. It was just that everything was dark. I was so scared; I started to run to get away from the darkness. I ran so hard and so fast, until I couldn't run any more, and I fell down. I started to cry, cry like a little baby, because I thought I was going to die. I just fell on the floor and thought that this was death. I was so scared. And then I felt a hand on my shoulder, and He said, "My son, you are not dead. You will now begin to live."

Tears began to roll down Pastor Nolasco's cheeks as he continued.

> I turned, and it was the most beautiful and peaceful face I had ever seen. It was Jesus. He was smiling at me. I wanted to look away,

because I was a bad person. I had always been a bad person. I never prayed to him; my family never went to mass—nothing. I wanted to look away, but I couldn't. I just kept looking at Him. He was bright and smiling at me, and then he said, "The victory is yours." And the more I looked at him, the more everything started to be bright again. I realized that I was standing at the other end of the airstrip. My men were surrounding me, thinking something bad had happened to me, but I was happy. I had joy and peace. That day, I went home and told my father, "I'm done with this. I'm going to go serve the Lord." My father warned me that there would be people after me. They wouldn't let me leave. But I knew I had the victory. Jesus told me I would be victorious. So I took my wife, who was pregnant at the time, and I left. We went to the mountains to minister to the tribes there. I have been serving Him ever since. And Jesus was right; He has given me victory, every step of the way.

It was this encounter with Jesus that led Pastor Nolasco to learn more. He found the victory Jesus promised him in Prosperity Gospel teachings. Today, he preaches that victory everywhere he goes. During the time I spent at Iglesia del Dios Victorioso, I witnessed Pastor Nolasco declare victory over disease, poverty, immigration problems, custody battles, low self-esteem, and even demons that had taken over a woman's body. No matter what the problem was, the resolution was always victorious. Pastor Nolasco was victorious over everything. When asked about his practice of declaring victory, Pastor Nolasco joked that it was his trademark. But he said, "We can claim victory, we must claim victory, because Christ has already given us the victory. He gave me victory, and I have to use that anointing to help others be victorious."

But like all promises of prosperity, victory is not free. Victory is reserved only for those who have enough faith to live as if they have already been victorious. The main requirement of obtaining victory is believing that one already has it. The world of Prosperity Gospel Pentecostals is one in which they are constantly under assault and defeat is a constant threat. Attacks come from the spiritual world as well as from the real world. Their existence is filled with adversaries who can destroy their peace: landlords who can evict them, employers who can cheat them out of their wages, children who might rebel, spouses who are tempted to stray, police officers and immigration agents who might clamp down on them. There are natural and supernatural wars waging against them at all times, and as they live in the trenches, they need a God who can help them win these battles. The war they are engaged in is not one for conquest but for survival. This is the message they receive week after week, and it is the example that Pastor Nolasco lives out before them. No matter how far behind they fall, God will help them win in the end. In the face of serious challenges, believing what is not yet real truly does take faith. And it's a faith that members of Iglesia del Dios Victorioso are willing to display time and time again.

The confidence these church members have in God gives hope and motivation to all those who flock to Iglesia del Dios Victorioso. It motivates them to push forward and not give up. At the end of every meeting, whether it is a Bible study, prayer meeting, or worship service, the congregation is discharged with the words, *"En el nombre de Cristo, vallan bendecidos y"*—the congregation joins in with the pastor in unison—*"victoriosos!"* (In the name of Christ, may you go, blessed and victorious!).

Iglesia Pentecostal del Rey Divino in New York City

New York City is home to 8.4 million residents, almost 30 percent of which are of Latin American descent. New York is the city of immigrants: 40 percent of the city's white population, 45 percent of the black population, 59 percent of all Latinos, and 95 percent of all Asians are first- or second-generation immigrants. At one point, most Latinos in New York were of Puerto Rican descent, but that percentage has decreased in recent years. In 1990, almost half of all Latinos were of Puerto Rican descent. By 2015, most Latinos in New York City were of Dominican descent (28.7 percent), followed by Puerto Ricans (27.8 percent), Mexicans (14.9 percent), Ecuadorians (8.8 percent), and Colombians (4.0 percent), with immigrants from other Latin American countries numbering 15.8 percent.[20]

Iglesia Pentecostal del Rey Divino (Pentecostal Church of the Divine King) is located in New York's Lower East Side, though it did not begin there. Like Iglesia del Dios Victorioso, there is no clear history to the origin of the church. The only record available is the oral history transmitted by the pastor and some of the older members. The church was established during the rise of the Prosperity Gospel movement in the 1940s, not long after the post–World War II wave of Puerto Rican immigrants arrived in New York. Established as a Pentecostal church, it was affiliated with a small Latin American council of Pentecostal churches headquartered in the Bronx. These churches are concentrated in the New York–New Jersey area, with some scattered throughout the East Coast and a few in California. There is an abundance of

Spanish-speaking Pentecostal churches in New York City, and many of these are Prosperity Gospel. Iglesia Pentecostal del Rey Divino stands out because of the age of the church and its members.

The pastor claims that Iglesia Pentecostal del Rey Divino started with a small group of Puerto Rican Pentecostals. The church met in midtown, some say in the Fiftieth Street area, but church members lived in the Lower East Side. The expansion of the subway system made it easier for people to commute, and more people began to move into the area. By the early 1980s, the Lower East Side was largely populated by Puerto Ricans and African Americans, in addition to struggling artists and musicians who were attracted by the low rents. The area was notorious for its high levels of crime and drug activity, which culminated in the Tompkins Square Park riot of 1988. It was right around this time that the members of Iglesia Pentecostal del Rey Divino agreed to purchase an abandoned synagogue and turn it into their church. The Lower East Side had historically been a Jewish neighborhood, but as the neighborhood declined, most Jewish residents left, leaving cheap land and houses of worship for sale. The church thrived and grew in the 1980s, working with the community and helping immigrants from Puerto Rico establish themselves in what was then a very poor neighborhood. The church pioneered anti-crime initiatives and offered recovery programs to drug addicts. The office of Teen Challenge, a popular drug rehabilitation program led by Pentecostals, was housed in the church for over ten years. In those days, the church served as the hub for out-of-state groups who wanted to serve the poor and needy. There are other Spanish-speaking churches within a few blocks of Iglesia Pentecostal del Rey Divino, but only this one is Prosperity Gospel and only this one remains vibrant, even as the members are growing in age.

Beginning in the 1990s, gentrification began to creep into the Lower East Side, and property became a hot commodity. In 1999, the current pastor, Reverend David Ramirez, took charge. Unlike the pastors of Iglesia Cristiana del Padre and Iglesia del Dios Victorioso, Pastor Ramirez did not come from a background of drugs and violence. Instead, he is a descendent of a Pentecostal "royal family" in the Dominican Republic. His aunt was an early immigrant to the United States, and she later returned to the Dominican Republic as the first Pentecostal missionary to their village. This was a significant accomplishment for a woman of limited education. The Pentecostal churches in the village attribute their faith to the Ramirez family; today, the pastor's family is known as *the* Christian family of the area. Pastor Ramirez was groomed for church leadership from a young age.

In 1983, he joined the U.S. Army, earning his residency through his military service. He then brought his wife and children from the Dominican Republic to Washington Heights, where his relatives lived. He was always active in churches, serving as a chairperson of committees and as an officer in different capacities. He was asked to co-pastor a church in the Bronx for six years. After that, he was invited to pastor a small immigrant church in Colorado, where the majority of the members were undocumented Mexicans. In 1999, Iglesia Pentecostal del Rey Divino asked him to return to New York, this time as a pastor. Upon his arrival, Reverend Ramirez found only twenty-two members left. There was no leadership when he returned, and the remaining members were barely keeping the building habitable.

Pastor Ramirez has never had seminary training, but according to him, "he studies hard and reads many books." He also listens to a lot of sermons; his favorites are classic sermons of Kenneth Hagin and Oral Roberts. He is a licensed electrician, which was his full-time job when I met him and the reason why he was often late to weekday church gatherings. This job allowed him to own a nice home in Staten Island, and he made it a point to tell me that he did not take a salary from the church.

Glimpses of Past Glories

Iglesia Pentecostal del Rey Divino is located a few blocks off of Broadway and East Houston Street. Around the church, Latinx families sit out on the sidewalk, enjoying the cool evening air while their children run and play. There are also trendy restaurants with live music and lines out the door on weekends. It is common to walk past young people dressed to party and people collecting cans to exchange for cash. The cars along the street are equally as varied. Nice European luxury cars are parked between old minivans, with front and back bumper guards to protect the nice cars.

On any given day, the streets are equally diverse. Groups of well-dressed white people socializing, others with headphones blocking the noise of the city as they go on a jog, some walking their small purebred dogs. Peppered in this mix are Latinx bodegas and community parks with Puerto Rican flags either painted on the walls or hanging from makeshift poles. The neighborhood is diverse in every way—economically, racially, and socially—but the encroachment of gentrification is hard to miss. The difference between the haves and have-nots gets clearer every day.

A seven-foot-tall metal fence surrounds the church itself. Three gates—two on the side and one in the middle—are normally locked with thick chains. But on the days of church events, the one in the middle is open. It is plainly evident that the building was a synagogue at one time. The Star of David and pictures of a scroll are still inscribed in the architecture. The only indicators of a Christian presence are a three-by-six-foot wooden sign with the name of the church and the pastor's name hanging over the Star of David, and the image of a cross. Like the other churches, this church is Christian Zionist, which is why members made no effort to remove the symbols of the synagogue.

The inside of the church has been left almost intact. Immediately in front of the entryway is a small chapel with ten wooden pews on each side. The space could probably hold one hundred people, but there were never more than twenty for Bible study and prayer meetings. The windows that were once there have been bricked over for security reasons; drawing back the curtains reveals nothing but brick walls. Carlos Fernandez, an elderly member of the church, told me that it was done a "long time ago" because people kept breaking the glass. There are bathrooms on either side, both of them clean but original—from the 1980s or earlier. The main sanctuary is on the second-floor meeting space, with a large Star of David prominently displayed in the front. There are no crosses in this main worship space.

The building is literally falling apart. Yellow caution tape forbids visitors from going to the balcony. The ushers inform me that snow from the previous year caused water damage to the roof, which partially collapsed, breaking some of the seats in the balcony. The church had collected enough money from the insurance company to fix the roof and make it waterproof, but there was not enough to make the necessary repairs on the inside. There are ceiling tiles that are barely hanging on, but no one seems concerned about the danger.

The setup of the church is identical to the others, though the stage is more formal, with a built-in pulpit. There is a drum set at the right of the stage and two keyboards on the left. There are microphones set up in the front and two electric guitars, one on the stage and one on the floor. At the center of the stage is a large pulpit. A few pews were removed from the front rows to make room for the prayer and healing area.

Everything in this space evokes a sense of decay—the smell of moist cloth, the water stains on the walls, the very dated shaggy carpets on the stage. It is clear that this was once a thriving church, as glimpses of past glories are still visible. Hundreds of well-worn bibles are stacked at the end of every pew and in the back of the church. The old paint and timeworn decorations indicate that at one time, there had been a thriving congregation worshipping there.

Living the Golden Age of Faith

Iglesia Pentecostal del Rey Divino intrigued me because its members are significantly older than those at the other two churches. There was only one person under the age of thirty who was not related to the pastor: Monica, the sixteen-year-old daughter of Elizabeth and Jorge, two of the church leaders. Elizabeth is responsible for opening the church and preparing it for services. Her husband, Jorge, works as a mechanic in Brooklyn, where they live. They commute to the church because of the ministry of Pastor Ramirez. They sense the power of his anointing and believe that this is where God called them to serve.

Gloria is a seventy-one-year-old living in subsidized housing on Houston Street. She has lived in the area for almost fifty years and has been part of the church for the last twenty. She is representative of the larger church membership. They are older, many of them walk with canes, and most of them have difficulty getting up the stairs to the sanctuary. Pastor Ramirez later confirmed that about 70 percent of the church members are senior citizens who have been "left behind" in the area, as younger Latinos have moved away from Manhattan or have joined other churches. He guessed that the official membership was over fifty, but attendance never exceeded forty during the time that I was there.

Everyone in the church greets me warmly, and they are excited to hear about the purpose of my visit. Much like their worn building, there is a sense of tiredness that emanates from the congregation. Their worship is expressive but routine. This does not imply a decline in energy, as they are every bit as energetic as other Pentecostal churches. The senior citizens in this little church can match the younger cohorts in other Prosperity Gospel Pentecostal churches in the energy and volume of their worship services. But the sense of "newness," the excitement that church members from the other Pentecostal churches exhibited, is missing here. Perhaps matured and experienced Prosperity Gospel Pentecostals have no need to justify themselves before God. Most of the members of this church knew the routines of worship and performed them well. There was a communal understanding that did not require justification. There were no new Christians that had to be taught. There was a freedom in their worship because it was exclusively for them.

There is Fernandez, the seventy-five-year-old member who told me about the windows being bricked over. He attends the church alone because his wife is a Catholic. There is Rafael Martines, a sixty-eight-year-old former superintendent of a nearby apartment complex. Rafael is now retired, but he still works odd jobs. He is the first one they call for any repairs at the church. There is Mercedes, an overweight, seventy-one-year-old grandmother who sometimes cares for her four-year-old granddaughter. There is also Felix, a divorced man in his fifties who works in sales. Felix lives in the Bronx and is the leader of the men's group. And then there is the pastor's family, which makes up one-third of the congregation.

Pastor Ramirez's brother is at every gathering, supporting him. With no official responsibility or title in the church, he does everything—from moving furniture to leading worship. Pastor Ramirez's mother and aunt (the missionary who brought Pentecostalism to his village) are also always present; their age does not permit them to attend the evening activities. They sit in the front with Diana Ramirez, Pastor Ramirez's wife, who is actively involved in church life. Margarita is Pastor Ramirez's sister-in-law, who, along with her husband, Omar, cleans the church, teaches the adult Sunday school classes, and collects the offering. The pastor's son-in-law is one of the bandleaders, playing the keyboard at a near professional level. His nephews are all part of the band, playing the guitar and drums. They are joined by the singers: the pastor's two daughters, one married with a one-year-old and the other one in college, and three of his nieces. Of the three churches, Iglesia Pentecostal del Rey Divino was the most formal. When the church members talked about their pastor, they always referred to him by his title and his last name: "Pastor Ramirez." In the other churches, members would call the pastor by his title and his first name or even just his first name alone.

Prosperity for the Mature

Prosperity in this church is different from the prosperity and victory of the other two churches. Most of the members are legal residents or citizens who live routine lives, speak English, and have no need for nice cars or bigger homes. For these ailing seniors, physical healing is not something that is preached or talked about frequently. During their testimony times, they do not testify about physical healing. Emotional or psychological healing are the main rewards these Christians seek. Sometimes they bring a piece of clothing belonging to a child or a grandchild, asking for a special anointing so that its owner receives a blessing when the item is worn. The many members who struggle to walk in, leaning on their canes, never ask for a miracle in their bodies. Pastor Ramirez was surprised that I asked about healing miracles. "They are very healthy for their age," he told me. According to the pastor, personal physical healing had *never* been requested during the times of prayer and healing. This is not, however, for lack of belief in the power of God to heal. Many of them told me about miraculous healing services they witnessed. Some of them attended healings conducted by Katherine Kuhlman, a prominent faith healer from the mid-twentieth century. In my conversations with church members, none of them ever stopped believing in healing. But at this stage of their lives, prosperity is mostly mental. It's the ability to stay optimistic as they watch their neighborhood, family, and friends move on without them.

The offering collection is routine in this church. Little baskets are passed throughout the church as someone proclaims prosperity for all those who give sacrificially. But during the healing time and the sermons, it is assumed that the parishioners already made their sacrifice. Their sacrifice is showing up at church. It is volunteering at the soup kitchen that meets in the church basement. It is dusting the pews and sweeping the floors. In this church, financial giving is not as important as the giving of one's time. In return, they don't ask for physical healing or large sums of cash. The good news they want to hear is that God has not forgot them.

God Knows We Are Here

At Iglesia Pentecostal del Rey Divino, "La Niña de Tus Ojos" (The daughter of your eyes) is a song that is sung repeatedly. It is a song by Daniel Calveti, a Puerto Rican singer. The lyrics describe a young girl who is forgotten by everyone but remembered by God. This is the church's anthem. It is sung almost every other week, and tears flow down wrinkled cheeks every time. It is a moving sight to see a group of seniors singing passionately. A group of immigrants whose home country is only a memory but whose new home has been transformed to the point that they no longer feel that they belong. Each day they see their neighborhood transform a bit more into something foreign. The song reminds the congregation that God gave them their name and loves them: "You saw me, when no one saw me. You loved me, when no one loved me." This song captures the reason why these Christians continue to come to this dilapidated building every week, bringing their gifts, material and otherwise, in the hope that God, and the world around them, will not forget them.

During prayer time, members of Iglesia Pentecostal del Rey Divino ask for psychological healing from such struggles as depression, fear, stress, and loneliness. They plead for family members who are in need of freedom and victory in their lives. As they are "filled with the Spirit," they claim victory over psychological challenges. What is most desired is exactly what the lyrics of their beloved song describe: being noticed, being special in the eyes of a powerful God. It is this social and psychological need that these members come to church to satisfy. And Prosperity Gospel Pentecostalism gives them the tools though which they can get the attention of God Himself.

That is why the relentless optimism of Prosperity Gospel Pentecostalism is alive and well at Iglesia Pentecostal del Rey Divino. No matter how invisible they become to their surroundings, all the members believe that God sees them. As gentrification erases their old neighborhood and threatens to erase them, Prosperity Gospel helps claim their place. They can make themselves visible in this world because they are visible to God. They never give up their faith because they know that what they want is what God wants. They simply have to stay the course to receive their blessing. This is not the only church in which parishioners do not ask for more money from God. No one in any of the churches ever asks for "more money"; they don't believe that anyone deserves "free money" from God. Miraculous meritocracy has no room for free money. One must work for everything, even the things that already belong to them. Instead of asking for more money, they ask for the ability to do the necessary work or make the necessary sacrifices to claim their victory and prosperity.

The Renewing of Their Minds

These three churches are a small sampling of the spiritual homes that Latin American immigrants have created across the United States. These immigrants have come to the agreement that Prosperity Gospel Pentecostalism provides the best framework to understand their lives. Sociologist Peter Berger famously claimed that "religion is the audacious attempt to conceive of the entire universe as being humanly significant."[21] Prosperity Gospel flourishes around the world because it has gone a step further and has made the entire universe personally significant. From weather patterns to potential legislation changes, the worldview of these believers teaches them that everything happens because God is working for their good as a result of their faithfulness. Theirs is a God who moves the world to cater to the faithful, and that belief has changed the way they view themselves. Churches have always been the central institution where these ideas are taught. These churches provide these immigrants with a social structure that simultaneously affirms their longings and provides them a framework by which to make sense of their reality. At the core of every religion is the desire to shape beliefs and behaviors for a greater purpose, and this is exactly what is happening at these three churches. The message that is persistently emphasized is that God wants prosperity and victory for the faithful. This idea is not only believed in the heart and minds but is lived outside the church. Beliefs have real-life consequences. The consequences of Prosperity Gospel Pentecostalism are the socialization of immigrants into entitled, hardworking, and moral individuals. Prosperity Gospel Pentecostalism empowers them to attempt what was once unimaginable. It comforts them when they are hopeless, and it leads them to take risks that they otherwise might have avoided. The most radical teaching these churches unintentionally passed on to their immigrant congregants is that contradictory thoughts can be held in harmony. In these churches, they can pray for heaven yet focus on earth. They can be victorious while facing real-life failures. They can live in America without considering themselves Americans. In these communities of dreamers, they are encouraged to dream for more than they can imagine, because when everyone is chasing the impossible, the unattainable seems within reach.

CHAPTER TWO

The Prescription for the Dream

Get Ready for the Harvest!

Pastor Gielis had built up this Sunday for months, preaching and teaching on the secrets of *la gran cosecha* (the great harvest) since the summer. He hinted at the tragic misinterpretation of the Bible that had led to poverty and defeat for many. But all that needless suffering was to end soon. Upon the revelation of his secret discovery, all who obeyed would experience true prosperity. On the first Sunday of October, Pastor Gielis promised to finally disclose the great secret.

The church was unusually full that Sunday. By the time he began preaching, there were no available seats in the main area. The ushers and some of the regular church members were standing in the back, having given up their chairs to visitors and long-absent members who had come back for this special occasion.

After an unusually long period of singing, Pastor Gielis slowly walked up to the podium. The room sat in silence, awaiting his words. He opened his Bible and came down from the pulpit to address his listeners more intimately. Looking pensively at the congregation he began to speak, but with a sense of hesitation in his voice. Missing his usual charismatic enthusiasm, he started his sermon like a doctor bringing bad news to the family of a patient.

"God has a rhythm," he said, as he drew a circle in the air with his index finger. "God has his own time. There is a biblical calendar and a worldly calendar. And unless you know the cycle of God's calendar, you will never prosper." He paused and looked out dramatically over the congregation. In total silence, he walked back to the pulpit. Pastor Gielis went on to explain that believers needed to adhere to God's timing or they would be out of sync with God and miss out on their blessings. The promises of God would pass them by if they were unsynchronized to God's seasons. He warned them, "You can be in the church for thirty years, you can be faithful and sowing seeds for thirty years, but if you don't know God's timing and God's seasons, you will never have a harvest. You need to know when God does things. You need to know God's calendar. That's the reason for all the poverty and sickness in this world."

The silence in the room was riveting. Parishioners' faces reflected a genuine concern, as if they had received a grave diagnosis. According to Pastor Gielis, the mistake responsible for their suffering hinged on the misalignment of two calendars, one human and one divine. The human calendar goes from January to December, but the secret, supernatural calendar goes from October to September. The tragic mistake—and big secret—is that humans have trusted in the wrong calendar to dictate their lives. The remedy is to reclaim the knowledge of the divine yearly cycles and to "work with God in His timing."

Pastor Gielis explained that the two most important months for God are October and April. According to his research, the Jewish people celebrated three major feasts during those months. The secret, then, to obtaining a life of prosperity and victory is in the ability to maximize growth during those two months—especially April, because it is the month when God liberates. In April, Christians celebrate the day Jesus resurrected from the dead and set them free from hell. In April, Jewish people celebrate Passover, the liberation from slavery in Egypt. According to his theory, the resurrection of Jesus Christ took place in April. Therefore, those seeking new life, financial freedom, or relief from disease *must* capitalize on the month of April because it is the month that God is most likely to set them free. April, he shouted to the congregation—"¡Es el mes de la cosecha!" (It is the month of the harvest!)

Many in the congregation stopped taking their copious notes in order to stand up to cheer and clap. They celebrated as if they had already been granted a precious gift in being entrusted with this secret. They were as happy as if they had already received the harvest. But in Prosperity Gospel, knowledge is never enough. There is always a system that one must work through to receive a blessing.

Pastor Gielis calmed the crowd as he stood behind the podium. He explained that October is God's month for new beginnings. It is in this month when Jewish people traditionally celebrate Rosh Hashanah (the New Year) and Yom Kippur (the Day of Atonement).[1] Therefore, October is the month God has anointed for getting rid of the old and starting anew. But Pastor Gielis proclaimed a new and surprising revelation to verify God's timing:

> This was the month that Christ was born! Did you know that? Jesus Christ was not born in December; he was born in October. Nobody knows the exact date, but we know that it was October, because Christians in the beginning celebrated the birth of Jesus along with the Jewish New Year. God entered the world in October, the Jewish

New Year, because He was doing a new thing. It was Emperor Constantine who changed Christmas to December 25 in the year 325, because he knew that if Christians continued to celebrate Christmas correctly, the children of God would prosper and be too powerful. Constantine could not allow that, so he changed Christmas. And to this day, there are so many failures, so much sickness and poverty, because Christians kept living that lie.

At this point, many in the congregation began shaking their heads in disbelief. They had just learned for the first time that Constantine the Great, the first Roman emperor to convert to Christianity, had shifted the celebration of the birth of Jesus from October to December in a calculated move to retain power. The congregation rarely challenges these types of government conspiracies because they come from countries where governments tend to do such things. Yet this was quite a claim. Constantine had somehow gained knowledge of this divine way of creating wealth and devised a plan to keep this knowledge from the masses. The congregation was engrossed. They had been victims of a grand conspiracy to rob them of their inheritance. Here was yet another explanation for the suffering they had experienced, but they were being offered a potentially new cure. Pastor Gielis continued listing "new things" God did in the month of October. Jesus was baptized in October. Jesus began his public ministry in that month. Many of the greatest miracles in the Bible were performed then.

All these assertions he stated as truth. He offered no sources, and the congregation demanded none. The pastor's authority was enough. Pastor Gielis had the congregation convinced that October was a magical month for prosperity and new births. But in Prosperity Gospel Pentecostalism, blessings are never free. The Jewish people not only commemorated these holy days with celebrations but also honored God on these days by bringing gifts and offerings. As an example, Pastor Gielis pointed to the biblical account of the Day of Atonement, when the Jewish high priest would take the offering of the people and bring it before God. If the offering was accepted, there would be great celebration, since it meant that their sins had been forgiven and they had earned another year of God's favor. The people's main responsibility during these holy times is to bring their offerings to God. The key lesson was that bringing offerings to God at the appointed time always results in blessings. Here, Pastor Gielis is able to simultaneously reinforce the Prosperity Gospel formula and rationalize its failure. For everyone in the congregation who were faithfully giving their offerings without receiving any blessings, the timing of their offering explained their lack of prosperity. They were supposed to bring their best and most symbolically important gifts to God in the month of October in order to activate yearlong prosperity.

Like a lawyer presenting his final argument before the jury, Pastor Gielis came down from the stage again and walked closer to the people, asking them, "Why do you think Jewish people are so few but they are so rich? Why do you think that Israel is one of the smallest nations in the world but they are one of the most powerful ones?" In Prosperity Gospel, wealth and power are always signs of God's favor. This rationale indicated that Jewish people prospered throughout history because they knew of God's timing. They were not fooled by Constantine's December Christmas scheme because, as Pastor Gielis reminded the congregation, Jews do not believe in Jesus and do not celebrate his birth. So they continued to practice as God had instructed them in the Hebrew scriptures. This cycle is embedded in God's will, so that even those who do not believe in Jesus can benefit from it. It is much like the warmth of the sun or the cool of the breeze. God sets it in motion for anyone who is at the right place at the right time. Like the laws of physics, these principles hold up, regardless of personal beliefs. And the results are guaranteed, with scientific accuracy. That is the power of God's secret calendar and the Prosperity Gospel formula.

Pastor Gielis stood still and silent; he looked down at his Bible. The congregation waited eagerly for his next move. Moments passed in suspenseful silence. Finally, as he lifted his head to look at the congregation, he spoke softly and with great emotion into the microphone: "My brothers, your health, your prosperity, your success, it's not a coincidence. We control it by joining in on God's seasonal cycles."

Pastor Gielis walked even closer toward the congregation, shaking his head as if thinking them unconvinced by the secret knowledge he told them. He reminded them to look at the natural world to understand God's order. He pointed to the changing foliage as a sign of God's calendar. Fall is the time for harvest and for gathering. Spiritually, harvest is a time to gather everything that God has given—specifically, material things. Since modern people no longer grow crops, they must gather their finances and decide how much to give to God. That is the seed they must plant. Pastor Gielis used the analogy of lawn preparation to explain why his congregation had to bring an offering on this very day. In order for people to have green lawns in the spring, they have to aerate, fertilize, and seed their laws in the fall. He called out some of the landscapers in the congregation to concur with him. Prosperity, health, and success were available to anyone who planned carefully and followed the formula meticulously. God designed this method for prosperity from the time of creation, and it is exhibited in nature. The conclusion is for the people to sow seeds now in order to have a harvest in the spring.

Looking intently out to the congregation, Pastor Gielis pleaded with them, "It is in your control. It is up to you. It all depends on you, not on God. Whatever happens to us happens because of *us*. Whether we fail or succeed, whether we are prosperous or poor, it's all up to us, not up to God." Whereas Max Weber's Protestants believed that God predestined everything that happened to them, no such view existed in Prosperity Gospel Pentecostalism.[2] There is no mystery behind the evil that befalls people in Prosperity Gospel Pentecostalism. Its teachings make it very clear that God only desires goodness and flourishing for his people. He desires it so much that he created a world order where individuals are bound to prosper if they only follow the plan. Any poverty or suffering came as a result of not living under God's will; poverty and suffering correlate with sin.

The pastor went on to describe how believers can take control of their lives and end their suffering by making a covenant with God. He explained that in the Hebrew Bible, there is a long list of individuals who made covenants with God. He cited Noah, Abraham, Isaac, Jacob, David, and Solomon. All these men made a covenant with God by bringing sacrifices to an altar. Pastor Gielis assured his eager listeners that bringing sacrifices to God on that day would be a step of faith toward their newfound mystical knowledge of God's calendar. They too could make a covenant with God and ensure their destiny. But this covenant was time sensitive. It was an offer they had to seize on at that very moment. "There will be a double portion of favor upon you in the next six months, culminating in a miraculous harvest next April. That great harvest in April will build up to an even greater harvest at the end of God's year, next October."

Pastor Gielis shook his head again in frustration, as if the congregation were still not convinced by his message. After composing himself, he took a deep breath and spoke calmly, pleading,

> Brothers, I want you to have this. I want you to prosper. I tell you from personal experience. About four or five years ago, I was at a conference, and I had no money on me. Nothing. The preacher had a beautiful message, and it was very powerful. I remember it was extremely powerful. And as he finished, he called for an offering, and I had nothing to give. I was sitting there with the most powerful people in the faith, they were all bringing their offerings, getting in on the

> blessing, and there I was, sitting at the right hand of Morris Cerullo, and I had nothing to give. I had four or five dollars in my pocket, but that was for food. But the Spirit was moving very powerfully, so I had to give. I gave everything except $1.50. I needed that for a Diet Coke. Because there were three days left to the conference, and I was not going to have any money, I wanted to buy a Diet Coke to get me through those days of fasting. I went and I gave everything I had. And on that day, I learned that when a man of God filled with the Holy Spirit calls for an offering, you better not hold back because something will happen. God still shows me to this day. He reminds me, "Remember what I did with those few dollars? How much I blessed you because of those few dollars? I could have done much more if you had offered more. I can do much more for you." I will never forget that. I will never miss another chance to prosper. When a man of God calls for an offering, pay attention. I am telling you now that today's offering to God will make something miraculous happen in April. I know if God can do it for me, he will do it for you.

At this point, an hour and a half had passed since Pastor Gielis had started preaching, and every person in the room was captivated by the message. He signaled for the musicians to play some background music, and the ushers passed out offering envelopes. He commanded the congregation to ask God how much they should give. He assured them that no one would know the amount that they gave. This was a personal covenant between them and God, and no one would judge them based on how much they brought forward. Pastor Gielis encouraged them to use the white envelopes the ushers handed out. Yet he reminded them again and again that the sacrifice they brought would determine the next six months of their lives. "These are the seeds you are sowing for your harvest next year," he reminded them. "How big do you want your harvest to be?"

The rustling of bodies and the creaking of chairs immediately filled the church. People throughout the congregation looked through purses and pulled out wallets as they prepared their offerings. Some ran to the grocery store across the street to get cash from the ATM. As background music played, Pastor Gielis asked for those who had their offerings ready to stand up. When he noticed that some people were still sitting, he quickly said, "Who doesn't have money to bring for their offering? Do not be ashamed. Who doesn't have money for this offering? Put your hand up." One young man raised his hand, and Pastor Gielis quickly walked over to him and gave him a $20 bill out of his own pocket, which the man put into his offering envelope. With a roll of his own cash still in his hand, the pastor asked around to see who else needed money. No one else took his offer. Once most of the people were standing, he called for everyone with an offering to come and stand in the prayer area in front of the stage. "I want everyone to raise your offerings to the air," Pastor Gielis said. "You hold your offerings, and you lift it up. This is *your* covenant with God. Close your eyes and repeat after me: 'Here is my offering, Lord! Abundance will be mine in six months! Six months, Lord. I will have my prosperity. In six months, I will live the abundant life! I make this covenant with you now, Father!'"

Everyone stood tightly together with their envelopes lifted high. Almost every eye was closed, and most were streaming with tears. Some people were murmuring prayers; others were shouting this claim at the top of their lungs. As the music got louder, Pastor Gielis began to speak in tongues. Bodies began to fall back, as they were unable to control the power of the Spirit. In this way, humble immigrants stood before God to claim their prosperous and abundant life. In their minds, they had punched their ticket to their American dream.

Formula for the Abundant Life

That sermon encapsulates all the elements that make Prosperity Gospel Pentecostalism attractive to its followers: the impartation of secret knowledge for prosperity, a conspiracy by an evil emperor centuries ago that explains their suffering today, a personal testimony from their charismatic leader, and a self-empowerment message that allows them to take concrete action to remediate the errors of their ways. In just one service, immigrants are provided with both an explanation of their current predicament and a way out of it. This is part of the reason why Prosperity Gospel has spread around the world. It provides a simple explanation for people's suffering and offers an immediate solution.

Prosperity Gospel Pentecostalism does not teach that money grows on trees, but it does teach how to grow those trees. The way to reach the abundant life is to apply a very precise formula. The basic blueprint for prosperity and abundance in Prosperity Gospel Pentecostalism is simple:

Faith + Action = Blessings

In other words, God will reward anyone who has faith *and* takes action based on that faith. A version of this formula is universally present in most religious systems. Worshippers believe that a higher power can do things for them (faith), but they must do something (action) to gain their deity's favor. This can be anything from excessive dancing to sacrifices to less obvious actions, like internal pursuits of holiness; whatever the particulars, believers all over the world labor to please their deities to obtain miracles.

The core belief of Prosperity Gospel Pentecostalism is similar to that of other religions. Followers believe that their God can give them what they want, and if they can get His attention through a sacrificial monetary offering or some other act of faith, He will bless them. The premise is that God is all powerful and is moved to exercise this power by a believer's actions.

Though the formula for prosperity is simple, the nuanced definition of each variable in the formula is highly complicated. It is in the definitions of the steps of this formula that the paradox of Prosperity Gospel is able to thrive. The variables *faith* and *action* are subjectively defined and are sometimes contradictory, as is the result: *blessings*.

Faith

Faith in Prosperity Gospel Pentecostalism is not defined by Christian theology but by psychology. The emergence of modern psychology in the twentieth century transformed the ways in which we understand human behavior and highlighted the power of the human mind. Sigmund Freud introduced the idea that people could be captive to repressed memories that were detrimental to their well-being. Personal failures of every type were traced back to past experiences that kept individuals under a state of psychosis.[3] The treatment for these deleterious effects was psychotherapy, which included counseling sessions with professionals who would help individuals make sense of their past in order to increase their sense of well-being. Psychotherapy would help set individuals free to achieve what was otherwise impossible under previous psychological distress. Freud's ideas were revolutionary. In generations past, religious institutions held the power to explain human challenges. Many of the disorders that modern psychology sought to treat were diagnosed as demon possessions or other forms of spiritual maladies. Anxiety and depression were the result of a lack of faith. As the Western world entered the modern age and religious explanations of physical disorders gave way to scientific ones, Freud rose to fill the gap. He legitimized the idea that invisible mental forces have power over human behavior. According to Freud, these forces exist in the human mind and could be channeled for the good of the person if only the person had the awareness to do so.

Religious groups joined the therapeutic movement soon after its birth by offering spiritualized versions of psychotherapy and self-actualization.[4] But Christians did not adopt these ideas from psychology alone. Religious groups in American had started advocating for the power of the mind to overcome sickness in the nineteenth century. Phineas Quimby (1802–1866) was a spiritual healer from New England who believed that the source of all diseases was the mind. Quimby's teachings became known as New Thought metaphysics. This movement consisted of both religious and nonreligious groups who shared the belief that the mind could generate practical effects in real life—even in matters like illness or getting a job. It promoted the idea that individuals—through their thoughts—had power over their destinies. One of Quimby's patients, Mary Baker Eddy, went on to found the Christian Science movement. The most significant clergy to bring these ideas to the mainstream was New England pastor E. W. Kenyon. Kenyon attended the Emerson School of Oratory at a time when most faculties were proponents of the New Thought movement. He was deeply influenced and shaped by that experience and, by the late nineteenth century, began preaching on the power of the human mind to accomplish all things. Kenyon taught the practice of positive confession, by which believers could speak things into reality.[5] Kenneth Hagin, one of the founders of the Word of Faith movement, was known to have preached Kenyon's sermons verbatim.[6] (This controversy is known as "the Kenyon connection.")[7] By the 1950s, clergymen like Norman Vincent Peale popularized positive thinking for the masses. Peale preached that with a reprogrammed mind, an individual could accomplish anything. Peale brought New Thought metaphysics to mainstream culture and validated it for American Christianity. In the 1960s, Peale was praised by evangelist Billy Graham as one of the most influential Christian leaders in America. He gained renewed fame in 2016, after President Donald Trump cited Peale as his most influential spiritual leader. But Trump was not the first president Peale had influenced. He was also named as a source of inspiration and influence by presidents Richard Nixon, Gerald Ford, Jimmy Carter, Ronald Reagan, and George H. W. Bush.[8] When Peale passed away in 1993, he was eulogized by President Bill Clinton as "an optimist who believed that, whatever the antagonisms and complexities of modern life brought us, anyone could prevail by approaching life with a simple sense of faith."[9] The faith president Clinton alludes to is positive thinking, which is the basis of Prosperity Gospel Pentecostals' definition of faith.

Kenneth Hagin and Oral Roberts—early champions of Prosperity Gospel Pentecostalism—gained fame popularizing positive thinking and taking it to new extremes. Their brand of Christianity began redefining faith as positive thinking (though they did not use that term), and they empowered followers to believe that they were in charge of their own destinies. They emphasized faith in *what God can do for them* instead of faith in *God*. Prosperity Gospel Pentecostalism is an instrumental faith. Whereas traditional Christian faith commands unquestioning obedience and loyalty for the sake of God, faith for Prosperity Gospel Pentecostalism is an instrument by which one gains favors. The more strongly one believes that God will grant blessings, the more likely those blessings will be granted. Believers would be encouraged to wake up in the morning with an expectation that God would perform a miracle in their life that day. Televangelist Joel Osteen teaches his followers to get up every morning and proclaim positive words over their lives. Although traditional definitions of faith are sometimes mentioned, Prosperity Gospel emphasizes a definition of faith that has not always been part of Christianity.

It is through this definition of faith that Prosperity Gospel Pentecostals are ushered into a reassuring sense of entitlement. Faith means always thinking positively and always believing that things will work in their favor. They do not only wish for new cars and larger homes; they *expect* them. I call this practice *relentless optimism*. No matter how pessimistic their situation, they are convinced, and must often convince themselves, that things are looking up. Yet their optimism is neither artificial nor forced. As people experience conversion and are socialized into the "logic" of Prosperity Gospel Pentecostalism, they truly become happier and more at peace with their life because of the confidence they have that things will work out as long as they follow the right formula. They are no longer helpless at what fate throws at them; rather, they are active participants in their destiny. This is the source of their optimism.

When I interviewed Feliciano, a young man working at a Thai restaurant and a member of Iglesia Cristiana del Padre, I asked, "How do you know you are blessed?" Without hesitation, he said, "I just have to look out my window. I have three cars out there, all for me. And I didn't have to pay for any of them." There were truly three cars outside. One had been given to him by his boss, but the transmission was broken and it was useless without thousands of dollars in repairs. The second vehicle was his roommate's thirty-year-old car, which was too unreliable to use on a daily basis and had failed to pass inspection five years ago. A church member who was on vacation and would be returning soon had loaned him the third car. In reality, Feliciano had no working car of his own and no prospects for acquiring one. Yet in his mind, he had been blessed with three cars. He was relentlessly optimistic, even in the face of a pessimistic situation. Through his faith, Feliciano was always able to put a positive spin on his situation.

For Gerardo of Iglesia Cristiana del Padre, a twenty-seven-year-old single man who has been living in the United States for ten years, "faith" meant believing that he should start his own landscaping company. His faith was strong, his confidence in the success of his new venture unshakable. With a winning attitude, he maxed out his credit cards in order to buy the proper equipment. He also borrowed $5,000 from two church members who eagerly gave it as an investment, equally confident that they would reap a return for loaning Gerardo the money, both financially and spiritually. His faith was not enough to bring prosperity, however, and Gerardo's company went bankrupt the following winter.

After Gerardo defaulted on his loans and was forced to sell everything he had purchased for his business, he moved from the three-bedroom home he had purchased in the suburbs during the housing bubble (when subprime lending made it possible for an undocumented day worker to purchase a home) to a roach-infested one-bedroom apartment with five other men in the city. He slept on the living-room floor with an old blanket. He became a day laborer, working any job he could find. One might think that he would be discouraged and depressed under such conditions. At the very least, one might assume that he would lose faith in Prosperity Gospel Pentecostalism.

Gerardo, however, is still active at a Prosperity Gospel Pentecostal church. It is a different church from the one I first met him in because of his broken relationships with the members of Iglesia Cristiana del Padre who had loaned him the money to start his landscaping business. (The investors were upset at Gerardo for failing at his landscaping business, though when I spoke to one of them, he confessed a sense of shame at his own failed investment. In his eyes, it was partly his own unfaithfulness that caused God to withhold financial prosperity.) Even after his failed business, Gerardo was still applying the Prosperity Gospel formula for the prosperity he still believes is God's will for him. Most surprisingly, he still believes that he is living an abundant life. In his mind, he has not been defeated; in fact, he believes he is better off than before because he had learned a lesson and could now better apply the Prosperity Gospel formula for the future. Gerardo is actively trying to convert his roommates. He insists that if they become Christians, they could all get rich and move out of that apartment. During one of our meeting in his apartment, he asked me to testify before his roommates that he had once been "blessed" and had been the owner and operator of a large landscaping company.

"Tell them," he told me. "Tell them how God had blessed me before. I had my own company, a house. I had so much work I had to hire other people. God is good. When you are faithful and follow his will, God blesses you."

To him, his failed business venture was not a failure of the Prosperity Gospel formula because the formula *cannot fail*. Gerardo, along with other Prosperity Gospel Pentecostals, is relentlessly optimistic because his God always gives victory over challenges, and defeat is never a possibility. This optimism is fueled by the fear underlying the paradox of Prosperity Gospel. The formula cannot fail because future blessings are only around the corner. To suggest otherwise is to demonstrate a lack of faith, and lack of faith is a one-way ticket out of God's will. A negative thought, as doubt is often framed, could derail everything they had done to earn their blessing.

Action

The action that is supposed to follow this faith (positive thinking) is even more important; it is the key that unlocks everything. It is more important because it is the proof, to God and to others, that their faith is real. In the Prosperity Gospel formula, action can simultaneously be defined as doing something and doing nothing. Action can include tithing, going to and being active in church, displaying emotions excessively, speaking in tongues, bringing new people to the church, and taking risks in life in order for God to "have an opportunity to work." A financial sacrifice is only one of many ways they can take action. Action can also come in the form of patience. The most extreme example of inaction as action is the cancer patient who will faithfully wait for God's healing and not seek medical treatment. I encountered no such case in my research, but in order to manifest positive thinking, sometimes a believer must do something grand, and sometimes a believer must do nothing at all.

Ana, a single mother from Iglesia del Dios Victorioso, once asked for healing for a lazy eye and was told by Pastor Nolasco to wait and go on living as usual because her patience was a demonstration of faith. Her act of faith was to not worry about her lazy eye and believe that God's healing was coming because the Lord had already fixed it. Pastor Nolasco often talked about the time it took for seeds to grow and bear fruit. He reminded his parishioners that once the seeds were planted and watered, they had to wait. This is what people like Ana and others had to faithfully do. The act of faithful waiting plays a decisive role in whether a believer receives his or her healing. If Ana were overly concerned about her lazy eye (which was still in the same condition years after I saw her) and kept asking for healing during the prayer time, her repeated request for a miraculous healing would be interpreted as a sign of her unfaithfulness, evidence that she failed to believe the healing took place the first time Pastor Nolasco prayed for her, thereby derailing the healing. She had to do nothing. However, inaction is hard to rationalize as action, and many Prosperity Gospel Pentecostals become understandably restless. I found few believers who truly waited patiently for their result. In the case of Ana, when a guest preacher and healer came to her church, she went up and asked for the alignment of her lazy eye. This is a case where believers do not take the pastors' words indiscriminately. They make sense of them and do what is necessary. Instead of waiting for their bad fortunes to miraculously turn, they take action. In Ana's case, she was taking every opportunity to find healing. It's hard to wait patiently when you think hope is in reach.

Most of the time, the action that is required is not waiting but taking actual steps with real-life consequences, since those actions are often financial in nature. It is this requirement to take action in the Prosperity Gospel formula that has garnered the most criticism. Those outside the faith view this practice as a scam that fleeces the poor and the gullible. If the Prosperity Gospel movement were a set of internalized spiritual behaviors, it would probably draw little public attention. But its doctrines require believers to act—and, more specifically, to give money. This is the image that most people have of Prosperity Gospel churches because televangelists emphasize the giving of money as the act of faith, demanding that viewers send financial donations in order to receive blessings. Though Prosperity Gospel Pentecostalism is more nuanced than a religious pyramid scheme, it is true that the action step is the most costly to religious believers. This is what sets Prosperity Gospel apart from the positive thinking movement epitomized by Norman Vincent Peale and others. Prosperity Gospel Pentecostals must give to get. Positive thinking alone is not enough.

The action they must take is controversial because true religious action in this formula is never about doing the bare minimum. Actions that get the attention of God are always impressive and dramatic. When one brings an offering, it has to be a *sacrificial* offering. Prosperity Gospel preachers have been accused of using this action to swindle the poor by insisting that they give more money to the church than they can afford. While this might be true of televangelists, it doesn't happen in these immigrant churches, where clergy and laypeople share life intimately. None of the parishioners I encountered suffered financially because they had donated too much to the church.

They did not give to the church to the point of hurting themselves or their families, regardless of what the pastors said about sacrificial giving. After all, only the individual could decide what was considered sacrificial to them. The acts of faith most often performed are those that benefit the individual. Whenever they did make financially risky acts of faith, it was an investment in their own ambitions. That is, they were a lot more likely to buy houses or cars that they could not afford than to give large sums of money to the preacher. For Gerardo, action meant risking everything he had to start his landscaping company. For the church members who loaned him the money, action meant loaning Gerardo the $5,000 to support his act of faith. Hence, all parties involved in the failed company were acting on faith: they were investing with an expectation of personal gain. In practice, actions almost always benefit the actor, not someone else and certainly not the preacher. At the core, Prosperity Gospel Pentecostalism is inherently individualistic.

To outsiders, these acts of faith might seem like spinning a roulette wheel—especially the relentless optimism and the hope that blessings are "just around the corner." But to Prosperity Gospel Pentecostals, it is not a gamble at all—it is empowerment. There is no indication of chance or uncertainty in the results of their actions (that would be a sign of unfaithfulness, a negative thought, which would sabotage the formula). They do not give money to the church or take business risks in the hopes that their number will come up and they can cash in big. They do not—or at least they are not supposed to—leave it up to chance. Instead, they offer their investments fully confident (through positive thinking) that their desired results will come to pass because God is faithful. This is not unlike the hope (and the problem) of chasing after a dream. Whether they are aspiring movie stars or entrepreneurs starting a new business, they invest fully of themselves, believing that they will succeed no matter the odds. One simply has to try, keep trying, and wait. When other paths to the American dream are blocked, Prosperity Gospel Pentecostalism offers these immigrants an alternative road. They are empowered to take control of their own destiny, and they gain a sense of much-needed dignity from the thought that they are actively participating in their own self-development. For a community that is marginalized and powerless, this form of self-control is transformative. Their faith offers them much-needed confidence and certainty in an otherwise uncertain world.

Prosperity Gospel Pentecostalism is a practical faith. The doctrines and practices are sensible and designed for daily use. Even the most difficult parts of this faith can be adapted for simple use. As such, the sacrificial acts followers are required to perform to get God's attention are sometimes too much to attempt all at once. These actions can be taken in installments. Their God may not grant free miracles, but He accepts layaway. When believers cannot take large risks, they can take several small ones over time. Their actions are cumulative, and in time, God will notice and answer their prayers accordingly. This also means that every offering and every small action is a tremendous act because each one builds on the previous one, and no one ever knows what will activate God's blessings. That's why offering time is always significant. No matter how much money they bring, that amount could be the one that makes all the difference.

For Prosperity Gospel Pentecostals, abundant living is a sign of spiritual achievement and an entitlement to the faithful, but it is never a free gift. Prosperity is dependent on the industriousness of the believer. Therefore, the more a person can offer in the form of talent and resources, the more likely he or she will be "blessed." Believers are encouraged, then, to work hard—both in the natural sense and the spiritual sense. The heart of Prosperity Gospel Pentecostalism is meritocratic. People get what they deserve, and God's favor is bestowed based on merit, not grace. The immigrants in these churches know that hard work alone is not enough. They know that even the most successful person needs some help. For them, that help comes in the form of a miracle. They don't believe that hard work alone will grant them a life of abundance, but they *do* believe it will lead God to perform a miracle that will open the door to their prosperity. This is miraculous meritocracy.

A strong work ethic is a recurring theme in the church's teachings and is the reason parishioners rarely pray directly for money. Since part of the Prosperity Gospel formula requires them to work for it, they pray for opportunities to work toward their prosperity. In their understanding, one must give to God in order to receive something in return. "God cannot multiply something from nothing," Pastor Gielis says. "You have to give Him something to multiply!" That something could be money, but it also could be your willingness to work.

Miraculous meritocracy carries with it all the challenges of a capitalist meritocratic system. In this model, those who have more spiritual, social, and financial resources are able to invest more resources to work the formula, leading to a system that reproduces the inequalities of the status quo. The rich and powerful have more time and resources to work the formula, which they credit with their success, thus leading to a causality dilemma: Are they rich because they applied the formula, or are they able to apply the formula because they are rich?

This is one of the paradoxes of Prosperity Gospel Pentecostalism. Though followers count on miraculous interventions for prosperity, they believe that they must work hard to earn their miracles. The prosperity formula always works, and their God never fails. Their relentless optimism helps them rationalize every outcome of their formula into a success. Whether they are succeeding or not, they remain positive and faithful that a reward will come soon. They only have to put forth more effort, more sacrifices, more risks, and more offerings. Pastor Nolasco used the biblical parable of the sower found in Matthew 13. A farmer scattered the seeds across his land. Some were eaten by birds, others fell on shallow soil, and others were chocked by thorns, but some fell on good soil and produced a crop "a hundred, sixty or thirty times what was sown." The action these Christians take is like the sowing of the seeds. Some seeds will never sprout, some will grow and die, and some will be taken away, but some will grow into a hundredfold harvest. That is why they follow the Prosperity Gospel formula. It is simple: the more one sows, the better the chances of a big harvest.

Blessings

Faith plus action leads ultimately to blessings, both tangible and intangible. This is the part where subjectivity and relativism rule most prominently. Since abundance and prosperity are defined in the believers' minds and not in concrete measurable reality, individuals can subjectively interpret the results of the formula. The "blessings" can be something major, something minor, or nothing at all. The believer is both free to interpret the results *and* responsible for viewing them positively. After all, a negative interpretation or a negative thought is a sign of doubt, which invalidates all the seeds that were previously sown. A lack of fulfillment of one's wishes, for instance, can be interpreted as God delaying the result in order to teach an individual patience or to prepare the individual for something better. If one were to interpret the lack of a desired result as God's failure to answer, the negative interpretation would be blamed as the actual reason God did not answer. The believer did not hold a view positive enough to remain stalwart regardless of outcomes; hence, the believer did not have enough faith to deserve the blessing. Prosperity Gospel Pentecostalism does not offer the option of a negative interpretation for the outcome of the formula—its God rarely says no. It sets strict limits of interpretation because the actual foundation of the faith is positive thinking, which leads to a paradoxical worldview.

Even if the congregants do not achieve the actual results they requested, their actions can still earn them the side benefit of increasing their spiritual reputation. It is part of the actions they are banking for a future blessing. They persevere in their work and sacrifice because everything is banked to make a miracle happen. This is what miraculous meritocracy is all about: excessive and intense action throughout their lives to receive blessings. Progress toward holiness—as defined by an abundant and prosperous life—is achieved by those who do the most spiritual work most consistently.

The Paradoxes of Prosperity Gospel Pentecostalism

Like every medical prescription, there are side effects. The power and attraction of Prosperity Gospel Pentecostalism is found in its paradoxical logic. This faith gives immigrants the framework by which to hold dual and often contradictory ideas. It empowers them to chase the dream, but it also thwarts it. Paradoxical logic allows them to make sense of their lives.

The Prosperity Gospel Pentecostalism formula—faith plus action equals blessings—is both true and impossible. The conflict between beliefs and practices often leaves Prosperity Gospel Pentecostals trapped in two endless cycles. The first is *the paradox of the means as the ends*. The worldview they must adopt in order to apply the formula for prosperity is in and of itself a form of prosperity. While the formula might seem to lead to a result, the belief in the prosperity formula is already the desired result. The second paradox is *the paradox of the means derailing the ends*. Because positive thinking is the faith that is required, any doubt about the outcome of the formula is the very reason why the formula will not work. As a result, Prosperity Gospel Pentecostals are trapped in an inescapable web. Either they fully believe in the formula, which means that the formula already worked, or the formula did not work because they didn't fully believe in it.

Rhetorically, Prosperity Gospel is "begging the question," proving itself true by the argument that it is already known as true. Philosophers refer to this as *petitio principii* (assuming the initial point), circular reasoning whereby the formula is true simply because it is. Christians have a long tradition of using this principle to talk about their faith. One of the most common examples is "the God of the Bible is real because the Bible reveals the true God." One must assume that the first part is true for the whole statement to hold true. In Prosperity Gospel, the logic is "God blesses only the faithful with prosperity, therefore all those who are prosperous are faithful." The doctrine has no room for doubt. The only option is to consistently believe. Prosperity Gospel Pentecostals must stay relentlessly optimistic no matter what they face. They are more susceptible to this type of logic because they want to believe. Often, they have to believe. The hope gained through Prosperity Gospel Pentecostalism is the only means to face an uncertain world. They believe it before they apply it not only because it is required by their teachings but also because they are out of options.

This faith places all responsibility for success and all blame for failure on the believer. One will only get the desired result if proper faith and action are taken. And one must not only have faith that the desired result will come to pass but also have faith in the way one chooses to apply the formula. Even though countless possible results are viable, followers must believe that they have correctly discerned the right path and the correct actions that will lead to their prosperity. An error in any of these highly subjective variables can derail the formula from its desired result, but the formula itself forbids the evaluation of the problem that disrupted the formula from the desired result. If a parishioner were to complain, the protest itself would be considered an act of unfaithfulness. Consequently, the actor would have sabotaged his or her own result. The same holds for doubt. Doubting the efficacy of the formula automatically aborts its effectiveness.

That is why the preachers, and certainly God, are always free from blame. If one does not get the desired result, it is because that individual had insufficient or imperfect faith, or perhaps performed insufficient or imperfect actions. No one can tell which one it is when one cannot exist without the other and the very questioning of the formula makes it fail. This is how entangling the logic of Prosperity Gospel Pentecostalism can be—that the process of discerning what went wrong is what went wrong. Questioning or even wondering if God will truly bring about the desired result is a sign of unfaithfulness (negative thoughts), which proves that there was never sufficient faith (positive thinking) in the first place. But then, admitting one's lack of faith is *also* a faithless act of negative thinking. The old saying, "It takes money to make money," is also true in Prosperity Gospel Pentecostalism. Here, it takes (real and mental) prosperity to be prosperous.

The second paradox of the Prosperity Gospel formula poses a greater challenge. This is *the paradox of the means derailing the ends*. It reveals itself when the formula is applied for material prosperity. Gerardo—the young man who invested everything he had and borrowed money from two church members for his landscaping company—is a prime example. His faith led to the conviction that God wanted him to start his own business and would grant him prosperity through it. He was confident that failure was not an option and took action accordingly, investing everything he had (and much that he did not have) into the company.

He started in the spring and was overwhelmed with work. His prosperity was evident when he invited many friends to Golden Corral to celebrate. He was so busy that one of the guys who had loaned him his seed money began working with him part time. In the beginning, he began arriving late to church or had to leave immediately after the service. But later, he started missing church entirely. By the end of the summer, he had stopped attending completely. As winter settled in, his landscaping work ceased. By December, Gerardo was selling his equipment to pay bills for rent and utilities. I asked him about the business. "I got away from God," was his immediate response. He claimed the formula for prosperity had failed because he stopped going to church. Had he remained faithful by attending church, God would have blessed him with long-term financial success. But he strayed from God, and prosperity was taken away. In his mind, it was his fault that he did not prosper. And because it was his fault, he believed that it was also within his power to make the formula work again.

This is the paradox in which Prosperity Gospel believers are trapped. The more time they spend in church and doing spiritual work, the more action they can apply to the formula for prosperity. Yet the more work they do to gain God's attention, the less time they have for paid work. It is not uncommon for church members to turn down overtime that requires them to work on Sundays or any other time that conflicts with church gatherings. Thus, they are trapped in the paradox whereby the more they apply the prosperity formula (attending church, spending time with their families, giving their money to charity), the less likely they are to engage in activities that can make them prosperous (working overtime, saving money, accepting extra work).

When Prosperity Gospel Pentecostals leave the church, they rarely leave because "it did not work." Most often they leave because the demands are too high, though these demands are not financial. The tithes and offerings are always in cash, and there is no easy way to track church members' giving. None of the churches I visited kept track of anyone's financial giving, and there was never any direct pressure to give; the offering was always an invitation, not a demand. The pressure on church members was self-imposed for their own desire to prosper. In Christian stewardship, individuals are invited to bring their time, talents, and treasures to God. These Christians can readily bring their talents and their treasures, but time is the greatest challenge. Being a good Prosperity Gospel Pentecostal is akin to a full-time job. Believers do not have enough time to devote to the formula to fully satisfy the requirements; they are unable to attend all the activities in the church in addition to the personal time they must devote to prayer, Bible reading, and evangelization. The real-life demands of work and family are too great. Sometimes individuals leave the church without any explanation, only to reappear months later. They are always accepted without judgment. Sometimes taking a break means stepping down from active leadership but continuing to attend the church without any responsibilities. In Iglesia de Dios Victorioso, the youth pastor was on a break during the time of my visit, uncertain as to when he would take up that role again, yet he was there every Sunday, worshipping with his family. Individuals who take a break from the church always speak of a time when they will come back and work the formula properly. They hang on to the formula because it gives them the confidence to face the world. They hang on to the possibility that they can and will someday be able to apply this formula again and make themselves successful. The Prosperity Gospel formula is like a rich distant relative they hope will help them in times of trouble but whom they do not call on until absolutely necessary. In the meantime, they live with the confidence and the sense of entitlement they learned from Prosperity Gospel Pentecostalism even when away from the church.

The Formula That Fulfills Itself

As part of the paradox of Prosperity Gospel, adherents believe they will get what they ask for before they even ask. And while this may not be exactly what they want, it is what they need: a feeling of autonomy over their own future. After all, it is no small task to muster the confidence to demand things from the almighty. Every request they bring before God is motivated by a lack of peace, an abundance of fear, and an irrepressible sense of helplessness. The Prosperity Gospel formula is an antidote to this fear and powerlessness because it requires positive thinking. Applying the Prosperity Gospel formula is an act of self-empowerment. Only those who believe they have some control over their future would attempt to influence it through their faith and actions. The faith required for this formula to work is positive thinking, which is incompatible with fear or uncertainty. Learning Prosperity Gospel Pentecostalism is getting rid of fear, uncertainty, and powerlessness. Believers only apply the formula for prosperity when they have internalized that self-confidence. Regardless of what they ask for or receive, they have already reaped the benefits of Prosperity Gospel Pentecostalism. They already feel better and are confident in facing their future with the promise of God on their side.

Physical miracles are more difficult to interpret. Healing from serious illness is an all-or-nothing proposition. That is why healing minor aches and pains is routine. One of the most frequent miracles performed at Iglesia del Dios Victorioso is the healing of head and back pain. Pastor Nolasco performs a common miracle among Pentecostals. "The leveling of uneven arms and legs is as common as eating a sandwich here," he told me. He performs this healing by asking individuals with back pain to stand in front of the congregation and extend their hands out to their sides. He then guides them in bringing their palms together while keeping their arms straight. The fingers would often be misaligned, indicating that one arm is longer than the other. Pastor Nolasco would point out the uneven arms as the reason for the back pain. He would then pray and shout for miraculous growth of the shorter arm. The same exercise would be performed again, this time showing every finger aligned. Sometimes this was done on the legs, with the person sitting and lifting both legs. Pastor Nolasco often called people up front for specific healing, saying, for instance, "God has told me that there are three people here today in need of relief from back pain. Today is your day! Come forward quickly!" Every time he said this, more than the number of people he called for would go forward for healing, but everyone walked away with their healing.

Daniela, a single mother of two preteen girls, recounted her healing experience on a cool Southern California Sunday evening outside Iglesia del Dios Victorioso. That morning, she had come forward during healing time for her back pain. Daniela had harvested vegetables when she was a child, traveling across the United States from farm to farm, picking cucumbers (and other crops) with her family for ten cents a barrel. Her family needed her to fill hundreds of barrels a day. Those years of harvesting placed great strain on her back, and she had been living with that pain ever since.

Daniela did not have a religious upbringing. She visited Iglesia del Dios Victorioso after her friends invited her. She had heard about the healings and how good people felt after worshipping, and she longed for the joy her friends experienced. The previous Christmas, she finally accepted an offer to visit, and she has been a faithful Sunday attendee ever since. She enviously watched people get healed week after week but doubted whether that could happen for her. The call issued that morning, however, had been too much to resist. Pastor Nolasco had asked for people who needed healing from back pain, and he specifically asked for "you, who doubted whether God could heal your back pain. God wants you to come now!" Daniela heard it as a message directed to her. But that was not the only sign. As a newcomer to the church and to Pentecostalism, she had always sat in the back because she wanted to watch the action from a distance. But on that Sunday, the ushers led her to a seat toward the front. The moment she sat down, she told me, she felt the power of God. She knew that God had something special for her. Occurrences that most people take for granted are often infused with divine meaning in hindsight.

As Daniela described her experience, she laughed about how foolish she must have looked falling backwards when Pastor Nolasco touched her. She was quickly caught by the ushers and covered with a blanket. She sobbed uncontrollably and shook on the floor. "I had never done that before, but I don't know why that happened to me. God was healing me and releasing all the curses and breaking all the chains in my life. I knew I was healed right away!" As the healing session ended, the ushers helped Daniela up, and Pastor Nolasco asked her if she was healed. "Yes!" she cried out. "Thank you, Father! I am healed." The band broke out in music and celebration.

As we sat outside the church, waiting for the evening service, I asked her if she still felt pain in her back. She said, "Yes, it still bothers me a little. But I feel *much* better. I know God has healed me. I feel much better about myself and about my life." The back pain was still with her, but she felt better and happier. She already expected a miracle when she sat in the front of the church (faith/positive thinking), and when an opportunity to go forward arose, she took it and "made a fool" of herself (risky action). It only made sense to believe that healing had taken place.

Whether the healing in her back was real I cannot say. But having seen Daniela the weeks before and spoken to her after her healing, I could visibly see a happier and more confident woman. In the weeks after, she always sat in the front of the church and became a lot more involved in the ministry of the church, often volunteering during services. Whether she received relief from her back pain was almost irrelevant; what she had truly longed for was happiness and a general sense of confidence. The performance of her healing before the congregation meant that God had taken notice of her. All the work she had done to apply the Prosperity Gospel formula had paid off. She now experienced the joy her friends experienced—the very joy that had motivated her to visit in the first place. She was now an insider, one of the privileged ones. That inclusion was probably more comforting than any actual physical healing, and it helped her stay positive. Regardless of any physical changes, she now had a concrete experience that motivated her to remain faithful no matter what. One can imagine that for a woman used to manual labor from childhood, as well as the challenges of single parenthood, a cathartic weeping accompanied by the pleasure and encouragement of those around her can go a long way toward healing—body and soul.

Complete Partial Knowledge

Regardless of her current pain level, Daniela *knew* that she was healed. This confidence in their own spiritual intelligence leads Prosperity Gospel Pentecostals to have what I call *complete partial knowledge*. Peter Berger referred to the plausibility structures that make belief more likely.[10] A plausibility structure is the sociocultural context for systems of meaning within which some beliefs are more credible. Living under constant fear, the threat of deportation, and the helplessness to make significant changes to their current condition are all part of the social condition that leads to the higher plausibility of Prosperity Gospel. These believers claim full comprehension of things that they honestly admit to knowing little about. For instance, they claim to know what it is that God intends to give them and how He intends to do it. They determine the correct *result* on which to focus their *faith* as well as which *actions* are required for it to materialize. The only variable in question is the timing. They have complete knowledge of what they need to do, how they need to do it, and what exactly will happen once it is done, but they do not know when it will happen. This final uncertainty is important to their logic because the things they are certain about must often change or be reinterpreted. A firm time by which God must act would go against their logic.

Eduardo is a fifty-eight-year-old Dominican immigrant who moved to New Jersey twenty years ago. He is part of a late-night restaurant-cleaning crew in New York City. After restaurants are closed and the cooks are gone, Eduardo and his coworkers go in and scrub down the entire kitchen. He attends Iglesia Pentecostal del Rey Divino in Manhattan every Sunday, sitting in the back. He is one of the most animated worshippers, but he rarely goes up front (only once, during my time there, did he walk up to give his testimony during testimony time; other regular church members went up almost weekly). On the Sunday before our interview, Gloria, one of the elderly members of the church and an usher, prophesied to Eduardo that he would use his spiritual gift of healing that week. Not considering himself a healer, he was surprised. But he believed in Gloria's prophecy because she had "the anointing," according to Eduardo. The following Wednesday, Eduardo went to clean a new restaurant, and there was a young man on the cleaning team whom Eduardo had never met. He described him as a nice guy from Chile, but not a Christian because he cursed. As they were cleaning, the young man said to Eduardo, "I feel bad. I feel really bad, man." Eduardo told him to drink some water and eat something; maybe he would feel better. After some time, the young man came back, complaining again that he felt sick. Eduardo heard God say, "Pray for him!" But he doubted, and he did not want to do it. Eduardo describes his hesitation to pray with this man as "the enemy," planting a seed of doubt in him, making him question whether God has power and, more importantly, making him question whether *he* has the power of God. As these doubts crept into his mind, Eduardo found himself "rebuking the doubts" in order to make them go away. He reassured himself that he *did* have the power of God. The next time this coworker came to him, Eduardo was ready. As soon as he complained about being sick, Eduardo seized him by the hand and said, "Do you believe in the power of prayer?" The man said, "No, I don't believe in that stuff." Eduardo answered him with confidence: "You don't believe, but I believe, and I prophesy in the name of Jesus that you will be healed. So close your eyes. Close your eyes right now. Just close your eyes and think that you are OK. Think that Jesus has made you well. Start thinking about being well right now." At that point, another coworker who had been vacuuming turned to look at the spectacle. Eduardo said to him, "Turn the vacuum off and close your eyes!" As the men stood there with their eyes closed, Eduardo began to "cast off evil spirits and the spirit of sickness in the name of Jesus." He proclaimed to his sick coworker that he was now healed.

After they opened their eyes, Eduardo and his Chilean acquaintance both felt dizzy because, Eduardo surmised, they had exchanged supernatural power. They went back to work. Soon after, the Chilean coworker came to Eduardo, saying that he still felt sick. Eduardo told him to "reprimand that spirit, because you have already been healed. You are healed! Stop thinking of yourself as sick." The next night, Eduardo saw this man again and asked if he was still sick. The man said no, he had been healed. According to Eduardo, this coworker professed faith in the prayer and agreed with him that it had worked. He thanked Eduardo for the healing. As Eduardo shared this story with the congregation, he was visibly moved by the fact that his prayer had "worked." Tears rolled down his cheeks as he emphasized Gloria's prophetic powers and interpreted the initial failure of his prayers as attacks by the devil. It was a test from God to see if he would continue to pray and seek his coworker's healing. The take-home lesson was that one had to believe things into reality.

Prosperity Gospel Pentecostals speak with total confidence that God will make them successful. But they admit that they often have no idea how or when. This unknown timing is the only part of the formula that retains an element of mystery. Still, they are fully confident of what they *do* know. And this confidence, for Prosperity Gospel believers like Daniela and Eduardo, is an answer to prayer before they even pray. Their journey is their destination. Their confident faith leads them to apply the Prosperity Gospel formula, *and* the positive thinking makes the Prosperity Gospel formula work. So, essentially, the formula can do anything—except fail. The prosperous and abundant life they desire is already realized in their minds.

What Is a Prosperous and Abundant Life?

Prosperity Gospel Pentecostals believe (1) that it is God's will that the faithful be wealthy and healthy, and (2) that positive thinking and acts of faith are required on behalf of the believers to "move God's hand" to grant this prosperity and health.

But even for those who faithfully believe this, real financial prosperity is rare. The majority of the members live below the poverty line and have difficulty making ends meet, even with multiple jobs. Many live in multifamily dwellings in order to afford the rent, and some depend on food pantries to feed their families. Yet the abundant and prosperous life, a trademark of Prosperity Gospel Pentecostalism, is promoted weekly: at Iglesia Cristiana del Padre, church members are dismissed every week to go out into the world to "fly like eagles" and to "run and not grow weary"; members of Iglesia del Dios Victorioso are sent out into the world already "blessed and victorious"; and members of Iglesia Pentecostal del Rey Divino are reminded that no matter how lonely they may feel, they have a heavenly Father waiting to shower them with love—in the form of health and prosperity. For all these Christians, the definitions of prosperity and abundance are a lot more nuanced than the average observer might think. Prosperity is not about finances alone. What does it mean to soar on eagle's wings when you are at the bottom of the ladder? The paradoxical logic can only be sustained for a short time if no real benefits are derived from it.

The prosperous and abundant life means a life lived in confidence with a sense of divine entitlement. It is a mental state of being. Prosperity Gospel Pentecostals who pursue the abundant life already believe that they are living their American dream, because to pursue the dream at all is the real miracle. The great majority of them came from communities where upward mobility was impossible. The social and economic class they were born into was likely the one they would stay in. For them, being in America is already a step up. The ability to dream of a better life is an achievement in itself. That is why for them, the dream lives even if it never materializes. The state of mind is more important than the material; the ability to think that one can be prosperous and victorious is often more important than obtaining any measurable evidence of prosperity. When these immigrants call their home countries, they are reminded that they are better off than those who stayed behind.

When reporting on the Prosperity Gospel movement, media sources often miss this distinction, focusing instead on the financial promises offered by Prosperity Gospel leaders. Adherents are then characterized as naive victims at best and gullible fools at worst. But critics would miss the point of Prosperity Gospel if they thought that it was *only* about money. The principal currency of exchange between these believers and their God is not money. That is, the members of these churches are not attracted to the movement because of the promise of money, and they do not remain with these churches in the hope of attaining it easily. Even while struggling financially, the majority of them are thankful for what they have. Indeed, financial struggles are not the greatest challenge they face, as every member of this church is able to find work. Gerardo, the young man from Iglesia Christiana del Padre, repeatedly told me, "There's a lot of work in this country for people who want to work." In the years I've known him, he never had a single full-time job but was always employed doing odd-and-end work.

Similarly, the caricature of pastors as sleazy scammers or deceptive charlatans out to get money from their innocent, unsuspecting, hardworking members for the purposes of self-gain is a mischaracterization. Church members are generally more sophisticated than they are often given credit for. They are equally as skilled as the pastors in applying the logic of Prosperity Gospel Pentecostalism, and they know how to instrumentalize their experiences and their situation in order to create a favorable narrative. They are able to discern when to reject or reinterpret facts, and they can apply their own internal logic in order to define and justify their existence. This is what they learn by sitting in these churches week after week.

Although miraculous financial prosperity is a promise given weekly, parishioners rarely go before God to ask for financial miracles. This is no different from many religious organizations, whose ideal claims are constantly presented before the congregation but whose actual reality is different. There are churches across America whose mission is preached week after week.

Whether they exist for biblical orthodoxy, peace, social justice, racial reconciliation, or traditional families, the gulf between their ideal and their reality is wide. Prosperity Gospel churches are no different. It is true that, when summoned, church members will present their tithes and offerings for the promise of financial blessings. They will also testify before the church about the financial miracles they experience. But during the time of my research, I did not record a single incident in which a church member asked the pastor or the leaders of the church to pray for a financial miracle. Not a single individual in all my interviews ever claimed to have prayed for money. They did ask for work opportunities and favorable relationships with their bosses that might lead to an increase in their salaries, but never for easy or free money.

Like religious people in many communities, Prosperity Gospel Pentecostals do not take the teachings of the pastor wholesale. These are thoughtful believers. Though they hear about miraculous debt cancellations and money spontaneously appearing in bank accounts during sermons, they do not naively walk around expecting these miracles to happen in their lives. Even as they express full confidence that God *can* make money appear in their wallets, they do not rely on such occurrences. Instead, they are fully grounded in reality when they take these calculated risks of faith. They are aware of their limitations and rationally think through the best possible way to get what they want and act on the plan; this is not unlike the decision-making techniques of other successful people. This discernment process is a product of their belief. Prosperity Gospel Pentecostalism teaches and forces them to constantly think through the logic of their actions because the consequences are profoundly significant.

As for the "health" part of "health and wealth," during my research I never met anyone who stopped using medications because of a spiritual entitlement to health. During the two times that special healers were present at the churches, they included a disclaimer before they began to preach and heal. Clearly and repeatedly they said, "Do not stop taking your medications unless your doctor instructs you to do so." The healers pointed to biblical accounts where Jesus had cured people and then asked them to go show themselves to the temple priest, the equivalent of a doctor in those days. They even included contemporary stories about how doctors were converted to Pentecostalism because of the miraculous healing they saw in people under their care.

The prosperous and abundant life is filled with hard work. These are not people who freeload from God, because Prosperity Gospel Pentecostalism does not work that way. There is a formula they must follow in order to earn their prosperity. They are drawn to Prosperity Gospel not because of the freebies but because of the hope. They want to cling to the hope that if they work hard, they will be rewarded. And it is not only a hope for future rewards. Prosperity Gospel Pentecostals believe in meritocracy, but life has taught them that hard work alone is not enough. They come to Prosperity Gospel because it gives them the hope and the reassurance that their hard work is not in vain. When meritocracy falls short, God will give them a special boost. This is what I refer to as miraculous meritocracy.

If it is hope, not money, that attracts believers, what do they hope for? It is the same hope shared by all people—the hope of a better life—and it is especially relevant to immigrants. After all, hope is all they brought with them as they risked their lives coming to America. The abundance and prosperity that these churches promise is ultimately an *intangible* blessing. The prosperous and abundant life is the ability to pursue it. For the average Prosperity Gospel Pentecostal, the life of abundance and prosperity is a *state of mind*. A psychological state of happiness and an attitude of entitlement is inherent in the tradition. Prosperity and abundance are defined first and foremost in psychotherapeutic ways.

Trading Fear for Hope

In order to grasp the importance of therapeutic well-being in the lives of Prosperity Gospel Pentecostals, one must remember that the majority of the people in this book live under the constant shadow of authentic threats. The fear that their surroundings invokes for them is not psychological alone—it is real. Prosperity and abundance are a state of mind to combat real-life threats and fears. Ultimately, fear—not greed—is the chief motivator underlying their religious adherence. This was especially true in Virginia and California, where most church members were undocumented. Inherent in the risks of the undocumented life in the United States is the fear of losing children, spouses, and friends (not to mention jobs and homes) through arrest and deportation. These immigrants live with a constant sense of uncertainty that is hard for the average person to fathom. When these parents put their children on the school bus, they do not assume that they will see them at the end of the day. These are fathers who leave for work and, as the result of a minor traffic violation, could be shipped off to jail and placed in line for deportation. These are mothers who entrust thousands of dollars with friends or family to care for their children in case they are deported. Most of them have told me that they have saved money to pay a coyote to smuggle them back into the country in case they are deported. They order their lives around a mind-boggling amount of uncertainties. During my time in Southern California, I encountered police checkpoints twice. My out-of-state driver's license and rental car gave them reason to examine me in more detail. As a nonwhite immigrant, even with all the proper documentation, the anxiety from being confronted by the police lingered. I never witnessed a raid by immigration agents, but during casual conversations after church, worshippers would share news of the latest raids, whether at a large Latinx supermarket in California or at a poultry-processing plant in rural Virginia. Rumors of raids on churches and other common places of gathering circulated with some regularity. Members of these churches often knew of the latest raids before the media reported them (if the raids made the news at all). Many times during my research, especially in California, church members received calls on their cell phones from acquaintances, warning them of police checkpoints on specific roads. Once, a leader at Iglesia del Dios Victorioso spotted a church member who had been absent for a long time from the pulpit. The leader called out to him jokingly, "Long time, no see! We thought you got taken!" The meaning was clear, and the congregation responded with knowing laughter at a reality in their lives.

But even those who are in the country legally experience the fears most often felt by racial and ethnic minorities and those living in poverty. There is the threat of homelessness, of being sick without health insurance, of being unable to provide basic necessities for themselves and their families. As outsiders, they face discrimination and abuse, along with the challenges and fears of living in a foreign land where they do not speak the dominant language. Most of them live in constant anxiety of the unknown. Even the Puerto Rican and Dominican Pentecostals in New York City—most of whom were U.S. citizens—still fear the social ills associated with poverty and urban life. Drugs, alcohol, divorce, and violence to them or their loved ones—these are universal problems, but their fears are magnified by their feeble economic safety nets. Their world is a constant message that this is not "their" country. And this message has only intensified since the 2016 presidential election. In addition to worrying about government agencies, immigrants of Latin American descent also worry about violence from white supremacists. Their church serves as the rejoinder to that message and that worry.

Prosperity Gospel teachings offer hope while simultaneously reinforcing fear. The preaching and teaching in these churches capitalize on the fears of the people, especially two primary ones: the fear of missing out on a profoundly important opportunity, and the fear of losing the benefits that one deserves (due to unfaithfulness). In the sermon excerpt at the opening of this chapter, the great motivation for bringing an offering and making a covenant was not love or respect for God but fear of missing out on "the great harvest" of a seasonally moody God. And if a person lets this chance pass, his or her entire future could be at stake. Thus, the paradox of Prosperity Gospel plays out again. Fear drives people to Prosperity Gospel, and fear of missing out on the antidote to this fear keeps them in the faith.

Congregants do not want to miss out on God's favor because this might be their only chance. They need to stay "in the know," as insiders, for a chance at a better life. Prosperity Gospel Pentecostals are clever observers of the world. They know that wealth does not come by hard work alone. In their native countries and in the United States, wealthy people usually have insider knowledge, sometimes legal and sometimes not; they know a politician, an investor, or some secret connection that can lead to wealth. Prosperity Gospel Pentecostals know they lack those contacts in the real world, but their churches tell them that their God is their ultimate ally. Those who are ignorant of God's will and his secret methods for success are miserable and hopeless. When talking about people outside their churches, congregants often take an "us versus them" perspective, describing "them" as uncertain and fearful—a state they were eager (and grateful) to avoid because those of "us" were blessed and victorious. Pastor Gielis often preached that sinfulness was essentially living outside God's will. Yet the penalties of sin he described were not eternal torment in hell but an earthly life of poverty, failure, sickness, and depression. Prosperity Gospel Pentecostalism turned otherworldly rewards into this-worldly demands and turned otherworldly punishment into this-worldly poverty. The gravest consequence of sin is missing out on the opportunity to prosper. Poverty is not a punishment, but living without an opportunity to prosper is the worse sentence anyone can receive.

The road to perdition is paved with ignorance. This is one of the greatest sources of fear for Prosperity Gospel Pentecostals. They fear what might happen to them if they were to slip outside God's will. One of the frequent songs sung at Iglesia del Dios Victorioso is "¿Que Seria de Mi?" (What would be of me?):[11]

> What would be of me if you had not reached me?
> Where would I be today if you had not forgiven me?
> I would have an emptiness in my heart.
> I would stumble without a way, without direction.
> If it was not for your grace and for your love.

Chorus:
I would be like an injured bird that dies on the ground.
I would be like a sheep that thirsts for water in the ocean.
If it was not for your grace and for your love.

The ever-present undercurrent to songs like this is that it is still possible to end up as that injured bird, thirsty sheep, or empty heart. And the sermons, songs, and teachings of Prosperity Gospel Pentecostalism focus heavily on the responsibility of the believers to avoid this state—to act in accordance with God's will for the sake of their well-being. Any sin, any misstep in their lives, can jeopardize their blessings from God. This is distinct from some of the other fundamentalist Christian traditions, in which eternal punishment from God is the main motivator for avoiding sin. Prosperity Gospel Pentecostals are not consumed by a fear of God's wrath but a fear of being overlooked by God. Their God is not full of rage; their God is a bias God, choosing to bless only the most deserving. They do not fear what God might do to them; they fear that God might do nothing for them. This fear becomes a powerful form of social control. While the requirement for perfection may seem as much a source of anxiety as the fear of divine punishment, the difference is that the believers think that they are in control of achieving this perfection. Whereas the wrath of God is something they must escape by refraining from bad behavior, the perfection required by God is something they must pursue through hard work.

Prosperity Gospel Pentecostals are taught that prosperity is not only thwarted by sin but also possibly hindered by inaction or mistakes, regardless of good intentions. Pastor Nolasco of Iglesia del Dios Victorioso often told the parable of the talents found in Matthew 25:14–30, in which a man gives three of his servants different amounts of money and goes on a trip. The two servants who were given the most money invest their share for a profit and are richly rewarded upon the master's return. The third servant, who was given the least amount of money, criticizes the master and appears afraid of him. He buries his money in order to return it to the master intact. The master proclaims the third servant "worthless," tells him that he should have at least put it in the bank to earn interest, and banishes him for failing to turn a profit. Through this parable, Pastor Nolasco warned people about "burying" their money. Though burying (or saving) money does not violate any divine laws, even by Prosperity Gospel standards, it can lead one to miss out on blessings. Pastor Nolasco argued that people would do better to invest what little they have in the work of God to "multiply souls" (meaning that the church, using their donated resources, could spread and reinforce its message to others). Herein lies the puzzle that every Prosperity Gospel Pentecostal faces. Their faith teaches them to work hard, which leads them to accumulate more wealth. But that same faith also requires them to use that money, or "invest it," for the work of God in order to receive greater blessings. The more they have, the more they are expected to give away. It is the paradox of Prosperity Gospel Pentecostalism. In this way, the prescription of the illness is also its cause.

CHAPTER THREE

Changed by the Dream

"I Belong in This Country"

"Things were bad for me in Mexico. The person I was there," said Juan Pablo, fighting back tears. "I was a dead person, and I just wanted to die." The deep brown eyes of this twenty-four-year-old filled with tears as he recounted his life story to me. Born in Tijuana, he experienced an unsupervised childhood in which his father was largely absent and his mother worked multiple jobs to support his brothers and sisters. At the age of thirteen, he started using drugs and began stealing to maintain his addiction. He was soon expelled from school. At seventeen, he was uncontrollable. His mother kicked him out of the house, sending him to San Diego, California, to live with his aunt. His drug use continued, but he got into less trouble on the streets because he knew that the consequences of criminal activities were more severe in the United States. "I overdosed and almost died a few times; my aunt had to send me to the emergency room. But I still didn't stop," Juan Pablo said, shaking his head disapprovingly.

Eventually he married, hoping that things would change. After his daughter was born, he refrained from his addictions for a while, but he was soon using again. Everything culminated one cold winter night: "I had so many problems and was so desperate that I just wanted to die. I had nothing, I owed money to everyone, everything was going wrong at my job, and my wife had left me and taken our daughter. I was all by myself. I just wanted to die because I was guilty of it all. It was all my fault." Juan Pablo decided to end his suffering by jumping into a river. On an unusually cold San Diego evening, Juan Pablo found a river and jumped. He remembers treading water at first, but his legs grew numb because it was so cold. He began to sink, but just as he was about to drown, he cried out to God: "If you save me now, I'll pay you with my life." He immediately felt a force pull him out of the water. This force dragged him all the way to shore. He is sure that it was supernatural because he was totally spent. As he lay on the shore, some stranger passing by spotted him and helped him out of the water, eventually taking him home.

The near-death experience transformed Juan Pablo. "It was like the bad part of me died in that river." He interprets his suicide attempt as a form of baptism. After that day, he never drank, smoked, or used drugs again. The proof of his changed life was that his wife moved back in with him after a week. However, Juan Pablo had not fulfilled the promise he made as he was drowning. He had not "paid God back with his life," he admitted; he had neither attended a church nor made any profession of faith.

A few weeks after his suicide attempt, he was stricken with a severe illness, which reluctantly led him to call his brother for a ride to Tijuana, where he could afford to see a doctor. Juan Pablo and his older brother had never gotten along; they had fought bitterly during their youth. Later, his brother had converted to Pentecostalism, and Juan Pablo confessed his jealousy of his brother's life. "He was living the American dream and I was trying to kill myself!" It did not help that his brother constantly pestered him with stories of healing and faith. As a good Pentecostal, his brother wanted to share the prosperity he had found, but Juan Pablo was not ready to hear it. As they were driving to Tijuana, his brother once again began to talk to him about faith and invited him to a prayer meeting at his church that night, telling him that he could be healed of all things physical and spiritual. This infuriated Juan Pablo even more because he knew that he had not kept his promise of giving his life to God. His anger raged against his brother, and after they saw the doctor in Tijuana, they drove back without exchanging a single word.

When Juan Pablo returned to his house, he felt prompted to ask his wife, Florencia, if she wanted to go to a prayer meeting. To his surprise, she agreed, and without asking for any details, she got ready to go. Juan Pablo was shocked. They had been culturally raised as Roman Catholics but had never attended Mass and had always been hostile toward religious institutions. He doesn't remember their having a single conversation about religion, but since his wife agreed, Juan Pablo called his brother, who gladly picked them up.

When they arrived at Iglesia del Dios Victorioso, Juan Pablo remembers Pastor Nolasco coming out to meet him before he even entered the church. He greeted him by name and told Juan Pablo that he had been praying for him. Juan Pablo was moved that a stranger was showing such genuine concern for him. The prayer services at these churches are always preceded by a sermon, and on this day, Pastor Nolasco preached on God's power to save and the transformation everyone could experience through Jesus. These words fell on Juan Pablo's ears with great conviction:

> All the things he preached were about me, and I started thinking about that because it was really all about *me*. Then at the end, they asked people to go to the front for special prayer, and three of us went up.

> There was a person with diabetes and another sick person and me. I was in the middle. Pastor Pedro [Nolasco] told this little old lady to come pray for me. When she put her hands on my head, my heart started beating, beating really hard. I could hear my heart: Ta! Ta! Ta! Ta! Ta! I felt my chest was about to explode. And then I fell back, and I started to cry like a little baby. I couldn't help it. I didn't want to because I was the only one who had fallen, but I couldn't help it. I cried out, "Thank you! Thank you, Daddy!"

At this point, Juan Pablo pauses to choke back tears before explaining that it was the first time in his life he had ever uttered "daddy" (*papá*). His father had left before he even learned to speak, and even when he saw him afterwards, Juan Pablo never addressed him as his father. And that is how for the first time in his life, this large, six-foot-tall, masculine man cried for his daddy. He describes his conversion physically: "I felt my heart melting. Really, it felt like it was *melting*. And when I got up, it was as if I had a new heart. Everything about me was new. I think God finished what he started with me on that river. I was a totally different person."

Juan Pablo undoubtedly became a different person. He was transformed from a drug-addicted, alcoholic day laborer who neglected his wife and young daughter to a responsible father, husband, and leader of a construction team. He had become involved in the life of his daughter, and at the time of my interview, his wife was expecting another baby. His boss entrusted him daily with a company van and a stack of cash to go out and hire day laborers and manage them on construction jobs. This complete turnaround came about in an amazingly short time. Only seven months had passed since he jumped into that river with no hope.

"Do you feel like your home is here or back in Mexico?" I asked him as we neared the end of our interview. He closed his eyes for a second before replying:

> My home is here today because this country gave me God. I'm first of all a Christian now. Not Mexican or anything else. But I belong here because God wants me here. In Mexico, I was without God, and I'm not that person anymore. I can't ever go back. In Mexico, I have no church, no pastor, no anointing, no power. My blessing is here. This is where God wants me. I think I'm more at home here because this is where I met God. This is where God has blessed me and where He will make me prosper. In Mexico, I have nothing. Here, I am under God's blessing, so I belong here now.

For Juan Pablo, his conversion experience transformed him in a way that made him unable to ever go back to Mexico. Part of his identity was now bound to the church he calls home. His life goals and hopes of the future now depended on his proximity to his church, his pastor, and the teachings he was receiving weekly. Before he was a Prosperity Gospel Pentecostal, his presence in the United States was one of convenience. He came because he was sent here and he had work here. After his rebirth, he had a divine reason for being in this country. His presence in the United States was no longer a convenient one; it was part of a universal plan that God had planned for him. Part of his conversation led him to that conviction, and he could never go back to Mexico. "So you consider yourself an *Americano*?" I asked him.

Juan Pablo laughed and said, "No," thinking it was a joke. But he quickly corrected himself. "Well, I never saw it that way, but *si pertenezco en este país* (if I belong in this county), then I am an American, right?" Is he?

The Paradox of an American

One of the most popular definitions of an American finds its roots in French American writer J. Hector St. John de Crèvecoeur in 1782: "What then is the American, this new man? . . . He is an American, who, leaving behind him all his ancient prejudices and manners, receives new ones from the new mode of life he has embraced, the new government he obeys, and the new rank he holds. He has become an American by being received in the broad lap of our great *Alma Mater*. Here individuals of all races are melted into a new race of man, whose labors and posterity will one day cause great changes in the world. Americans are the western pilgrims."[1] Implicit in this definition is that an American is an immigrant, someone who came from a distant land and possesses "ancient prejudices and manners" they must abandon. It is anyone in pursuit of the American dream. Anyone who leaves the old world and starts anew, a blank page by which to write one's future without hindrances of the past. This "new man" is a better person because his "labors and posterity will . . . cause great changes in the world." Implicit in this definition is also the idea that this new man will make the world a better place. This definition of an American captivated the public imagination and still persists in America and around the world. However, it has a history of being contradicted by the reality of those who live in this country. The characteristics of an American have been paradoxical from the start.

The romanticized definition of an American implied that any person could live up to his or her fullest potential in this newly created nation, yet in practice, it included only free white men. The tension between the ideal and the real could not be sustained. A legal American was defined by law in the Naturalization Act of 1790, the first statute to codify naturalization law for the United States. According to the act, citizenship was limited to "free white persons of good character." This legal definition of an American is marred by issues of religion, ideology, and—most importantly—race. This definition was upheld long after the Civil War, as other immigration and naturalization laws continued to exclude people by ethnicity or race. Crèvecoeur's painting of the American omitted the fact that it applied to whites only. Immigrants did come with new hope, but there was no "melt[ing] into a new race of man." Instead of leaving their ancient prejudices and manners, they introduce them into their new nation. History demonstrates that not all were "received in the broad lap of our great Alma Mater."

Americans were in reality defined by the color of their skin. African slaves who had been in America for over a century when Crèvecoeur penned his definition were not considered Americans; rather, they were property. Non-European immigrants faced exclusion from legal protections and formal inclusion into the United States. Their physical looks legally barred them from becoming Americans. This racial exclusion remained long after Crèvecoeur's observation. The Page Act of 1875 and the Chinese Exclusion Act of 1882 barred immigrants of Chinese descent from entering America. Even into the 1900s, skin color was still a determinant of certain rights.

Cynical observers might claim that America was hypocritical from the beginning. There is some merit to this criticism, since America always aspired to higher moral standards than it displayed. The clearest evidence is its celebration of freedom while the millions of enslaved Africans toiled under brutal conditions. But hypocrisy implies deceit and intention. The ideal was always aspirational, much like the prosperity and success that Prosperity Gospel Pentecostals desire. America claimed for itself an ideal that had not yet been realized. But while the aspirations and the reality were different, the belief that they would one day align was sincere. Throughout its history, America has always been a land of contradictions. The paradox of Prosperity Gospel Pentecostalism is inherently American.

Less influential than race, Americans were also defined by a distinctive ideology. America was founded on the "self-evident truths . . . that all men are created equal, that they are endowed by their Creator with certain unalienable Rights, that among them are Life, Liberty, and the pursuit of Happiness." While this promise did not hold true for the nonwhites who lived in this country, it proved effective at inspiring a generation of immigrants around the world who came to live out that dream. Many clung to that ideal and left everything behind in order to enjoy that life, liberty, and happiness.

For better or for worse, Crèvecoeur's definition of an American is stuck in the public imagination. The essence of his definition has been ingrained in the American consciousness and often materializes in legislation and institutions within and beyond the United States. This definition was further rooted in the American consciousness by the Christian narrative that helped reinterpret the founding of America. Protestant Christians escaping Europe viewed their new lives as an opportunity from God to create a new world order in order to make the world more Christian. Much like Christopher Columbus, whose first name literally means "Christ bearer," these immigrants came to America with a divine authority to claim land and souls for their God.

The notion that Americans (as defined by Crèvecoeur) have a special right granted from God to live in freedom and happiness has taken different shapes and been given different names throughout the history of this nation. Alexis de Tocqueville used the term "American Exceptionalism" to describe the special position America held in the world as the first modern democracy.[2] During the westward expansion of the nineteenth century, European immigrants justified their claim for western territories along with the slaughter of Native Americas as a divine order from God through the idea of Manifest Destiny. America as a "shining city on a hill" has been used as a metaphor by presidents from John F. Kennedy to Ronald Reagan to Barack Obama. At the core of these beliefs is the notion that Americans are entitled by a divine deity to make themselves and the world a better place.

"Endowed by Their Creator . . ."

The Prosperity Gospel movement originated in a country where the national psyche has been programmed from its inception to believe in divine entitlement—that any American has a God-given right to enjoy certain freedoms and privileges—at a time when most people in America were not. The paradox of Prosperity Gospel is the paradox of America—a nation that claims for itself ideals that are far from its reality. Prosperity Gospel is the natural outcome of this national psyche. The parallels are plain. American ideals demanded from their Creator the right to life, liberty, and the pursuit of happiness (originally drafted as "the pursuit of property").[3] Similarly, Prosperity Gospel Pentecostals believe their God wants riches, health, and success for them. The therapeutic ethos found in Prosperity Gospel Pentecostalism is the modern definition of "the pursuit of happiness."[4] The Universal Church of the Kingdom of God in São Paulo, Brazil, is the largest Prosperity Gospel church in the world. Its motto is "Pare de Sufrir" (Stop suffering), and it has amassed billions of dollars in assets globally with the mission of ending psychological suffering. In the age of anxiety, Prosperity Gospel is an attractive drug.

The pursuit of psychological and emotional fulfillment is central for modern Americans. The success of the positive psychology movement is evidence of a culture desperate for joy. Positive psychology affects every industry, as well as politics, the arts, religion, the military, education, families, and parenting. It is a relatively new field within the discipline of psychology, which claims to study the conditions necessary for human flourishing. Practically, positive psychology is a utilitarian and individualistic philosophy. Its end goal is to empower individuals to increase their happiness and avoid suffering, which are the ultimate goals of Prosperity Gospel.

The logic of positive psychology and of Prosperity Gospel Pentecostalism are identical. Positive psychology offers its devotees "scientific" methods for achieving happiness and living a flourishing, meaningful life. It is a form of "gnostic meritocracy." Prophets of happiness impart secret knowledge to followers who must apply its methods for fulfillment. Followers of positive psychology must work hard to obtain the happy life they desire. They must do things such as think positively, engage in activities that build on one's joy, and seek out positive relationships. The assumption in positive psychology is that the end goal can always be achieved as long as the person performs the right acts. Prosperity Gospel Pentecostalism is the spiritualized version of positive psychology. The responsibility for happiness and prosperity rests on the individual. Both are creations of an inherently American milieu.

The dream of prosperity and success is not a unique American creation. While many religions, Christianity included, offer stark warnings against greed and materialism, religions around the world have constructed gods that can alleviate poverty and suffering. The devout make pilgrimages and sacrifices in the hope that it will bring about relief from material suffering. Prosperity Gospel goes further by offering a God who can grant all things and who wants all good things for the faithful. It is this sense of God-on-our-side entitlement that makes Prosperity Gospel Pentecostals unique. The materialistic and psychological focus on the attainment of blessings in the here and now makes Prosperity Gospel the gospel of the American dream.

Once a vision of political freedom or of a simple, peaceful life, the American dream today is understood almost exclusively in terms of material success. For much of its existence, the American dream was deeply tied to spiritual, moral, and political aspirations in addition to economic prosperity. But the American dream that these immigrants dream of is one that became popular around the same time as Prosperity Gospel. It is a post-1960s American dream that involves upward mobility and focuses on the dream of homeownership and material goods.[5] It is the dream that coincided with the end of westward expansion and the growth of the suburbs. Prosperity Gospel Pentecostalism is genuinely a product of its time.

Today, American popular culture is saturated with stories of rags to riches. From the financial tycoons of past centuries to celebrities today, the stories Americans are most hungry for depict the underdogs who succeed against all odds. Politicians, even those from privileged backgrounds, must frame their stories of success as one of rags to riches. They must Photoshop their history into the myth of the self-made individual. The ability to worship freely—the dream that motivated Puritan immigrants—is almost never heard of as an example of achieving the American dream today. Life, liberty, and the pursuit of happiness are now translated into an enjoyable and comfortable life, freedom from financial struggle, and the pursuit of happiness through these material things. This is the pursuit of that "new man" Crèvecoeur wrote about nearly 240 years ago. An American is someone who will give up past prejudices in order to live the way he or she wants to live, enjoy the things he or she wants to enjoy, and experience personal contentment to the fullest of his or her abilities. These are the rewards that Prosperity Gospel Pentecostalism offers, which is why its practice is part of the Americanization process.

Assimilation as Americanization

American sociology has long been concerned with the great changes that faced this nation at the beginning of the twentieth century—urbanization, industrialization, and immigration. Between 1880 and 1920, roughly twenty-four million immigrants entered the United States at a time when the total U.S. population was only about seventy million.[6] Such a large wave of immigration would not be repeated until the late 1990s. The constant flow of immigrants forced scholars to look seriously at the ways these new citizens were being weaved into the fabric of American society.

Sociological discussions of assimilation have been central to the study of race, ethnicity, and minority groups since the early 1900s. When writing about assimilation in 1921, sociologist Robert Park and Ernest Burgess stated,

"Not by the suppression of old memories, but by their incorporation in his new life is assimilation achieved. . . . There is no process but life itself that can effectually wipe out the immigrant's memory of his past."[7] Assimilation was thus viewed as a linear process by which immigrants shed the characteristics of their home and transformed into a homogenized generic type of American.

This classical theory of assimilation centered on the white Anglo-Saxon Protestant ideal as the end goal of the assimilation process. Sociologists described the process by which immigrants move closer to the mainstream by altering practices and behaviors to become more white and more Protestant.[8] It was commonly believed that in order to get ahead, immigrants needed to overcome their "deficiencies," which were defined as their differences from the majority culture. Religious and charitable groups dedicated themselves to helping immigrants purge beliefs and habits that were not conducive to white middle-class American life. Historically, the Native American boarding schools established throughout reservations in the United States existed to strip away Native American practices. The groups who ran these schools, often Christians, did it as their civic service and their mission to help Native Americans. In those days, "assimilation" and "Americanization" were used interchangeably.

Alternative theories emerged to argue against "straight-line" assimilation theory. Racism and exploitation reproduce social disadvantages found in racial minority groups, preventing them from achieving upward mobility assimilation.[9] Alternatively, segmented assimilation theory claims that discrimination, segregated communities, and other urban conditions influence immigrants' ability to assimilate into a white mainstream or toward an ethnic and racial underclass.[10] The general test of assimilation, of how "American" an immigrant has become, depends on the immigrants and their children reaching parity with native-born whites.[11] The progress of immigrant assimilation remains gauged on whites as the reference group.[12] In almost all cases, the theories of assimilation expected immigrants to completely abandon their previous traditions. Some even argued that by the seventh generation, all traces of ethnic distinctiveness would disappear. These ideas failed to take into consideration the African Americans who had been in the country for many generations but had yet to reach parity with whites.

Assimilation and its meaning has always been contested. W. E. B. Du Bois's *The Souls of Black Folk* was an early work that pushed against the traditional assimilation theory by focusing on black Americans.[13] Originally published in 1903, it is as relevant and important today as it was a century ago. In this seminal work, Du Bois rightly challenges the old paradigm of Americanization as defined by Crèvecoeur. The idea that one could give up past identities and adopt a new, generic American identity was wrong. Instead, Du Bois wrote about the "double consciousness" that black Americans experience. They live with two identities, "an American, a Negro."[14] The two conceptions of the self permanently struggle to make meaning of daily life. Du Bois championed the idea of multiple American identities, but his work was not taken seriously.

Scholarly work on assimilation continued to support the linear "Americanization" view until the 1960s, when research began to challenge the ethnocentric assumptions of the previous decades. Assimilation became a controversial term associated with ethnic superiority and racist notions toward non-Eurocentric cultures. Milton Gordon's *Assimilation in American Life* provided one of the first attempts to explain the different subtypes or states of assimilation.[15] Gordon argued that immigrants passed through a series of three basic stages: acculturation, structural assimilation, and material assimilation. However, his theories were based on the children of European immigrants, so they were not suitable for understanding the African American experience or the wave of nonwhite immigrants.

It was only after the Immigration and Naturalization Act of 1965 that a more racially diverse wave of immigrants began to enter the United States. These new immigrants were unlike the white European immigrants of the previous century. They came from different continents, increasing the racial and ethnic diversity of America. It is important to point out that the Immigration and Naturalization Act—and U.S. immigration policy in general—has never been an open welcome for all those who wish to enter. Immigration laws are formal legislation that defines who can be an American. The Immigration and Naturalization Act of 1965 allowed highly skilled workers to come to America in order to add to the productivity of the country. The law limited entry to those who fit the existing mold of hardworking, educated, and morally upright members of society. Most of the post-1965 immigrants came already having fulfilled that prerequisite. These new Americans bought into the modern vision of the founding ideals and were industrious members of society, but they were not assimilating because they were not melting into the white Anglo-Saxon Protestant core viewed as the ideal American. As a result, the straight-line assimilation theory was largely abandoned. After years of academic dispute, prominent scholars of immigration began asking, "Is assimilation dead?"[16]

Since the mid-1990s, new waves of scholars have answered that question. Assimilation is not dead, but it is different. New scholarship on immigration discredits the past understandings and offers a new perspective, in which the contributions of immigrants to the new nation are valued and a more nuanced understanding of becoming American is applied. Most notably, Alejandro Portes and Ruben G. Rumbaut offered the segmented assimilation model as an alternative to the straight-line assimilation model. They theorized that assimilation could take different trajectories, not always toward the same destination.[17] In their book *Remaking the American Mainstream*, sociologists Richard Alba and Victor Nee argue that assimilation is a by-product of purposive actions taken at the individual level to improve social and other life chances for self and family. Assimilation is, in other words, "something that frequently happens to people while they are making other plans."[18]

Latin American Assimilation

The assimilation theories for Latin American immigrants are more complicated than those for European immigrants. First, unlike Europeans, many Latinos in the Southwest trace their ancestry to lands before they became part of the United States. These Latinos did not immigrate, but they have a distinctively rich cultural heritage that distinguishes them from white Americans.[19] Second, their proximity to Mexico gives them easy access to resources to maintain their traditions. Also, since new Latin American immigrants are constantly arriving, ties to the native culture remain fresh. Because of this, some have generalized that as a group, Latinos face greater difficulties assimilating into mainstream America. Samuel Huntington declared in 2004 that "unlike past immigrant groups, Mexicans and other Latinos have not assimilated into mainstream U.S. culture," accusing them of slowly dividing America into two culturally different nations. Huntington makes this claim while ignoring the millions of white Americans of Latin American descent who had already assimilated according to his definition of an American (the use of language and upward mobility).[20] In fact, by Huntington's own definition, the majority of Latinos have already assimilated. The most complicated aspect of Latinx assimilation is not what they do but how they look. Latinos are a racially ambiguous group of Americans; they do not fit into the traditional black–white racial dichotomy that has dominated American culture since its formation.

The racial diversity within the Latinx population is a significant factor in determining whether linear assimilation has occurred. Unlike other groups,

Latinos are the most racially diverse ethnic group in America, including whites, blacks, Asians, indigenous Americans, and mixed races. Latinos are treated differently based on their perceived race; that is, black Latinos are treated as black Americans, Asian Latinos as Asian Americans, and white Latinos as white Americans. As a result, Latinos tend to view themselves as members of the racial group they most physically resemble. That is, black Dominicans tend to identify with African Americans, whereas light-skin Cubans identify with white Americans. This is why for many black, white, and Asian Latinos, being Latino or Hispanic is an "ethnic option" they intentionally choose to affiliate with.[21]

The ethnic option, however, is not available to brown-skin Latinos. The anti-immigrant sentiments that underpin America are not about immigrants but about dark-skin individuals. States have passed laws targeting undocumented immigrants that depend on the enforcer's ability to racially profile individuals. This method most adversely affects Latinos with darker complexions. These anti-Latino sentiments, as confirmed by the passage of these laws and the election of anti-immigrant politicians to prominent offices, further alienate the Latinx community from appeals to "become Americans." The complexion of their skin makes it more difficult for brown-skin Latin Americans to be accepted into the American mainstream. Because identities are dialectically constructed, these same Latinos also have a harder time imagining themselves as Americans. They do not assimilate because they cannot blend into white America.

The wave of Latin American immigrants in the 1990s poses a challenge to previous assimilation theories, which do not seriously engage the immigration status of the individual. There is growing evidence that legal status affects immigrants' experiences of integration.[22] Undocumented immigrants who live with the "threat of deportability" experience constant fear and mental stress.[23] This uncertainty further reinforces the "double consciousness" in these immigrants. They have a new identity in this country, but they cannot fully embrace it because they might be deported at any time. They must hang on to their old identity because they will need it if they are deported to their homeland. Living in the "in between" not only keeps them from fitting into old assimilation models but keeps them from desiring that form of assimilation. The majority of the church members studied in this project were undocumented. Most of them, regardless of when they entered the United States, arrived for pragmatic reasons. They are immigrants escaping violence or seeking better opportunities, and they have little interest in participating in American civic life. For them, there is little advantage in adopting American customs and traditions. The practices they choose to adopt and their selective integration are made on utilitarian spiritual principles. For example, they learn English because it gives them better economic opportunities, which leads to higher status in the church. Thus, learning English is part of their pursuit of holiness.

The Church as a Vehicle of Assimilation

Religion has always played a key role in the lives of immigrants. The United States is publicly as religious as most Latin American countries. Religion is publicly and privately infused in American life. Immigrants constantly experience the pressure to conform to American norms, including religious ones. Immigrants who are already religious often become more religious in the United States because of the cultural hyper-religious norms. Immigrant religiosity is not a residue from their home countries but a development of their new lives.[24] Their religious conversion is an act of assimilation into an inherently American religion, because the primary objective of Prosperity Gospel Pentecostalism is economic upward mobility.

Assimilation was almost always measured by upward social mobility, which itself was determined by a person's ability to minimize his or her cultural (and especially racial or ethnic) differences from the dominant group. In that light, attempts to assimilate immigrants and other minority groups were often viewed as forms of charity work by churches. There is much practical help that religious institutions provide immigrants: registering children for school, getting a driver's license, using public transportation, arranging medical assistance, and so on. Churches also offer English lessons as a means to "Americanize" immigrants for their own good.

The church, the central gathering place for Christians, is a hub for shaping identities. Like Juan Pablo, many immigrants find churches especially helpful in negotiating conflicting identities and defining new ones. In his study of immigrant Chinese churches, sociologist Fenggang Yang observed "the Sinicization of Christianity," in which the church successfully integrated Christian and Chinese identities in order to meet the psychological and emotional needs of its middle-class immigrants. Yang found that Chinese immigrants who converted to Christianity increased their levels of ethnic cohesiveness while adopting different aspects of mainstream culture. Immigrant congregants were more likely than non-converts to listen to and speak English, expose themselves to U.S. cultural patterns, and celebrate American holidays.[25] Yang calls this "adhesive identity," in which immigrants can simultaneously hold multiple identities and display them by choice. This pattern has been observed in other immigrant groups. Religious institutions provide minority groups a safe space where they can preserve their ethnic (and in some cases, religious) identities even while they and their children learn to incorporate into the larger culture.[26] The churches in this book serve that twin purpose. The Latin American immigrants who join them are passionately pursuing spiritual renewal. Yet as they are spiritually fulfilled, they are also socially transformed. Pentecostal churches have played this role in the past for Latinos.[27] What is uniquely Prosperity Gospel Pentecostal about this process is the logic they learn to help them be residents and foreigners at the same time.

As Juan Pablo's life story illustrates, something real happened to him when he converted to Prosperity Gospel Pentecostalism. He does not view himself as an American, at least not without my prompting. He is not trying to become American. In his worldview, there is no category or process by which he could or should see himself as an American. Like most first-generation immigrants in these churches, he does not care for that label. He and the others want to live their lives in peace and flourish in this country. Unlike their U.S.-born children, these first-generation immigrants have little interest in participating in the political process. However, through their spiritual experience—and specifically through Prosperity Gospel—immigrants like Juan Pablo have taken steps to become something different from what they were before. Unlike temporary workers, Prosperity Gospel Pentecostals tend to plant roots in this country. The social changes that occur after their conversion to Prosperity Gospel Pentecostalism lead them to more stable lives. Instead of dating or hooking up, they marry and start families. They stop renting and buy homes. They quit working for someone and invest in their own businesses. They no longer live from day to day but make long-term plans to live prosperous lives. Much like Juan Pablo, the average Prosperity Gospel Pentecostal is more likely to affiliate with institutions and organizations beyond his or her ethnic circle.[28]

Latinx immigrants who are active in Prosperity Gospel Pentecostal churches learn how to hold paradoxical identities and beliefs. This is the attraction of Prosperity Gospel Pentecostalism. It gives these immigrants the tools they need to make sense of their world. The paradoxical logic allows them to see themselves as their own versions of Americans without legally being in the United States. The end goal of church attendance is not upward mobility or assimilation; rather, they are in these churches to learn the rationale that will give them peace and confidence to face the challenges of immigrant life. By believing Prosperity Gospel doctrines, they intensify their sense of entitlement to live in this country. Even if there are those who will try to keep them from their American dream, Prosperity Gospel Pentecostalism empowers them to step out and claim that dream. They are reminded that they have a divine endorsement, and with God's help, they live out their lives. Like Juan Pablo, they pursue happiness and, in the process, become—at least in spirit, if not in law—more American.

To Integrate, Not Assimilate

Latin American Prosperity Gospel Pentecostal churches are both a safe haven where immigrants can freely express themselves and associate with coethnics *and* a place of inadvertent integration into American culture. I intentionally use the word "integration" instead of "assimilation" because these immigrants desire inclusion in American society, but they do not want to become Americans. They work, plant roots, serve their communities, build businesses, and pay taxes. They want the practical parts of being a citizen, but they have no need for a national identity. Like Juan Pablo, they do not identify as Americans. They have little interest in politics and civic involvement. They want to enjoy the goods of this nation and contribute to it, but they do not want to conform to the generic identity that the traditional definition of linear assimilation demands from immigrants. In the churches I visited, there was no intentional attempt to "Americanize" church practices or worship styles, and there was no attempt to use English or incorporate American themes into worship. On the contrary, immigration themes were highlighted; congregants were often reminded that they must work harder and have greater faith because life is more difficult for them as immigrants. Decorations and social gatherings often emphasized their native country and celebrated their countries of origin. During the World Cup, Pastor Gielis wore the jersey from Colombia's national team. Many of the church members did the same for their native countries. Like at other immigrant churches, stories of their native countries dominated public discourse. National pride was often on display at these churches. Immigrant worship spaces often double as cultural centers to promote and pass on the traditions of the old country to the next generation. These churches were no exception.

The sermons of Pastor Nolasco (of Iglesia del Dios Victorioso in California) often blended themes of success and persistence with those of ethnic pride. In one sermon on perseverance and faith, he recounted the difficulties he had faced in establishing his first church in Mexico:

> My wife was pregnant. We were homeless, living in the hallway of a person's house. And my wife was about to give birth, and we had nowhere to go. I was crying and praying, "Why is my wife sleeping on the floor? I did what you told me. Why is it so hard?" And it was hard on us. It was hard, and it would have been easy to quit. But I stayed faithful and removed all doubt from my mind. And *a puro coraje Mexicano* [by pure Mexican courage], we stayed in the fight, and we raised that church! So don't ever give up! Don't ever doubt that God will make it happen. Don't ever let the things of this world—poverty, pain, suffering—deter you from God's plan for you!

The congregation, most of whom were Mexican, broke out in applause and an eventual standing ovation. This clear incident of ethnic pride resonated with the worshippers. "By pure Mexican courage" is a saying I frequently heard from Mexican men while I was in California. One churchgoer used the phrase in reference to his ability to work even when he was sick. Another used it to refer to working overtime despite fatigue. Similarly, credit for the success that Pastor Nolasco achieved in his first church was divided between God and his own "Mexican courage." Through references to national identity, Pastor Nolasco teaches perseverance, grit, and optimism.

None of these churches had any form of outreach for non-Spanish speakers or any goal of integrating their church members with native English speakers. Iglesia Cristiana del Padre once invited an English-speaking guest preacher, whose sermon was translated by a Salvadoran man, but at Iglesia del Dios Victorioso and Iglesia Pentecostal del Rey Divino, guest preachers spoke only in Spanish. This was the case even when the guest preacher was more fluent in English than Spanish. The churches are filled with Latinx Spanish speakers, and there is no intention of using the language of the mainstream. This is an intentional choice. At Iglesia Cristiana del Padre, I attended a small prayer meeting at which every single person was fluent in English. Despite being more fluent in English than Spanish, the pastor and his wife prayed and conducted the meeting in Spanish.

Integration happens. The process is more subtle than hosting English classes and workshops on American norms and practices. The most powerful motivation for integration is through role models. The pastors and leaders of these churches are fluent in English (though they never use English in the churches).[29] They congregate in Spanish-speaking churches, but they live in the English-speaking world. The type of success that these leaders have achieved often requires engagement with the American mainstream. In the sight of the congregants, those who have achieved prosperity and success are those who have successfully adopted a white English-speaking middle-class lifestyle. Buying a home, starting a business (especially with English-speaking customers), and opening a bank account are all considered successful milestones in the Prosperity Gospel dream. For these church members, these milestones are signs that God is blessing them. Planting roots in this nation and integrating into its fabric is an aspiration for these Christians. The clear implication of these churches is that returning to one's home country too soon is a failure. This includes deportation. It is presumed that only those who are not protected by God must leave the United States. While these immigrants do not seek to assimilate, their faith compels them to engage in practices that lead to integration.

Their integration is social, but there is still a level of assimilation taking place. If assimilation is the adoption of ideals and practices of their new home, then assimilation takes places for them in the form of mental attitude adjustments. Prosperity Gospel Pentecostalism requires that adherents face each day with the confidence that the world is literally *theirs* because it was given to them by God. It is part of the rights endowed by their creator. This means living with a sense of divine empowerment as they tackle their daily challenges. This is the positive thinking that Norman Vincent Peale preached effectively to generations of Americans. These are the foundations that Martin Seligman adapted for a secular audience through positive psychology, calling it "learned optimism"—that one must always be positive about the world. These beliefs give immigrants the assertiveness, self-confidence, and boldness to take risks—traits that in themselves can take a person far in American mainstream culture. Most importantly, they give them the confidence to stand up for themselves and not shy away as marginalized or inferior people. This form of Christianity takes marginalized people and makes them believe that they belong at the top and in the center. Although they are never told to learn English, move out of ethnically segregated neighborhoods, or adopt white middle-class norms, church members already believe that these practices are correlated with success.

Hence, these immigrants are experiencing a different kind of assimilation. Their undocumented status, the proximity of their homeland, and the constant threat of deportation keep them uninterested in adopting new national identities.[30] They have little interest in becoming a "new man," in Crèvecoeur's sense. The idea of straight-line assimilation is colonialist and racist. It is not grounded in the reality of immigrant experiences. Migrants usually leave their homes in search of new and better lives, not because they see fault in their identities that can only be improved by adopting other cultures and norms. They invest in their communities and are committed to contributing to the common good because their faith demands it of them. But they have little desire to identify as "Americans." Immigrants throughout U.S. history have been proud of their ancestry. They started newspapers in their own languages and created communities where their cultures would be preserved. Yet they were thoroughly invested in the good of this nation. In every practical way, they are Americans. This is the paradox of Prosperity Gospel Pentecostalism on display.

When they think of national and religious identities, the Prosperity Gospel Pentecostals I encountered never saw themselves as anything other than nationals of their countries of origin. Pastors Ramirez and Gielis, for example, identified themselves as Dominican and Colombian, even though they had spent most of their lives in the United States. These immigrants rarely spoke of assimilation or thought in terms of such a process. Instead, like Juan Pablo and most Pentecostals, they spoke of their *conversion*—the moment the Holy Spirit descended upon them and made them new persons. And though they still may not have looked like white Americans, they certainly did not feel much like their old selves, either.

Toward an Explanation of Prosperity Gospel Conversion

The majority of Latin American Protestants are converts, and almost half of those converts are former Roman Catholics.[31] A high rate of conversion among immigrants is not unique to Latinos, yet the rate of conversion away from Roman Catholicism does not necessarily imply dissatisfaction with the Catholic Church. Many Latin Americans were ever only minimally and culturally Catholics. Most immigrant churches have similar percentages of new believers; sometimes as many as half of the members in an immigrant church are converts.[32] Immigrants need stories to make sense of their new lives, and religion offers an attractive narrative.

Conventional wisdom would point to the practical advantages new immigrants gain by adapting to the worldview of a majority group as the primary motivation for conversion. This is especially true for immigrants whose churches can offer them mainstream American religion within a safe, culturally familiar space. Religious groups offer benefits that are rarely found in society at large. An immigrant church is a community of co-ethnics who are familiar with the immigrant culture and are ready to offer material assistance and valuable networking opportunities. In one study of Korean immigrants, their religious needs (making sense of the world), social needs (experiencing a sense of belonging), and psychological needs (having a sense of comfort) were inseparable. The satisfaction of one simultaneously met all three.[33]

One might assume that the religious, social, and psychological needs of Latin American immigrants would best be served by Catholic churches, since Catholicism is the faith of their homeland. Large Spanish-speaking Roman Catholic churches are present near Iglesia Cristiana del Padre, Iglesia del Dios Victorioso, and Iglesia Pentecostal del Rey Divino. The Spanish-speaking Catholic communities surrounding these churches are three to four times larger than those of the Pentecostal churches. The Catholic churches also serve as unofficial Latin American cultural centers, hosting festivals and other cultural events. Lastly, whereas these Pentecostal churches are largely independent, the Catholic churches are deeply connected to extensive networks that supply a multitude of resources—from community resources to Spanish-speaking priests and spiritual retreats. In towns where it is hard to find services, consulates and free clinics often borrow space from local Catholic churches to host events. If these Latin American immigrants were seeking to satisfy their social needs, the rational choice would be a church practicing the faith of their native land—Roman Catholicism—where their religion and traditions would be reinforced while they received necessary services.

Yet the immigrants I encountered chose to convert to a faith that is not only different from their traditional beliefs but also marginalized, both socially and theologically, from mainstream culture. Neo-Pentecostalism might be popular and widespread, but these churches were traditional Prosperity Gospel Pentecostalist, and they had not softened their message for a wider audience. The idea of getting rich through one's faith is not readily accepted in the larger public. Famous Prosperity Gospel neo-Pentecostal preachers reject that label and emphasize other forms of prosperity as superior to financial prosperity. But it is not the financial emphasis alone that is condemned; the belief in spiritual powers and demons; the practices of glossolalia and miraculous healing; and the falling down and lying on the ground in a trancelike state are frowned upon by the general population. In 2008, former Pentecostal Christian Sarah Palin was mocked by the media when a video surfaced of a preacher praying that she be kept safe from "every form of witchcraft," a common phrase in Pentecostal churches. At Iglesia del Dios Victorioso, pastors and leaders spoke often against witches and witchcraft. Within a month of attending that church for my ethnography, I witnessed the exorcism of a witch.[34]

There are theories that explain the growth of doctrinally stricter churches with practices that seem more fitting for fables than for modern America.[35] But these explanations fail to shed light on the reasons why Latinx immigrants are converting to Prosperity Gospel Pentecostalism specifically. These immigrants convert to these ethnic churches to learn a specific set of skills that will help them thrive in America.

A Different Kind of Conversion

Pioneers of the sociological understanding of conversion have defined it as the process by which "a person gives up one perspective or ordered view of the world for another.[36] Weber described conversion as a shift in worldview, the renouncing of ancient church authority, and the embracing of ascetic rationalism.[37] In traditional evangelical Christianity, conversion is defined as the moment a person chooses to declare Jesus Christ as his or her Lord and Savior and promises to live according to this new allegiance.

Conversion to Prosperity Gospel Pentecostalism is different. Conversions in these churches are not driven by a desire for change but by a necessity to survive. Most worship services I witnessed lacked the traditional evangelical altar call—the moment when people are invited to "accept Jesus." That is not to say that this step was unimportant. All three churches conduct regular evangelistic activities in which church members go in teams and knock on doors in Latinx neighborhoods, offering people the opportunity to become Christian. Most of the people they encounter are already some form of Christian. The "missionaries" usually offer a prayer and move on. This is a pragmatic faith, and conversion is undertaken for utilitarian reasons. People change their perspectives because it is advantageous to their situation.

Conversion of Latin American immigrants into Prosperity Gospel Pentecostalism is further influenced by their immigration experience, which gives rise to their religious lives in the United States in many ways. Their uprooting, coupled with the isolation and marginalization of a new land, pulls them toward the form of Christianity that can bring them happiness. Conversion and adoption into Prosperity Gospel Pentecostalism is an adaptation strategy for survival in America and is its own form of assimilation.

Practices that are done from a state of well-being are often different from those done under distress. Most of the converts I encountered in this book believe they were saved from a real threat. To them, salvation is not a metaphor for an otherworldly reward. Their conversions are never a spiritual experience alone; there is always deliverance from some material affliction.

Most often, it is deliverance from certain types of suffering. Pastors Gielis and Nolasco were saved from a life of drugs. Juan Pablo was literally saved from drowning. In other cases, I met converts who were saved, or had a loved one saved, from bad relationships, sickness, or violence. The religious experience of those who live at the margins is utterly different from those who live in privilege. The daily need for a savior is tangible for only one group.

Much like Juan Pablo, their conversions often give new meaning to every aspect of their identities, not just the religious one. They see their new life as a way to reinvent themselves. When white middle-class people convert to a white evangelical Christianity, they will likely continue to hold the same socioeconomic status. Their political identities might change, but their social and cultural circles will likely remain unchanged. For the Latin American Prosperity Gospel Pentecostals in this book, they do not view their conversion as an intellectual or emotional decision. Rather, it involves a total life transformation—from life goals to relationships to the way they approached their work. Everything is transformed by the conversion, and everything is constantly being fine-tuned. This is the role of the Prosperity Gospel Pentecostal church. These churches place a constant emphasis on helping believers experience what is called "second baptism," the moment when believers are filled with the Holy Spirit as evidenced by speaking in tongues or miraculous healing. This is a traditional Pentecostal practice. At a Prosperity Gospel Pentecostal altar call, believers are summoned not to make a decision but to an experience. Their first physical encounter with God is considered transformative. When asked to single out the moment they became Christians, members of these churches pointed to the moment when they were filled with the Holy Spirit (normally with some type of physical manifestation, such as crying or shaking), not to any decision they made or a prayer they uttered. This is the crucial difference between a religion of experience and a religion of knowledge. Traditional forms of Christianity, both conservative and liberal, are preoccupied with doctrines. Lines of inclusion and exclusion are drawn around adherence to the right beliefs. Pentecostalism draws its boundaries through experiences. This baptism of the Holy Spirit serves not only as a marker of their real conversion but as a marker of their continuous transformation.

Of more importance than the conversion experience to Prosperity Gospel Pentecostals (and, according to Max Weber, to all Protestants) is their *certitudo salutis*, or "certainty of salvation." Weber insisted that the promise of one's salvation was the central driving force behind all religious systems of meaning. In other words, it is the people's need to assure themselves—and others—that they are truthfully "saved" that leads to their religious actions. The need for tangible evidence of one's salvation is what Weber named "the Protestant ethic." Protestants must use every aspect of their lives—both public and private—to reflect their transformation in Christ. This ethic dictates the vocations they choose and the ways they manage their private affairs. Weber contended that for Protestants, the sign of God's grace on them was their diligent work and the purity of their lives.

For most Pentecostals, the first evidence of one's salvation and God's blessing is being filled with the Holy Spirit. Experiencing the Holy Spirit physically assures them that God is genuinely with them. The physical manifestation of their faith also reassures others that they are saved. All believers who receive the Holy Spirit, as demonstrated by speaking in tongues or excessive expression, are regarded as holier people. Believers who have spiritual gifts that allow them to heal the sick, prophesy about the future, and probe the mind of God are considered special individuals. For Prosperity Gospel Pentecostals, their *certitudo salutis* is found in their ability to sustain and reproduce the experience they had when they first received the Holy Spirit.

Because their conversion is almost always associated with a form of liberation, the assurance of their salvation is found in their ability to remain liberated. This liberation can be lived out in many ways and might include staying sober, recovering from illness, turning around a misbehaving child, or even divorcing an abusive spouse. There is evidence that Prosperity Gospel Pentecostalism is effective at liberating individuals from certain ills. Scholars have found that Prosperity Gospel Pentecostals in Latin America, when compared to their non-Pentecostal counterparts, usually dress better, speak a more formal form of Spanish, use English more often, and intentionally save more money and have more opportunities to save—making them more self-reliant.[38] Also, like many other conservative Protestants, the faithful Prosperity Gospel Pentecostal is expected to attend church at least two times a week: once on Sunday and at least once during the week for a Bible study or prayer meeting. (Members who only attend Sunday services are rarely counted as truly faithful or promoted to the leadership circle because once-a-week attendance is not considered sacrificial enough. Prosperity Gospel Pentecostalism requires sacrifice worthy of God's attention.) In addition, most church members are informally encouraged to socialize primarily with fellow Prosperity Gospel Pentecostals, significantly reducing their non-church recreational options. Since they are also required to abstain from drinking, smoking, and illicit drug use, more money can *theoretically* return to the family. All the requirements that Prosperity Gospel Pentecostalism places on them help them remain liberated from the harm they sought to escape when they converted.

I claim that they can "theoretically" save money because while Weber's Protestants would have invested or saved their money, Prosperity Gospel Pentecostals have other requirements for their extra income. In addition to this evidence of salvation (liberation from addiction, distress, and abuse), Prosperity Gospel Pentecostalism adds even more tangible evidence of *certitudo salutis*: wealth and health. Adherents associate God's blessings with the material wealth of a person and their physical well-being. Taking this to its logical conclusion, Prosperity Gospel Pentecostals judge God's opinion of a person by his or her financial success, physical health, and mental well-being. And in this way, the more they desire holiness, the more they have to work to achieve wealth. Proximity to God requires successful families and careers. The more they want from God, the more they have to sacrifice. This is where the paradox of Prosperity Gospel Pentecostalism leads to a cycle. They are told to plant "seeds of prosperity" into ministries, which could be giving money to a televangelist, sending a child to a Christian camp, or even helping a church member financially. Two church members gave money to Gerardo to start his landscaping company because they had to take a risk by helping a fellow believer achieve his God-given dream. Though not loaning the money to Gerardo would have been the safe thing to do, they needed to apply their disposable income to the Prosperity Gospel formula.

Sometimes the formula requires them to invest in companies bound to fail, and sometimes it demands that they buy things to "bless" others. To receive the assurance of salvation is to continuously apply the Prosperity Gospel formula. Even if the dream does not come true, they are compelled to give the impression that it succeeded by surrounding themselves with material things that might give the impression of victory, even if these are things they cannot actually afford. The paradox of Prosperity Gospel Pentecostalism both ensnares and empowers. It traps them because they have to believe and act as if they are already prosperous for their prosperity to materialize, but it empowers them because believing they are rich is already a form of capital. The ability to apply the formula is already a blessing. While a dream might only live in fantasy, the chasing of that dream has real-life implications. The truth is that most Prosperity Gospel Pentecostals spend the entirety of their spiritual journey in pursuit of that assurance. For many of them, that is enough.

CHAPTER FOUR

Dreaming of Prosperity at Home

"This Church Saved My Family"

On a sunny Tuesday morning, Cristina sat in the children's play area at one of the many fast-food chains in her neighborhood outside San Diego. The morning rush was over, and things were quiet. Her two-year-old daughter happily played in the background as Cristina talked about her life. "No one ever taught me any values about the family, but I knew that when I married someone, I was going to be with that person forever, that he was going to be the father of my children. It was more like the things I learned from fairy tales," she said. Cristina always wanted a fairy-tale family because her upbringing was far from it. Her mother believed unions with men were done only out of convenience. Cristina remembers her mother explicitly telling her that when a woman gets tired of a man, she should leave him, a philosophy her mother exemplified. At the time of the interview, her mother was living with her latest boyfriend, while her father was living on the East Coast with another woman and her children.

Cristina followed her mother's example and started living with her boyfriend, Diego. They soon had a daughter, but it was not the fairy tale she had imagined. She does not even remember when they moved in together, it was that unremarkable. She had begun spending more nights at his house than at hers and eventually moved in with him. Diego was no prince; in fact, he was an alcoholic and a periodic drug user. His struggle with addiction and finances led him to leave Cristina and their infant child for three months. It was during those three months that members of Iglesia del Dios Victorioso reached out to support Cristina. After she started attending the church, the men of the church sought out her estranged boyfriend, and surprisingly, he started attending the church as well. For a couple of months, the only time they saw each other was at church, and they rarely spoke. Yet the church community prayed for them continuously. Cristina reported that the women of the church would gather with her to pray for her family every week. Pastor Nolasco and the leaders would sometimes ask Diego into the office to pray for him. There was no forceful pressure to reconcile, no probing into their private lives; "they just prayed for us," Cristina said.

"The pastors kept telling me to believe in God. They told me to claim my family before God."

One weekend, a guest preacher was invited to preach a special event on marriage, which culminated on a Sunday-morning sermon emphasizing the importance of God's role in holy matrimony. The preacher summoned the men to repent and to take up God's calling to be good husbands and fathers. Cristina does not remember the specifics of the sermon (when I asked Diego, he could not recall the details of that sermon, either), but it was "powerful"—so powerful that it broke Diego down and reduced him to tears. During healing and miracle time, Diego sought out Cristina and hugged her. He sobbed uncontrollably while he held her and pleaded for forgiveness. Cristina told me: "He cried like I'd never seen him cry before. He had never cried the whole time I had known him. But he cried and asked for my forgiveness in front of everyone." They approached the preacher together, asking for forgiveness from God and promising repentance. Soon afterwards, they completely changed their lives. They stood in front of the church again, this time for their holy union before God. At the time of my interview, they were preparing to celebrate their one-year wedding anniversary. Tears filling her eyes, Cristina struggled to get out her next words: "And next month, we will have another baby. This church really saved my family. I really believe it. Coming to this church, both of us being here, really saved us."

"Society's Last Hope": The Centrality of the Family

For traditional Christians of all denominations, the home is a microcosm of the church,[1] with the traditional family serving as a reflection of God's relationship to humanity. As a justification for this connection, Pastor Ramirez regularly quotes the bible, which claims that the family unit reflects Jesus and the church.[2] A family unit is viewed as a mini-congregation and the relationship of husband and wife; children and parents are viewed in light of God's relationship to humanity. The centrality of the family has been a notable characteristic of Latin American culture for centuries. The churches described in this book are representative of most Spanish-speaking churches in America in their strong emphasis on the importance of the family. However, none of the churches ever offered an explanation as to why the family is central in Prosperity Gospel Pentecostalism, and none of the pastors ever offered biblical citations in defense of the nuclear family. The traditional nuclear family is taken as an assumption, much like belief in God and Jesus. Even in the midst of political debates on gay marriage, the topic was never addressed from the pulpit because it was far from their reality.[3] Church members were expected to model the ideal married father, mother, and children (usually more than two). Yet stories of relationship breakdowns are not hard to find in Latin American Pentecostal churches. A cultural and spiritual emphasis on traditional families does not make a community immune to the problems that plague families everywhere. But these churches' message of hope and insistence on healthy marriages could also attract troubled couples in search of restoration, like Cristina and Diego. The paradox of Prosperity Gospel holds true at home as well. The ideal they profess can contradict the reality they live, and the harder they try to create a good marriage, the more difficult it might be to sustain one.

Much like the rest of society, many individuals at Iglesia Cristiana del Padre, Iglesia del Dios Victorioso, and Iglesia Pentecostal del Rey Divino have been personally affected by addiction, divorce, adultery, or abuse. These issues are not unique to immigrant communities, but the challenges of living in the margins often magnify these problems. Members of these churches are constantly reminded that the world is chaotic and forces, both spiritual and social, are trying to destroy their dreams, topple their families, and lead them away from their faith. They are told that "in the world" (as opposed to in God's kingdom within the church), divorce rates are high; irresponsible fathers leave families destitute; and the absence of fathers leads young men to gangs, drugs, and even homosexuality—all of which will ultimately condemn them to hell. Much like many of the behaviors they consider unacceptable, they never talked about them in terms of theological absolutes. It was assumed that everyone in these churches unanimously agreed that drugs, alcoholism, domestic abuse, and homosexuality were unacceptable.

Though these pastors might exaggerate the dangers that unchurched families face "out in the world," church members nevertheless have reason to worry. Recent trends delaying the age of marriage, an increase in cohabitation before marriage, and the dramatic shift in the proportion of children born outside marriage are all serious concerns for Pentecostals. African Americans and Latinos have the highest number of single-mother households, and divorce rates are increasing when compared to other races.[4] The families who attend Latin American Prosperity Gospel churches represent this trend. While the religious messages they hear herald strong families, the congregants themselves do not represent it.

Pastors at these churches strongly emphasize combating the social ills that plague church members' families. They teach that by stewarding their families, church members can be faithful to God and reap spiritual and personal prosperity as well as help to redeem society. For them, there is a causal relationship between the success of traditional families and the well-being of society. Pastor Gielis in Virginia, for instance, often emphasized that the family is God's avenue by which He intends to bless all of humanity. His wife, Veronica, who is known as "la pastora"—the female version of a pastor—described the general feeling of the church: "When you have a healthy family, you have a healthy society."

The importance of the family was most prominently displayed and emphasized, however, at Iglesia Pentecostal del Rey Divino in New York, where two-thirds of the congregation are related to the pastor, and members of his immediate family are all in public leadership roles. Week after week, the congregation could see this "faithful and anointed" family, as one of the church members described it, serving God together. Lest anyone forget, the pastor often made a point to remind everyone that it was his family onstage. These reminders were everything from an off-the-cuff remark to the keyboard player followed by jokingly explaining to the congregation, "I can talk to him like that because he is my son-in-law," to breaking out in an impromptu prayer thanking God for his daughter and her beautiful voice as she finished performing a song for the congregation. It was well understood that God's blessings in the pastor's life were at least partially due to the unity of his family. Interestingly, the average church members do not benefit from this precious commodity for themselves. Other than the pastor's extended family, there was only one other nuclear family at Iglesia Pentecostal del Rey Divino. That couple was also in public leadership roles, confirming that the family was a commodity that raised one's status.

The members of these churches are well indoctrinated into this view of the family. Ana, a single mother from Iglesia Cristiana del Padre, said, "I think the family is the foundation for humanity. I believe that all human beings need to have a family to learn, to develop, to have foundations in life, to be able to succeed, because the family is highly important for people to succeed outside." In the same vein, Francisco from Iglesia del Dios Victorioso said, "To me, the family is the most important, the most sacred, thing the Lord has given us. We have to take care of it. It is fundamental for all human beings and for the world." During a child dedication (a ceremony similar to a child baptism except that they do not perform the actual baptism) at Iglesia Pentecostal del Rey Divino, Pastor Ramirez emphasized the importance of the family: "Not only are our children our future, but they are the future of our society. We must raise them in our families, make our families strong!" Ironically, he said this to a single mother who was dedicating her daughter alongside her mother (the child's grandmother), who was the actual church member. The single mother never attended before or after the ceremony, and the father was never seen or mentioned.

The link between a healthy family and a healthy society is a common belief for conservative Christian traditions. However, Prosperity Gospel Pentecostalism carries a more personal incentive for maintaining a healthy family: God will grant prosperity and success only to families that reflect his standards—one father, one mother, and multiple children. In Latin American Prosperity Gospel churches, having a family and raising obedient children are sources of social capital. Status in the church is often established through the family. Official leaders of Iglesia Cristiana del Padre, Iglesia del Dios Victorioso, and Iglesia Pentecostal del Rey Divino must display the appearance of nuclear families in reality or in aspiration. Those who desire leadership roles must do the same.

In all these churches, one's efforts and successes in obtaining and managing a nuclear family are the most important indicators of nonfinancial prosperity—and understandably so. In communities where influences beyond one's control put extreme pressure on marriages and children rebel against parents, the unified, loving family is an accolade that can elevate some members above others.

In adherents' desire for a successful family, however, we see the first paradox of Prosperity Gospel Pentecostalism at work. Like financial prosperity, a nuclear family is an actual status marker for a "victorious life." It is a sign that one is truly faithful and evidence of the kind of faith that will bring about God's blessings. Yet the nuclear family is also one of the things that the faithful seek from God, for reasons of personal fulfillment and well-being. That is, a nuclear family is simultaneously the means to success, the sign of success, and the desired state of success. The family is the faith, the action, and the blessing—every component of the Prosperity Gospel formula. It is both the goal and the path by which to obtain that goal.

The Ideal Marriage

For these churches, a good family can start only with a godly marriage. Like most traditional Christians, Prosperity Gospel Pentecostals believe that husbands and wives must be faithful to each other in monogamous and supportive relationships and that they must relate to each other as did Jesus Christ and the church—Jesus Christ giving sacrificially to the church, and the church following in faithful obedience.

In the three churches I studied, marriage was not understood as a separate institution from the family. For many congregants, *marriage* and *family* were interchangeable terms; when asked to talk about the institution of marriage, for instance, responses always included discussion of children and extended family. This is consistent with other research on Latin American families.[5]

When asked about the values of marriage, Sandro (from Iglesia Cristiana del Padre) said, "Love. Love is the most important value—love for your wife, love for your children. Love needs to be first." Gerardo said, "Men and women need each other. Like God designed, men cannot live without women, and women cannot live without men. So they need to come together in marriage and have children and bear fruit." Analia said, "Marriage is God's plan. I'd like to get married and have a family. . . . When I'm responsible enough to start a family, I'll get married." Paulina, a single mother, said, "Marriage is very important. I'd like to be married and have a complete family someday because right now, I'm not complete."

Since marriage is of such importance to their understanding of family, the mate-selection process is also guided by the doctrines of Prosperity Gospel Pentecostalism. All the single adults interviewed considered their potential mate and the family that would follow as a reward from God only if they remained faithful. They lived in that paradox where marriage and family were both a spiritual reward and the required elements for such a reward. Those who wished for marriage must be faithful to God through tithes and service, then patiently wait for God to bring their spouse. The formula for obtaining financial prosperity, then, is the same formula that yields a spouse. Faithfully tithing, maintaining a positive attitude, and confidently believing that they will meet the spouse that God has already chosen for them is the key to obtaining the perfect marriage.

There is little room for lifelong singleness in this plan; God wants marriage for everyone. By default, singlehood is viewed not as a curse but as a withholding of God's blessings. This foundational belief was widely accepted. At Iglesia Cristiana del Padre, Lorena's story illustrates how the Paradox of Prosperity Gospel can play out in an individual's search for marriage. One Thursday evening, a few single young adults had gathered at the church to plan some group activities. What began as a brainstorming session about eating out or going to the movies eventually moved on to the topics of relationships and marriage. Lorena began to share her own experiences. The only unmarried leader at Iglesia Cristiana del Padre, she is a successful real-estate agent with the title of "evangelist" at the church. She met many nice Christian men and dated a few, but she is still waiting for the husband God has prepared for her.

Lorena recounted a dream in which God showed her the man she is to marry, though she confessed that she did not like what she saw. Still, she believes it is her responsibility to obey God by not doubting her dream. Hence, this thirty-six-year-old has rejected multiple men who have asked to begin courtships with her. She purchased a house two months before this meeting, and the church was invited to the blessing of the home, during which the pastor prayed for her future husband and family. Having done all she knows, then, to prepare for her future marriage, she continues to wait for the man in her dream, as she shared with the group of single young adults:

> I want to get married and start a family. I really want to have children. God has even given me a house to start my family. I've prayed a lot for God to bring me my husband. I don't know why He is not bringing him yet. He showed me exactly what he looked like and all the ways we are going to serve God together. He showed me in a vision that this man would be my husband, and I believe it. I claimed and affirmed it in faith; I've already given Him thanks. But God probably knows that I'm not ready yet. He is probably still preparing my husband to be ready for me and to start a family because it is such a big responsibility. So I have to stay faithful, keep giving to the Lord, keep serving, and he'll [her future husband] come when he is ready.

Lorena must faithfully cling to the Prosperity Gospel formula in order to find success. Any deviation from the plan, she believes, will result in the shattering of her dream for marriage. Yet at the same time, she believes that her dream has not come true because of an imperfection within her (or in her future husband, since his unfaithfulness could also affect their fate). She is not yet ready, and God is still preparing her. When I asked what she was being prepared for, she answered with her best guess of the source of the delay: "I've been in leadership positions all my life. I've worked for myself, and I have managed other people, even in the church. I started this church with my pastors, and I'm under the authority of my pastors, but I'm also a leader. So I need to learn how to be submissive. My husband needs to be ready to be a strong man of God who can lead me and lead the family." This comment illustrates the second paradox of Prosperity Gospel doctrine—that the means sometimes derails the ends. Lorena's success and exemplary faith has led to leadership positions in the church, which is a sign of success and blessings. Yet according to her rationale, that success is also what is keeping God from blessing her with marriage. Being blessed with a husband required Lorena to tone down her leadership and "be submissive." At the same time, toning down her leadership could be interpreted as unfaithfulness, an abandonment of the Prosperity Gospel formula, which would cause God not to bless her. This is the bind that turns into a paradox for many Prosperity Gospel Pentecostals.

Lorena hinges the fulfillment of her dream on her readiness to submit to her future husband. The wife's total submission is necessary for a successful marriage and family in Prosperity Gospel Pentecostalism. This is a trait that her pastors constantly emphasize in sermons and exemplify in their lives. When preaching, Pastora Veronica constantly turns to her husband for confirmation and credits him for the insights she shared in the sermon.

The Ideal Hierarchy

According to Prosperity Gospel Pentecostalism doctrines, the family is a sacred institution, second only to the church. They are the only two sacred institutions found in the Prosperity Gospel world, all other establishments belonging to "the world." They are the two institutions that can serve as the "sacred canopies" for Prosperity Gospel Pentecostals, two places of refuge where one can be free to express and live out the beliefs that are rejected by the outside world. The hierarchy that exists in the church must be replicated in the home for the family to be "right before God" and qualify for blessings. The father must take on the role of the pastor, the mother must be the assistant to the pastor, and the children are the equivalent of the congregation that the "pastors" of this "church" are responsible for nurturing and raising in the faith.

The ideal hierarchy prescribed for these churches is not very different from that of other Christian traditions. The family structure and management style are arranged according to traditional Christian principles, which desire to show the world that God's ways are superior to those of a merely humanistic worldview. What is different for Prosperity Gospel members is the explicit teaching that a righteous family is a primary way by which the faithful can activate the Prosperity Gospel formula and thereby obtain what they desire. That is, the ideal family is not only the sacred sphere in which to enjoy God's blessings but also the avenue for earning even more. When things go wrong with the Prosperity Gospel formula and problems seem unsolvable, the restructuring of the family is one option for potentially gaining ground. That is, family problems or the problems of individual family members can be blamed for sabotaging the Prosperity Gospel formula.

The pastors of all three churches, along with the claims of all the Prosperity Gospel leaders they invoke, define the ideal model of a healthy Prosperity Gospel family as one in which a husband and a wife have several children within the bonds of Christian marriage, and the entire family is actively serving and participating in all church activities. In this ideal family, the father must be the primary breadwinner and the clear leader. Proper family life must be modeled after scripture, and the biblical passage most often quoted to support this view of male headship is Ephesians 5:22–23: "Wives, submit to your husbands as to the Lord. For the husband is the head of the wife as Christ is the head of the church, his body, of which he is the Savior."

All the pastors in this book cited this passage. They argued that Spirit-filled men who are responsible for the physical, emotional, and spiritual needs of their families must lead households. Assisting the head of the household is a "suitable helper," as Eve was to Adam in the book of Genesis. This helper is a Spirit-filled wife and mother who supports her husband and submits to his authority. Central to this definition of an ideal family is the requirement that both husbands and wives attend every church meeting and are actively involved in ministry, along with their children. Conforming to this ideal assures Prosperity Gospel believers of God's blessing and His response to their prayers. In this way, having a marriage that is actively engaged in ministry is one step toward attaining blessings from God.

The submissive wife is central for the family to work. Both Pastor Gielis and Pastor Nolasco often spoke against irresponsible fathers and abusive husbands. But the pastors also spoke against defiant wives because they break God's plan for the family. During an interview, Pastor Nolasco (of Iglesia del Dios Victorioso) told me the story of a woman who came to him, asking for his permission to divorce her husband. She was fed up with his selfish machismo. Pastor Nolasco knew the couple well and offered her a solution: "Okay. Get divorced if you want. But let's punish him first. This way he'll know what he's missing once you are gone. From now on, for one month, I want you to keep the house clean, cook him all his favorite meals, have his lunch ready before he goes to work, make him everything he likes to eat, and welcome him home nice and pretty every day after work. Then after a month, you can get a divorce and leave him. That'll really teach him and make him suffer."

The wife readily agreed to the plan. A month later, the pastor said, he called her and asked, "Do you still want to go through with the divorce?" The wife responded, "Ay no, pastor! Let's punish him another month!" The husband had completely changed after the wife started fulfilling her household duties. He began to hold doors open for her, bought her flowers, and treated her the way he used to when they were dating. Pastor Nolasco claimed that the couple is still in the church and are now both faithful and happy. Their successful marriage was credited to the wife's willingness to submit to—and, more importantly, serve—her husband. I asked Pastor Nolasco to introduce me to this couple multiple times, but he never did, which leads me to suspect that this story was more a parable than a real story. But I included it here because it illustrates his view of the family.

Submission alone, however, is not enough. The wife and children must acknowledge the authority of the husband to others. This can be as simple as a mother telling her children "Go ask your dad" when they want her permission for something. Or it can be as intense as a wife's public confession of her previous disregard for her husband's God-given authority. After returning from a Christian women's conference, Marta, the hairdresser from Iglesia Cristiana del Padre, testified that during the first two days of the event, she did not receive anything from the Spirit because of her sin: rebellion against her husband. Her rebellion took the form of bossiness and making decisions without asking for her husband's approval. It was only after she confessed and repented from her insubordination that the gates of heaven opened and she was blessed. She received healing and comfort in ways she had never experienced before, including the healing of a weeks-long toothache. The obtainment of that healing during the women's retreat further convicted her by revealing that all the problems her family had had—including the decline of her business, her children's academic difficulties, and her five-year-old daughter's attention problems at school—were all attributed to her unwillingness to submit to her husband. Her logic, as she told the congregation, was that when she became the "head of the house," her entire house was thrown into disarray. It was only by the restoration of the rightful "head"—her husband, Alejandro—that order and blessings would return to her family. She went on to confess to and be reconciled with her husband on that Sunday, promising to never challenge his authority again. The couple embraced in tears as Pastor Gielis and Pastora Veronica prayed over them while Marta and Alejandro's three children gathered around. It was a moving scene for the church to witness, yet it was even more powerful as an educational tool: the lack of a wife's submission can mean the lack of blessings for her entire family.

The hierarchy of family order in Prosperity Gospel churches requires that traditional gender roles be observed. Much like the average Latino, men from

Iglesia Cristiana del Padre, Iglesia del Dios Victorioso, and Iglesia Pentecostal del Rey Divino do not and are often not expected to contribute to household labor. Housekeeping, childcare, and meal planning and preparation are viewed as a sacred vocation endowed by God upon women. In the home, the husband-father is responsible for disciplining the children, making major decisions for the family, and treating his wife with kindness. Pastor Ramirez of New York points to himself and the men in his family as role models, crediting his spiritual and financial success to his godly view of manhood and the way he "serves" his wife. When I asked married men in these churches, including the pastors, if they helped their wives with the household labor, they all responded in the negative. However, they were not domineering about it; the majority expressed remorse for their lack of involvement. Even though they knew that their gender roles were clear and divinely ordained, they still felt as though they should help around the house. Many tried hard to think of a time when they had done household labor and expressed disappointment in themselves for not having done more.

The wife is additionally expected to care for her husband as she cares for her children and her home, often picking his clothes for the day and packing his lunch. For the wives, cooking and caring for their husbands is a reflection of their obedience to God's plan for the family and purpose for their lives. Pastor Ramirez explicitly said this when I asked how his wife was involved in the ministry, since when compared to the wives of the other two pastors, she had a less visible leadership role in the church. He responded that "her ministry is taking care of me so I can minister." God's calling was for her to make it easier for him to preach and lead the church.

The Ideal Parenting

The good Prosperity Gospel wife must be the primary childcare provider at home. Her first role after wife must be mother, as her children play a central role in her spiritual identity. There is a heavy burden for married women who have no children. A wife is expected to stay at home, with no outside responsibilities unless they are limited and can be justified as a form of ministry. Pastora Veronica, for example, sells Avon products and occasionally teaches English at a local community college at night. She justifies these activities as opportunities to interact with nonbelieving women. She is intentional about focusing on women, as her husband is the one with authority over men. It's her work of evangelism. A woman's paid work is usually limited to an extension of her gendered vocation. That is, a woman typically works in childcare, cleaning, and other jobs that overlap with her calling as a mother and wife. Rarely do women have paying jobs in which they work in an office or supervise men.

The emphasis on the mother's role in the lives of the children does not, however, excuse a father's absence. Pastor Nolasco frequently blamed uninvolved fathers for the problems in society. Men and fathers bear the blame for social problems in Prosperity Gospel Pentecostalism. It is the failure of the men that allows the devil to do ruin to the world. The pastors rarely blame women, perhaps because most of their churches are composed of women who are already carrying the bulk of the weight of family responsibilities. When talking about homosexuality, for example, Pastor Nolasco pointed to the absence of fathers as a main cause. Though men are never told to participate in the practical work of child rearing (bathing, clothing, feeding, homework), they are responsible for the spiritual development of their children, which includes teaching and discipline. They are the pastors of their homes. Pastor Gielis constantly reminds fathers that it is crucial for the head of the household to pray with the family. Men have also been encouraged to mentor their children, especially their sons, in order for them to learn how to become proper Christian men. Interestingly, when I asked Pastor Gielis *how* fathers are to mentor their children, he offered no specifics. He expected men who grew up with little male involvement in their lives to intuitively know the process of mentoring their sons. This often proved problematic in an immigrant church, where the parents' upbringing is radically different from that of their children. The parents literally grew up in a different world from the one in which they are raising their children. This is further complicated by the fact that most of these men were raised without fathers. As they become fathers in this new country with a new religious worldview, they are left to figure out fatherhood on their own. This is when the charismatic leadership of the pastor works to the benefit of the men. Fathers do not look toward one another for a model of a good father—they imitate their pastors.

I never heard sermons or specific teachings instructing church members to have children. However, in both Iglesia del Dios Victorioso and Iglesia Cristiana del Padre, the pastors were called upon to cast out demons of infertility for couples unable to conceive. In one instance, Pastor Gielis prayed for a young woman who then fell to the ground, shaking. As she began to speak in tongues while lying on the floor, he stood over her and spoke into the microphone: "There it is! There it is! Listen to me, everyone. By this time next year, she will have a baby!" He lifted his hands in the air and showed the palms of his hands to the congregation, saying, "God has done amazing things with these hands. God has done the impossible with these hands." Then, pointing toward the woman's husband, he said, "Be faithful! Give to God what is His, and He will give you what is yours." The implications were obvious. This was the pastor's way of saying that the ball was now in the husband's court. The pastor, and God, had done their part; the wife's womb had been opened. It was now up to the husband to properly and sacrificially give to God in order to unlock the blessings waiting for—and in—his wife.[6]

In these churches, the average couple has three children. While it does not appear that having many children is an obligation, nor is contraception viewed as problematic, the value of children is instilled via the positive reinforcements given to those families who have many children. Elaborate and highly celebratory baby showers at the churches emphasize God's gift of children as part of the prosperity of the family. Pastors casually state that children are a blessing from God. As such, infertility is seen as a disease requiring God's healing or, worse, a punishment from God. Biblical stories of miraculous fertility are often mentioned from the pulpit on Sundays, as in God blessing Abraham and Sarah with a child in their old age or God finally opening the womb of Jacob's barren wife, Rachel.

Nevertheless, church members' decision to bear children is primarily driven by their cultural expectations; the churches and their teachings have little direct influence in this matter, at least in the minds of the believers. When asked why they decided on the number of children they had, none of the interviewees offered theological answers. Instead, all of them based their answers on personal and cultural preferences, such as "I like kids," "I grew up in a big family and I want that for my children," or "I like big families." Even the few families who had only two children expressed a desire for (and sometimes disappointment for not) having more children. No one ever expressed a wish that they had had fewer children.

For those who are blessed with children, having a son is extremely important—both for cultural and theological reasons. Stories of the importance of the male child in carrying on the mantle of the family are abundant in the scriptures. The role of the male child was emphasized repeatedly in sermons, through biblical examples and real-life illustrations. At Iglesia del Dios Victorioso in California, Pastor Nolasco preached a sermon specifically directed at men on the importance of raising "godly men." An equivalent sermon was never preached for women. In talking about his son's baptism,

Federico, the pastor in Virginia, expressed his excitement to the congregation: "Freddy is my Joshua" (referring to the biblical character of Joshua, who led the Israelites after the death of Moses). "It's very important for me to see Freddy accepting the faith because he is the one I will hand the torch to; he is the one I am passing my anointing to." This was said in the presence of Freddy's two sisters, one older and one younger, who were also getting baptized on the same day. Neither the daughters nor the congregation seemed bothered by the pastor's statement. Though he seemed equally excited and moved for his daughters' baptisms, no special words were spoken about them.

There is nothing modern about Prosperity Gospel ideals for marriage, gender roles, and parenting. Some might consider such traditional views premodern and ancient, yet the postmodern aspect of their belief is the fluid rationality they use to bridge the gap between their ideal and their reality. Traditional logic would clearly show that their families are far from the ideals they aspire to. But since rational objectivism is irrelevant in their paradox, they are able to justify the disparity between their reality and their ideal. As I explain later in this chapter, there is a great deal of negotiation that Prosperity Gospel believers must perform daily in order to make sense of their complex lives.

The Pastor as the Ideal

In Iglesia Cristiana del Padre, as in many Pentecostal churches, the pastor, his wife, and his children—two daughters and a son—are the exemplary family after which parishioners are expected to model themselves. This is the uniqueness of Pentecostal congregations: members are not meant to take their cues from other believers; rather, they are socialized to be like their charismatic leaders. This is true both in their personal lives and in the way they order their family. In New York, Pastor Ramirez and his family make up the majority of the church and almost the entirety of the leadership. The pastor's family and extended family literally lead the whole congregation. Often during sermons, Pastor Gielis in Virginia talks about his daughters as examples of faithful children. He once even described how his oldest daughter healed him when he was immobilized by back pain: she placed her hands on his back, and he felt the healing enter him. He also speaks of festive prayer times with all his children—ages eight, six, and four—when they sing and dance together at home. In many of his sermon examples, Pastor Gielis points to numerous teaching moments that involve his children. Parents learn that by being faithful and working the Prosperity Gospel formula, God will miraculously turn their children into faithful little Prosperity Gospel Pentecostals.

More than in other conservative Christian traditions, Prosperity Gospel churches have women who are honored as leaders. Wives of pastors are sought out as spiritual guides, especially (but not exclusively) by the women of the church.[7] In Iglesia Cristiana del Padre, the pastor's wife is the second in command at the church, yet the superiority of Pastor Gielis over his wife is frequently emphasized. During her times of preaching and teaching, Pastora Veronica often quotes her husband and emphasizes his authority over her, which simultaneously validates her own authority over the congregation and emphasizes her submission to her husband. The rest of the church leaders, including the men, are under the authority of Pastora Veronica, and they have no reservations about following her leadership in the absence of Pastor Gielis. When her husband is preaching out of town, Pastora Veronica is the one who makes all the decisions for the church. She acts, and is viewed by all those present, as the clear leader in charge. When asked about the authority of Pastora Veronica, Gerardo, a single young man and longtime church member, reiterated her right to leadership. "She is anointed, just like the pastor. They have a very powerful anointing, and I respect the anointing they have in God. I have seen her preach and heal and speak in tongues. I have felt the anointing from my pastora. So I have no problem following her. She is leading me to the Word and the Spirit."

The notion that the pastor's family is the perfect ideal was evidenced in Yolanda, a mother of two teenagers whose husband serves in the military, who saw her family's faults only in light of the pastor's family. After a trip to Honduras with the pastor's family and other church members, Yolanda testified during church to the faults in her own family and expressed her aspiration that they become more like the Gielis family. Seeing the pastors' family pray and worship together made her desire that for her family as well. Because her family did not practice those spiritual exercises at such intensity, Yolanda felt that there was something wrong with them. She, like all faithful Prosperity Gospel Pentecostals, tries to follow the path to an ideal family. However, the stark realities of immigrant life can put up difficult roadblocks. Making their way around these obstacles requires some creativity and reprogramming of habits, and they deftly apply the relativism logic of Prosperity Gospel Pentecostalism to help them do it.

Negotiating the Latin American Prosperity Gospel Pentecostal Family

Some scholars have noted that the modern Latinx family structure in the United States is comparable to the U.S. family structure during the second half of the nineteenth century.[8] Today, Latinx families—especially first-generation immigrants—face economic and social challenges akin to those faced by European immigrant "frontier families," with a disproportionate number of men. This leads to fluidity of family roles and a greater reliance on extended families and friends.

At Iglesia Cristiana del Padre and Iglesia del Dios Victorioso, the ideal nuclear families they aspire to are in the minority. On any given Sunday, non-traditional nuclear families (cohabiting couples, single parents, independent singles, and those married but unaccompanied) easily outnumber traditional nuclear families by four or five to one. This ratio is more extreme at Iglesia Pentecostal del Rey Divino in New York, where, with the exception of Pastor Ramirez's family, there is only one nuclear family in the whole church.

For the average church member, there is no husband or wife alongside whom one can fully live out the expectations of Prosperity Gospel. The large majority of church families are mothers who are single or whose husbands do not attend the church. There are also some cohabiting couples, but no one investigates the details of these relationships, since it is common to live in multifamily homes, where rooms are rented out to other families or even to two or three individuals. It is hard to tell who is married and who is not in larger churches. At Iglesia del Dios Victorioso in California, I encountered the most difficult living situation: two families with a total of five children under ten years of age sharing a single bedroom in an apartment while the leaseholder's family occupied the living room and the other bedroom. The interview I conducted in this house was done on the balcony because there was no quiet space inside.

A visitor to these churches might be surprised to learn that the family ideal held by the churches' members is different from the reality. Even the married couples who are consistently there on Sunday do not always sit together as a family, partly because their responsibilities in the church keep them apart (the wives usually teach the children on Sunday mornings). A church visitor's first encounter is most likely with a single mother, a single man, a divorced person, or someone whose family remains in their homeland. The first two people I met at Iglesia Cristiana del Padre, for example, was a man whose family is in Colombia and the woman he was sharing a house with.

They were not married and were not together as a couple. It was cohabitation out of necessity and convenience.

In Pastor Gielis's own family, his mother-in-law attends church weekly, but her husband is always at work—even on Sundays. Pastor Nolasco and his wife, Cecilia, take care of their grandson while their unmarried adult daughter lives in Northern California with her boyfriend. A visitor would have to investigate the churches' doctrines in order to learn of their strict and traditional beliefs on the family and how far their ideal is from their reality.

Negotiating Headship: Suave Machismo

Like many Latin American families, the managing of the families in these churches is shadowed by the problem of male chauvinism, known as machismo. Both male and female members of these churches wrestle with the contradiction of simultaneously opposing and agreeing with the ideas of machismo.

Sociologist W. Bradford Wilcox found that conservative and evangelical Protestant men are more emotional and more dedicated to their wives and children than are secular or liberal Christian men. Thus, Wilcox theorized that conservative religion has a domesticating effect on men that makes them more sensitive to the needs of their wives and children. This creates a softer form of patriarchy. These "soft patriarchs" are not as authoritarian as mainline or secular husbands, and are more emotionally invested in and dedicated to their families. Other researchers have found that Pentecostalism has feminized machismo.[9] My research confirms that these trends are also present within Prosperity Gospel Pentecostalism.

Machismo has been a long-standing topic in the study of Latinx culture. Scholars from different disciplines have defined and theorized about this phenomenon, often with inconsistent and sometimes contradictory conclusions. Unfortunately, this attention has also led to superficial generalizations and a mix of negative and positive stereotypes, such as these: "male dominance, aggression, fearlessness, bravery, authoritarianism, promiscuous behavior, virility, excess use of alcohol, stoicism, reserved or restricted emotions and aloofness, sexism, oppressive and controlling behavior toward women and children, autonomy, strength bravado, responsibility, honor, respect and being a good provider and protector of women, children and the less fortunate members of society."[10] Researchers have known that Latinx families and the male gender roles assumed therein are diverse, and one must be sensitive to the different manifestations of machismo among different

Latin American cultures. Anthropologist Matthew Gutmann warns that the etymology of the term *machismo* "derives as much from international political and social currents as from cultural artifacts peculiar to Latin America."[11] There are, indeed, husbands who are domineering and patriarchal. But there are also men who are submissive and dependent on their wives for major decisions, and others who follow a more egalitarian power structure. Although most Latinos are aware of the problems associated with machismo, it is not a universal concern for everyone.[12]

Machismo is described by members of these churches in various ways. Some attribute it to a man who makes decisions without consulting his wife, while others define it as physical abuse. In general, most people describe the stereotypical *machista* (the personal noun) as a man who is unfaithful to his wife, rules the household autocratically, spends too much time and money outside the home, and is generally irresponsible toward his family. Machismo is repudiated by men as well as by women, and by all age groups. It is universally criticized by the members of these churches, many of whom grew up seeing their *machista* fathers abuse their mothers emotionally, economically, and sometimes even physically.

Both Pastor Gielis and Pastor Nolasco have explicitly preached against machismo, and they often describe it as a practice that keeps God from blessing families. One of Pastor Nolasco's most popular sermons at Iglesia del Dios Victorioso is titled "Man, the Head of Christ."[13] He preached it years ago, but many of the church members remember it and mentioned it to me. His title is from 1 Corinthians 11:3: "Now I want you to realize that the head of every man is Christ, and the head of the woman is man, and the head of Christ is God." I purchased the videocassette of this sermon, and the young man who sold it to me said it was one of their bestsellers. "It's a message for men," he laughed, "but many of the wives bought it for their husbands." In the sermon, Pastor Nolasco boldly chastises men who neglect their families and abuse their wives. He blames the lack of prosperity in these families on the irresponsibility of the men: "The families don't prosper, because men are not the heads of their homes. Men were created to be the head of women, but they have failed and abandoned their families. How can God bless something that is incomplete—that is broken? No, He will not bless the irresponsible *machistas*." Pastor Gielis similarly condemns machismo and singles it out as particularly harmful when asked about the biggest problems facing Latinos: "Machismo and domestic violence. Men don't communicate, and they just use violence. They think it's good that they are macho and they can do what they want. But women need to learn how to help men and change them. And men need to learn how to respect women and listen to them." When asked what women could do to change their *machista* husbands, Pastor Gielis fell back on the Prosperity Gospel formula: "They must be faithful to God and pray and keep giving to God and claiming it before God. God will change their husbands."

The scene at Iglesia Pentecostal del Rey Divino was a bit different. Pastor Ramirez described machismo as a problem from the "old country." He acknowledged that it was a serious social ill in the Dominican Republic and among many of the new immigrants in New York City. But he said that it was not much of an issue in his church because of the demographics of his congregation, mostly older and mostly women. He also attributes the lack of machismo to the spiritual maturity of the men. "The men at my church are more mature, they know God better, they are in the Word [they read the Bible], they have grown a lot, so they reject these *machista* ideas."

Iglesia Pentecostal del Rey Divino is the only one of the three churches where there is a true matriarch of the faith—the pastor's aunt—who brought Pentecostalism to their village. Yet the gender hierarchy is still present at this church. In all my time there, I never saw a woman step up to the podium onstage. Whenever a woman spoke, even the pastor's wife, she always spoke from a smaller podium placed at the level of the congregation. No women ever preached, prayed, or made announcements from the formal stage. This was true even for the music leaders. The all-male band walked up and down the stage to perform with their instruments. But the women singers, some of whom led the singing, stood in front of the stage, never on it. When I asked one of the female leaders why she never went up onstage, she said it was a *costumbre* for them—a habit.

As instinctive as it might be to conflate the male-dominated hierarchy encouraged by Prosperity Gospel Pentecostalism with an overbearing role for men, I found that men at these three churches go out of their way to oppose *machista* practices. For many of the fathers, they talk about not doing what their fathers did because they were *machistas*. Diego said he knew he had to clean up his act or he would end up a *machista* like his father. Gustavo, as I point out later, thinks of his role as a husband in opposition to that of his *machista* father. They rarely talked about "a Christian" definition of father or husband; instead, they talked about being non-*machista* fathers and husbands. Their identities as Prosperity Gospel Pentecostal husbands and fathers are shaped by their need to reject machismo, which forces them to tactfully negotiate their patriarchal mandates. This results in a softer form of machismo, a *suave* (soft) machismo. They must still lead and rule the house, but they do not do it by force. Instead, they lead by Prosperity Gospel doctrines. Their reason for leading, and the reason why their wives submit to their leadership, is their subscription to the Prosperity Gospel formula. In most cases, when the formula does not work, the blame falls with the one applying the formula. In families, it is the men's responsibility and therefore the men's failure when the family does not prosper. This makes the men less likely to blame their spouses and children for their misfortunes, though as I showed earlier, this does not keep wives from blaming themselves. The men, then, act out their *suave* machismo, not for personal power or ambition but because they want to prosper materially and spiritually. Their wives and children comply with this leadership for the same reasons, and also because they see that their husbands and fathers truly desire their well-being and prosperity.

Negotiating the Hierarchy

According to the ideal family model that the church promotes, husbands play the role of a "priest" in the home. Their responsibility is not one of breadwinner or decision maker alone but also one of spiritual leader. Much like a shepherd guides his sheep to green pastures, a husband-father must guide his family to spiritual growth. That is the ideal, but none of the husbands in Iglesia Cristiana del Padre describe themselves as completely fulfilling their priestly role. When asked to give examples of how they spiritually lead their families, the men expressed that family prayer was usually the most involved they got. They described their lack of spiritual activities within their families, and most admitted that their wives took the initiative to pray and read the Bible with their children. Alejandro, the father of three girls, said, "I pray before we eat and those types of things. But my wife spends more time with the children reading and praying. Especially with the teenage girls because they are older now."

The majority of the men understand the role of "priest" mainly as the one who is in charge. When the men spoke to me about their role in the family, they used the phrase "head of the household" most often. They never spoke of being priestly or pastoral in their homes, even though that is the role emphasized by their pastors. And, in actual practice, their role and understanding of "male headship" was more culturally than spiritually informed. After all, women are generally more spiritually active than men in most traditions of American Christianity, even in households where husbands are also active in the church.

Culturally, Latinx husbands expect their wives to submit and hardly expect them to dominate a marriage. Prosperity Gospel Pentecostalism validates these expectations by sanctioning that hierarchy through the Bible. The adoption of the Prosperity Gospel Pentecostalism ideal of male headship is a spiritual re-understanding—a softer application—of the patriarchal hierarchy these Latinx husbands retain from their cultural upbringing.

This softer version of male headship was most evident when it came to making choices for the family: all the married men consulted with their wives before making major decisions. As one husband explained, "Decisions are made between both of us, but the final word falls on the man. The men still have more authority. But you don't make the decision without consulting her first." When asked if he had ever had to enforce his "final word" authority, he responded, "In twelve years of marriage, I've never had to make a decision my wife disagreed with."

Women also qualify the authority they give their husbands. Yolanda believes that the husband must make the decisions, "as long as it is done with respect and love. That's the way it should be." Another wife said, "In the things of the Lord, yes, the man should be first. I want my husband to lead, but of course, he should ask for my opinion." In most cases, neither the husbands nor the wives were willing to concede all decision making to the husband alone. Ana, a single mother, believes a man should be the head of the household and be responsible for all decision making, but only when he is "responsible before God and is providing financially, in love, and provides for the home." Though their doctrines endow men with absolute authority, that power is not used in reality. Many husbands pointed out that making decisions *with* their wives and taking their opinions seriously were essential elements of being a good husband.

Part of the reason these men oppose autocratic rule is the shadow of machismo. Many of them suffered the oppressive reign of *machista* fathers and therefore resist (and retreat from exercising) full control over their families, in order to ensure that they do not replicate their father's mistakes. When asked about the relationship between his parents, Gustavo described his father's treatment of his mother as classic *machista*:

> Their relationship was a total domination by my father. For a long time, it was like that. It changed in the last four or five years, because he is much older, but he used to treat her like a total *machista*. He had the right to go out, have other women, waste money any way he wanted. But my mom could not do anything. It was always a case of domination. It affected me because I had that fear. I used to fear that I would relive the same cycle that my father did, that I would end up

being a *machista* like him. But I found that it was the total opposite. I realized that that type of life wasn't going to take me anywhere and that it was wrong to treat your wife that way. To me, that was a great teaching. So I don't resent my father at all. I still help him and send him money. But my brothers sometimes yell at me; they tell me, "Don't you remember what he did to us?" I can't say I thank him for it because that would be dishonoring my mother and all that she suffered. But I learned from him how *not* to be a husband and a father.

Other men reflect similar sentiments, such as Sandro (from Iglesia Cristiana del Padre): "My father was a selfish person. He was really selfish, because he was an alcoholic and he was a *machista*. He always thought of himself and never the family." Diego (from Iglesia del Dios Victorioso) told me, "[My father] believed that the man is the boss. He is the boss in the house, and you have to do what he says, because he says so. And if you don't, you are going to get it because he is the boss, and you didn't listen." Francisco (from Iglesia del Dios Victorioso) had a more absent father: "My father left us when I was nine years old. He was a drunk and a *machista*. He had women everywhere and was drinking and on the streets all the time. I never heard from him; not even my grandparents knew where he was. His own parents thought he was dead. I don't really remember him that much."

Many of the men from these churches have deep emotional scars from their *machista* fathers. The doctrines of Prosperity Gospel Pentecostalism endow them with the same amount of authority imposed by their fathers. But they avoid the full exercise of that authority it is closely intertwined in their minds with the role of a *machista*.

Negotiating Gender Roles

The ideal of the wife's full-time homemaker role plays out as vaguely as that of the husband's priestly role. Members of Iglesia Cristiana del Padre, Iglesia del Dios Victorioso, and Iglesia Pentecostal del Rey Divino face the same economic pressures as all American families of a similar socioeconomic background. Yet their challenges are complicated by their cultural and linguistic differences. For many of them, two incomes are crucial to maintain even the lowest of living standards. Because they live with the economic realities of America, their financial circumstances often overshadow the requirements of their faith. That is, the ideal they strive for is trumped by more practical and realistic needs.

At Iglesia Cristiana del Padre, none of the married women stayed at home full time with their children, despite the Prosperity Gospel ideal. Of all the single mothers, only one did not have a job. Her brother supported her because she had a newborn, but she was expected to rejoin the workforce as soon as the child was weaned. When her brother faced economic hardships, church members—including some of the leaders—urged him to get his sister back to work. When I asked Pastor Nolasco of Iglesia del Dios Victorioso to estimate the number of stay-at-home mothers in his church, he shook his head and said, "Very few. Very few. They might work fewer hours, but I think they all work." All the married women interviewed for this project were in the labor force except for those who were on a break due to recent or upcoming childbirths and the retired members of Iglesia Pentecostal del Rey Divino.

Pastor Gielis holds a secular job in order to support his family, but he often speaks of the day when he will quit his "worldly" job to devote himself to full-time ministry. Sandro and Yolanda come close to the model of prosperity but fall short of the ideal. Sandro works full time in the military reserves, and Yolanda works part time as a secretary. Yolanda was preparing to earn her real-estate license at the time. The church supported her in prayer and celebrated with her when she began working as a full-time agent a year later. Sandro expressed pride in his wife's success, and the church joined them in celebrating the future prosperity that was coming their way. No one pointed out that Yolanda would be moving even further from the ideal of full-time stay-at-home motherhood.

Yet working families at all three churches insist and often convince themselves that they are living up to the standards of their faith. Husbands and their working wives continue to "act out" and reinforce (to themselves) the ideal of a full-time stay-at-home mother and a full-time working father. That is, the working wife will downplay her job, often not even talking about working outside the home. She will focus on her role as a mother and a wife. These actions are justified through Prosperity Gospel logic: "God blessed me with this great opportunity to earn money, so I had to be faithful," said Yolanda, explaining her real-estate license. "God opened the door. I asked God, and He told me I had to do this for my family, that He would bless me through this job so I could provide for my children." Yolanda justifies her job as a means of being a better mother. The work of these women is basically an extension of their mothering. In the end, then, the full-time stay-at-home mother ideal, though lauded, can be technically replaced without church censure by a working mother as long as the emphasis is on the children's well-being.

Most of the women have jobs that supplement the income of their families, but they are reticent to refer to them as "careers." A childcare worker will say that she "watches children," even though it is her full-time job. A schoolteacher will say that she "teaches kids" instead of calling herself a teacher. These women describe their professions in intentionally specific gendered actions and do not self-identify by the professional title. Whereas a man has a career, a woman has only a job to make extra income for the family. Ultimately, their vocation is motherhood, even though they may work outside the home as often and sometimes as long as their husbands. Husbands also speak of their wives as mothers and wives but never as contributors to the family income. In addition, the wife is still expected to do the majority, if not all, of the housework.

The delicate negotiation of gender roles is present not only in Prosperity Gospel homes and workplaces but also in the church. There are a lot of confident women in these churches, and submissive wives often take leadership roles. These women are usually more active, show more knowledge of the Bible, and are more expressive during times of prayer than their husbands. Many of these submissive wives actively seek out children (often their own) and other women during times of prayer and pray for them, while their husbands remain passive. Women in these churches do not feel powerless because they are taught to submit. Rather, they feel they have a voice and are in control of their families and their lives. This public voice and presence are exercised weekly in church, most prominently during the time for prayer and miracles.

The involvement of the women could be somewhat explained by necessity. For example, at Iglesia del Dios Victorioso, the prayer and healing time at the end of the service is divided by gender. The men who desire to receive prayer gather to the right of the stage, the women to the left. Because of the makeup of the church, there are always more women than men asking for prayer, which requires more activity from the female leaders of the church to both pray for them and catch them and cover them when they fall. Their husbands, though also leaders, often remain seated with the children because there are not as many men to pray for.

Negotiating Conflict

Husbands who are not part of the church rarely object to their wives' involvement. In most cases, they do not even object to their "sowing seeds," as long as it is money from the women's own earnings and the family is not neglected.

However, there is evidence that Prosperity Gospel doctrines, when not fully embraced by both husband and wife, can sometimes lead to serious conflict and marital crisis.

In one case, when Francisco became a follower at Iglesia del Dios Victorioso and unilaterally decided to take up his role as "head of the household," he was met with strong opposition from his wife, which eventually led to divorce. At the time of his conversion, Francisco was a father of four who had been married for six years. He had been irreligious early on and married a non-practicing Jehovah's Witness. He described the marriage as strong and himself as a responsible father even before he was a Christian. Problems in his marriage began after his conversion, as his wife objected to the large amount of time that he was spending in prayer and Bible reading. She complained of neglect, but Francisco describes his ex-wife as a needy person of low self-esteem who demanded all his attention. He admits that before his conversion, his life had been completely dedicated to his wife and children, but all this changed after he became a Prosperity Gospel Pentecostal and began to "claim after God" and "pursue God" for victory and prosperity. He denies any neglect of his family, but he does admit to spending more time at church and in personal spiritual pursuits. He recounts the times when he would come home from work and sequester himself in his bedroom for prayer and bible reading, though his wife wanted him to help with the children while she prepared supper. He did not consider that neglect; he was satisfying a personal need for the benefit of his family. The final straw that brought on their divorce was when he started giving 10 percent of his earnings to the church.

This is a unique case, however, because even though he is now divorced, Francisco continues to serve in the church. He is not a public leader (at the front of the church on Sundays), but he serves in less visible roles, such as helping to record the services and run the sound equipment in the back. Although there are divorced people in all the churches, they are not usually involved in public leadership. It is also unique because, according to Francisco, the pastor condoned his divorce and applauded his faithfulness to God. He chose to love God over his wife, and that counted toward his faith and action, which would soon lead to prosperity and, according to him, maybe even a new wife.

Francisco is one of only two Prosperity Gospel Pentecostals I met who divorced *after* they joined the church. It is more common to meet people for whom the church saved their marriage. There were many who were divorced before they converted, such as most of the single mothers. Prosperity

Gospel Pentecostalism can help couples stay together. Close association with other families and support from fellow believers who have experienced similar problems could help. But a more immediate effect of belief in Prosperity Gospel Pentecostalism is relief (or the hope of relief) from the daily burden of immigrant life. Immigrant families face hardships at every turn. The culture is foreign, they face economic uncertainty, and their families are under constant stress. Joining a church that gives them hope alleviates some of the pressure and helps couples endure the afflictions of life with the hope that things will get better. The hope they get at these churches has real consequences for their lives.

Still, both Pastor Gielis and Pastor Nolasco say that visiting troubled families and working with couples on the brink of divorce occupy a significant part of their professional ministry. Even active members who attend church together can encounter domestic abuse and infidelity. But the very fact that they are part of the church explains why these couples are less likely to break up: there are respected leaders invested in the success of their marriage.

During my time at Iglesia Cristiana del Padre, I witnessed the breakdown of the first marriage ever performed at the church. Facundo and Carla had been married by Pastor Gielis in his basement about four years previous, before the church had a formal building. The couple attended church weekly and were often pointed out by Pastor Gielis and Pastora Veronica as the young couple whom they were mentoring. Their marriage began to suffer because of financial difficulties. Carla did not work and stayed at home with their daughter. Facundo worked full time as an auto mechanic, but because he lacked the proper licenses, he was unable to find a steady job. One day, Facundo found Carla in a grocery store with another man, and though she insisted he had only given her a ride to the store, Facundo believed that she was having an affair and physically attacked her. The storeowner called the police, and Facundo was arrested. When he was released several weeks later, he came to the church, and the men of the church prayed for him. Pastor Gielis also had a special service of reconciliation for the couple. Though they agreed to reconcile, Facundo soon left the church and separated from his wife. Thus, even in cases where a couple was at one time firmly committed to the Prosperity Gospel doctrines and mentored in the doctrines of the church, some of the challenges of marriages cannot be overcome by faith alone.

A Familiar Paradox

The paradoxes inherent in Prosperity Gospel Pentecostalism are a constant presence in the family lives of these Latin American immigrants as they strive to make sense of their existence in America. The paradox of the means as the ends requires that they have or think that they already have what they want in order to get it, and the path to getting what they want too often is what keeps them from getting it. Husbands must be the head of their homes while rejecting machismo practices. They must take charge without taking charge in order to live up to the ideal family. Single mothers must be good nurturers and homemakers for the blessing of a nuclear family, yet the fact that they must work to support their families disqualifies them from assuming the ideal motherly role. Lorena must be proactive to receive God's blessing of a husband, yet she must also be submissive to ready herself for a husband. She would have to reduce her leadership role, yet doing so would be a sign of unfaithfulness, which would keep God from giving her a husband. She, along with all the members of these Prosperity Gospel Pentecostal churches, must live with the tension of these incompatible options. They must constantly act as if they already have what they are hoping to obtain.

Yet for the sake of the many benefits they receive from Prosperity Gospel Pentecostalism, church members reconcile their faith and their lives with impressive success. What I describe as paradoxical is perfectly logical to their minds. The average member is not particularly concerned with the contradictions an outsider might find confusing or even troubling.

This is not to say that Prosperity Gospel followers are unaware of the tensions between their doctrines and their lived family experiences. Sometimes those who cannot hold the paradox in delicate balance might eventually leave the church. For those who remain, the riddle of Prosperity Gospel Pentecostalism rests on an unshakable foundation: relentless optimism. And this positive thinking trumps any potential flaw in Prosperity Gospel logic. Since God cannot fail to give them what they are entitled to, the possibility of never acquiring the ideal nuclear family is never an option in their mindset.

For the faithful, there is simply no conflict to resolve. Those who have yet to achieve the ideal family keep trying because their optimism is coupled with miraculous meritocracy. No matter how hopeless their situation, their hard work (in the form of service and financial giving to the church) can result in the miraculous receipt of their wishes at any time. They do not need to apply logic in their paradoxical beliefs; they only need faithfulness and patience. After all, miracles are not logical.

In the eyes of church members, the positive effects of the Prosperity Gospel doctrine are real. Cristina and many others, including Pastors Gielis and Nolasco, are visible reminders that Prosperity Gospel Pentecostalism can heal broken families. This is not new to those who understand the relationship between family and religion. Families who attend church frequently are stronger and healthier.[14] While there may be many explanations for this correlation, Prosperity Gospel Pentecostals have only one: God blesses them because of their faithfulness in and to the church. Followers place their faith in their pastors and fellow church members who show them that their faithfulness truly leads to rewards.

This is anything but wishful thinking. Wives' submission might be countercultural to the average American, but they believe, and have evidence in their churches, that it leads to successful marriages. It contributes to happier households and fewer conflicts for most couples. Men who were alcoholics and drug addicts credit God for saving them but credit Prosperity Gospel Pentecostalism's formula for guiding them and keeping them out of a life of addiction. Thanks to the church, their drug-free and sober life has divine purpose and entitlements. Regardless of the paradoxical beliefs and the unorthodox doctrines, the positive influence of Prosperity Gospel Pentecostalism is real. The dream of prosperity at home might be one dream that actually comes true.

Conclusion

The Dream of Meritocracy

"Dios es bueno, hermanos," Paulina said, as she took the microphone from Pastor Gielis and stood behind the pulpit. "God has been so . . ." she choked back tears as "Amens" echoed through the congregation in support and encouragement. "God has been so good to me. I have received more than I ever could have imagined. He has given me more than I could have ever asked for." The congregation waited in silence as Paulina prepared to give her testimony.

Over two years passed since I first entered the world of Prosperity Gospel Pentecostals through Iglesia Cristiana del Padre in Charlottesville, Virginia. I had been invited back to attend a special service as the church inaugurated its new and larger location. The church's place of worship was no longer a converted warehouse. An African American congregation was renting their space to Iglesia Cristiana del Padre in the late afternoons on Sundays. Paulina was honored with the opportunity to give her testimony at this special occasion. She stood before the congregation of over a hundred people. Many guests had come to celebrate. The room was full, and there were also children in the rooms adjacent to the meeting area. Unlike the original services I attended, Iglesia Cristiana del Padre now had simultaneous English translation for every part of the service because it was now an "international" ministry. Headphones were provided for all non-Spanish speakers, as the service was still unapologetically in Spanish. Paulina stood, full of emotion, yet confident, wearing a tan designer pantsuit; the original tag was still attached to one of the sleeves, perhaps intentionally to show the expensive brand. She looked out on the congregation while composing herself, then began to tell the congregation of her humble upbringing in Colombia.

She was uneducated and married very young. Her husband was physically and emotionally abusive. She was kept at home under the threat of violence while her husband was out womanizing. Life proved too much for young Paulina, and she tried to end it. She attempted suicide twice, at least once by slitting her wrists. She was found by a neighbor and saved in the nick of time. After each suicide attempt, her husband treated her better, but he soon went back to his old ways. When her daughter was born, Paulina realized that there was no future for them in Colombia. If her abusive husband did not kill her, she would have killed herself in another suicide attempt, leaving her daughter behind. She had no hope her husband would change, yet her family, steeped in the *machista* culture, had taken her husband's side; they believed she should quietly serve him and raise their daughter without complaint. This was not surprising, since her father had behaved the same way toward her mother. One day, with the help of her sister in Virginia, she took her daughter and got on a plane. Mother and daughter landed in Washington, D.C., and were immediately driven to a town outside Charlottesville.

Paulina's new life did not begin once she arrived in the States. Life was still hard. She lived in her sister's trailer with her sister's boyfriend and their three children. The place was crowded, and her sister pressured her to get a job. She also suggested that Paulina go to Iglesia Cristiana del Padre, where she heard new immigrants could receive help. And so, on her first Sunday in America, she did something she had never done before: she attended a Prosperity Gospel Pentecostal church. At the end of the service, unsure of what to do but extremely moved by the experience, she naively walked to the front when Pastor Gielis asked those who had a need to come forward. She did not know the Pentecostal tradition and was unaware that this was the time for healings and miracles. She recounted what happened when she walked up to Pastor Gielis:

> The moment he put his hands on me, I fell to the ground and it was as if everything I had been carrying was lifted up. All the abuse I had endured, all the poverty I experienced, all the negative things, the stress, the fear, the anger, all the bad things were lifted up. And I felt loved. I felt that I was loved for the first time in my life! I wanted to give my life to the God who loved me like that, and I did. I gave my life to God; me and my daughter, we both gave our lives to God on that day. When we did that, our new lives began. The curse of the past was destroyed forever. Since then, I have been blessed with prosperity and abundance.

By almost any measure, Paulina has clearly been blessed with prosperity, and I have chronicled her rise from rags to riches. It was only my second week at Iglesia Cristiana del Padre when Paulina and her daughter, Gabriela, arrived at the church for the first time. I remember briefly meeting the shy and confused woman with a young daughter so scared that she would not leave her mother's side to go with the other children. I wrote about them in my field notes, especially recording the distinctiveness of their humble Colombian village clothes. Their ignorance of Pentecostal church practices and mannerisms also made them stand out. The members of the church were welcoming and intentional about making them feel included. On her first Sunday, Paulina was quickly ushered to the area where other single mothers were sitting with their children, and the wives of the leaders of the church quickly sat around her.

Now, after two years, Paulina was standing on that pulpit as an exceptionally different woman. She has bought a car, pays her own rent, and manages two other women in the home-cleaning business she started. Her daughter, who had grown into an outgoing thirteen-year-old, spoke English fluently (even better than her Spanish), wore only brand-name clothing, and sent text messages to her friends on her heavily decorated smartphone. Most importantly, Paulina now had a title in the church. She was a teacher, the highest rank endowed on a woman with her credentials (single mother and lower middle class). This title allowed her to take up the offering, help teach Bible studies (but not by herself), counsel other church members, and speak before the whole congregation at length, as she was doing on that special Sunday. She also traveled with Pastora Veronica, leading workshops and retreats for women titled La Reina en Ti (The Queen in You), La Belleza de Adentro Hacia Afuera (The Beauty Inside Facing Out), and Aprende tu Destino por la Obediencia (Learn Your Destiny Through Obedience). A brochure at the back of the church promoting La Reina en Ti stated that the day would be spent in "practical teaching for today's women. Learning about finances, self-esteem, marriage, the Last Days, and much more." Most importantly, the women of the church looked up to Paulina because she held the title of teacher. This form of social capital raised her status significantly; she was endowed with dignity and respect.

In her testimony, Paulina was intentional in shedding light on the details of how she procured her blessings from God. She explained how this church and Pastor Gielis specifically taught her about the biblical principles of finance and God's will to have her prosper. As she learned the Prosperity Gospel formula, Paulina began to tithe even though she was earning little and was dependent on her sister and her boyfriend for many of her basic needs.

But more prosperity came to her as she "stepped out in faith," taking risky actions in the Prosperity Gospel formula. Her first act of faith was moving out of her sister's apartment. She explained that she had to move out because her sister "was living in sin" with her boyfriend, and God would not allow her to prosper her if she remained in that situation. She took a risk and signed a lease for her own apartment, and according to her testimony, she was soon blessed with many cleaning jobs, which helped her afford the rent. Paulina attended every Sunday service, Bible study, and prayer meeting at Iglesia Cristiana del Padre, and was an active participant in all the activities of the church. As she received more cleaning work, she began hiring other women to help with the business—first one person, then another. Her economic status began to rise. These younger women looked up to her as their boss. She spoke of generous bonuses she would receive from clients, always at a time when she needed it the most, always as an answer to her prayers, and always a direct result of her acts of faith.

Paulina had truly come a long way in only two years. She was confident, happy, and, compared to two years before, rich. But that is not why Paulina was asked to give her testimony on that particular Sunday. The sacrifices and acts of faith had earned her something: the greatest dream for many of the members of that church, and almost every undocumented immigrant. As Paulina was finishing her testimony, she pulled out a piece of paper from her Bible. It was a letter-size sheet of light green paper with a hint of pink on it. She carefully unfolded it and held it up to the congregation in silence. Then she said: "Hermanos, God is good to me. God is good to us. He listens to our prayers. He gives us more than we can imagine. I had everything I needed. He has already blessed me with prosperity. But last week I got this letter in the mail. My [immigration application] papers have been approved! They have been approved! God has blessed me with my [legal immigration] papers! I will be a citizen in this country!"

The congregation broke out in "hallelujahs" and "Amens," and the band began to play as an impromptu party broke out in the church to celebrate this announcement. Omitted in her testimony was the fact that Paulina's sister had previously been married to a U.S. citizen and received her citizenship years ago. She applied for Paulina's legal residency before she came to the United States, but it was only recently approved. This did not mean that Paulina would get her residency card right away. The letter, which she showed me later, was legitimate. It stated that her application had been approved, but she would have to wait for an interview, which could be a long time coming. Plus, Paulina had to wait six years after receiving her residency status before she could apply for U.S. citizenship. But those details were irrelevant on this day. She held in her hand an official letter from the U.S. Citizenship and Immigration Services office declaring that her application had been approved. She would one day be a citizen of the United States of America. It did not matter how long she had to wait, because patience was part of the formula she employs regularly. As the congregation settled down, Paulina announced a final proclamation to her testimony: "Tomorrow, Pastora Veronica and I will be searching for homes with sister Yolanda (a real-estate agent). I dreamt about this before, but I dream no more because my dreams have come true!" The congregation broke out in applause and cheers. Having received her papers for legal residency, Paulina will take the greatest step toward achieving her American dream—home ownership—the ultimate visible sign of her invisible blessings.

Paulina's story is rare, and is not the norm for most immigrants. Most do not obtain legal residency in this way—or at all. The fact that her non-Christian divorced sister was central in Paulina obtaining her residency was not mentioned in the testimony. It was only God, and God received all the credit. Yet the few wealthy people in the church are always lifted up as examples to the congregation. Her testimony was offered as an encouragement to the rest of the congregation: if they remain faithful to the formula, they too can achieve what Paulina did.

Their American Dream

This book is an attempt to enter and understand the world of Latinx immigrants as they try to make sense of their lives. How do people live and thrive under difficult and changing circumstances, especially when they are removed from their familiar surroundings and plunged into a different world? Their stories can be viewed as a reversal of Daniel Defoe's classic novel *Robinson Crusoe*.[1] Defoe describes the adventures of an English sailor who is cast away on a deserted island and has to make a life for himself without his usual comforts. Crusoe not only survived but thrived by his ingenuity and might. The lives of many of the immigrants I described are similar to that plot. Many come from small villages and are thrown into major U.S. cities, often overnight. They are left to survive in a world they have never encountered. Much like Robinson Crusoe, they not only survive but thrive by their ingenuity, their might, and, in the case of the people encountered here, their faith.

Their story is an inherently American one. It is the story of innovation, survival, relationships, and the religious foundations on which they have chosen to build their new lives. It is this hope that has led and continues to lead many to leave their homeland in search of a better life in America. For this group of Latinx immigrants, their faith has become the main tool by which they construct their world. What is intriguing is that the most effective tool in helping them become Americans is one that they adopted for a completely different reason. They sought out Prosperity Gospel Pentecostalism because of the hope and comfort they received from it. They sought the rewards promised by this faith because of physical, psychological, and spiritual needs. Their spiritual journey led them to create and pursue their version of the American dream. In the process, it gave them the characteristics and the hopes of the average white middle-class American.

I describe throughout this book that the life of abundance is not only a matter of being rich. For Prosperity Gospel Pentecostals, prosperity is a mental state of being, a life process. It involves a close following of the Prosperity Gospel formula and a sophisticated process of rationalization by which they make sense of their conditions when the formula does not work—or, as they would see it, when it does not work *yet*. Living in such an orderly and highly rationalized world requires extreme discipline and frequent reinforcement to remain faithful. After all, these Latin American Prosperity Gospel Pentecostals constantly face hardships in areas of life that most people would take for granted. Renewing a driver's license (for those who even have them) or helping a child perform well on an exam are, for them, acts of faith that require miraculous intervention, miracles that rarely happen to their fellow immigrants. For this reason, Prosperity Gospel Pentecostals must have their beliefs and their hopes reinforced constantly. They are not unlike other fundamentalist religious groups when they saturate themselves with faith; these fundamentalist groups retreat into their own worlds and cut off ties with any external influences that might challenge their beliefs.

Prosperity Gospel Pentecostals do not reach the theological and moral extreme of fundamentalists, but they do participate in some of their separatist practices. For example, the church hands out free CDs of most of the songs that are performed during church meetings, so that church members can listen and sing those songs on their own. Gustavo, the painter, plays videos of Pastor Gielis preaching at Iglesia Cristiana del Padre whenever he is at home. He told me that his television does not even have reception; the only reason he has a TV is to watch videotaped sermons of Pastor Gielis. Church members intentionally immerse themselves in Prosperity Gospel teachings as a way to maintain the world they have constructed.

To further enforce their worldview, they gather together with a community of fellow believers who sustain and reinforce Prosperity Gospel doctrines and lifestyles. They share their lives with people who are living out this faith. For most of the Latin American Prosperity Gospel Pentecostals I encountered, the church dominates their lives. Their primary reason for going to church is not to gain spiritual insights or growth; after all, the core message of the sermons is essentially (and intentionally) the same week after week. Every sermon emphasizes the formula for prosperity and illustrates how the formula can bring the desired result in different aspects of life. Thus, the church serves mainly as a place for Prosperity Gospel Pentecostals to act out their faith. It is the place where they "sow their [financial] seeds" and display great emotion in order to get God's attention. The church also provides them with friendships that will encourage them and support them, especially when they engage in risky behaviors. Making sense of one's life requires constant conversation and explanation from others, especially from the pastor. These interactions are especially important in the face of hardships. For these Prosperity Gospel Pentecostals, the church is more important than an ethnic neighborhood. They can live without compatriots or ethnic comfort foods, but they cannot maintain their worldview without a church. To believe in Prosperity Gospel doctrines and to keep applying the formula in their daily lives, especially in the face of failure, is difficult. Prosperity Gospel Pentecostals need other believers to sustain them in their journey. They need pastors and teachers to help them understand disappointments. They need role models to remind them that the formula works. Most importantly, they need a place where the intangible rewards of Prosperity Gospel Pentecostalism are real. The dignity and respect that Paulina received exists only within the church. The status she gained was real only within that faith community. In the church, she is viewed as a success. Beyond the safety of her church, she is merely a cleaning lady.

Because Prosperity Gospel Pentecostals must get God's attention with their actions, their behavior becomes increasingly calculated as they become more and more devoted to the faith. This is why the more mature Prosperity Gospel Pentecostals in New York had routinized their worship. Even after the novelty of the faith had worn off, their behavior continued, even if less energized. Every decision a church member makes must ultimately contribute to the formula for prosperity. That is why they are likely to cease activities they used to participate in before they became Prosperity Gospel Pentecostals. Past behavior, even if not necessarily negative, is typically abandoned because it does not contribute to the formula. This is because the proper application of the Prosperity Gospel formula is such an all-consuming affair that in order to apply it properly, they must abandon other activities. Many of the men who played soccer quit once they converted because soccer games usually conflict with church and do not gain God's attention. Women report watching less television, especially telenovelas (Spanish-language soap operas), once they convert. Other activities and relationships simply become unimportant or are removed from their schedules because of their busy lives in the church.

At the same time, this abandonment of past activities steers Prosperity Gospel Pentecostals to adopt behaviors that lead to their Americanization because they reflect the life of white middle-class Americans. They begin reading and studying Prosperity Gospel books, which are all written by Americans and which all promote a consumer-capitalist worldview. The examples and stories that are told in the books they read pertain to the lives of white Americans and some African Americans, but not to the lives of first-generation immigrant Latinos. They are more likely to learn English because it is a skill all the prosperous possess. Pastora Veronica from Iglesia Cristiana del Padre occasionally teaches a class called English for Success! at a local community college, promoted as a way to help immigrants build confidence. They are also more industrious in their jobs. They work harder and spend more time working, since they have fewer leisure activities to take up their time. Plus, they see extra work and extra hours as an answer to their prayers, which is hard to turn down unless it conflicts with a church event, which it often does. In addition, they start dressing more professionally. They take "a step of faith" and purchase the best tools for their jobs, including the latest cell phones. And, most importantly, they begin doing things that help them plant roots in the United States. Whether it is owning a home or starting their own businesses, Prosperity Gospel Pentecostalism orients immigrants toward economic and social upward mobility. It keeps them actively seeking their success.

These behavioral changes also transform their domestic life. The Prosperity Gospel home is organized like the church and is a place where the prosperity formula is enforced and acted out. The prosperity formula is emphasized in every aspect of the family, including raising children and making decisions. The goal is always more faithfulness, more sacrificial action to live an "anointed life," which means a life of security and abundance. In this way, they are not unlike other families. Children are taught to be obedient and to study hard in order to have prosperous futures. When hard work is not enough, they are taught that faith will bring about miracles to make up the difference.

Prosperity Gospel Pentecostalism flourishes in the here and now; that is why these Latin American Prosperity Gospel Pentecostals do not have a spiritual need to detach themselves from the world. They do not fear being corrupted by material things, because many of these secular things are the objects of their desire. The sacred canopy they create to shelter and reinforce their beliefs is not created to protect them from the outside world but to further internalize their transformation. Their positive thinking keeps them from the fear of the secular world, because fear is for the unfaithful. For this reason, they do not separate themselves from the world. Their children go to public schools and are encouraged to succeed in them, as the church offers no warnings against secular education. They do not publicly engage in U.S. culture war issues, as the majority of church members are oblivious to such conflicts, which are irrelevant to Prosperity Gospel Pentecostals. They are too preoccupied with their own daily battles for survival to fight the American culture wars.

Unlike the European Protestants who immigrated to America centuries ago, these Prosperity Gospel Pentecostals have no notion of a "chosen nation." Instead, there is only the idea of chosen individuals, and each Prosperity Gospel Pentecostal firmly believes that he or she belongs to this group. Like God's decision to choose the nation of Israel, they believe God chose them, not to form a nation but to possess special knowledge that can bring forth wealth and prosperity. Unlike other fundamentalist groups, Prosperity Gospel Pentecostals do not believe that they are under attack from the corruption of the world because of their victorious mentality. They believe that the world they live in is sinful and corrupt, but that does not deter them from their personal sanctity, unless they intentionally enter into relationships with those who are outside the church. As Paulina said in her testimony, she had to move out of her sister's house for her blessing to materialize because her sister was living in sin. The Prosperity Gospel God is intensely personal, and His blessings and curses are handed out individually. Followers have little concern about the power that culture and institutions yield in their lives. Educational and financial systems, governments, and laws are essentially irrelevant in their pursuit of blessings. Analia (of Iglesia del Dios Victorioso) told me, "Whether you are blessed or not, it is up to you; you can't blame anyone else. You have the power to be blessed." Their role in the world is not to call nations to turn to God. Instead, they convert individuals to believe in the prosperous and victorious life. That is why they are uninvolved in politics. They do not believe in obtaining things through the government, partially because as undocumented immigrants they do not qualify, but, more importantly, because their faith teaches them that they are responsible for bringing the changes they need, even when it involves their immigration status. That is why Paulina could stand before the congregation and give testimony to her achievement. It was *her* faith that helped her gain legal status in this country. Credit was neither given to her sister, who submitted the application years ago, nor the immigration laws that permit U.S. citizens to bring family members into the country. This was Paulina's achievement. Her faith and her sacrifice moved the hand of God in her favor.

Prosperity Gospel Pentecostalism and America

I have tried hard to present an impartial view in this book. As I learned about this group of Latin American Prosperity Gospel Pentecostals, I tried my best to describe their lives and their meaning-making logic. I have tried not to ask the larger question: Is Prosperity Gospel Pentecostalism good? But having described their world, I want to step back and look at that bigger picture.

As I have pointed out, few Prosperity Gospel Pentecostals ever get rich. Gustavo and Paulina are rare exceptions, and even they were not "rich" by American standards. Neither of them would classify as upper middle class, and many would question whether their success has anything to do with their faith. In both cases, there was an abundance of external factors that led to their success, all of which were beyond the control of any one individual. After all, there are many stories of immigrant success, many of which have nothing to do with religion or Prosperity Gospel Pentecostalism.

Skeptics may wonder how a faith based on a formula that is impossible to fulfill can possibly be good for anyone. How can "trapping" immigrants in the Prosperity Gospel paradox possibly be understood as a good thing? Many outsiders have viewed those who believe in Prosperity Gospel Pentecostalism with much condescension: they are fooled by the false promises of a charlatan preacher. Some may even wonder whether merely making these immigrants desire comfort and consumer goods is making them Americans at all. Christians also question the orthodoxy of this faith. Many find a lack of biblical support for Prosperity Gospel teachings. Plus, their emphasis on material wealth does not agree with the otherworldly aspect of most traditional religions. Theologians and religious scholars will continue to debate their creeds. From my ethnographical observations, I confirm that these doctrines and practices have real effects on the lives of immigrants. I would venture to say that the effect is more positive than negative.

Prosperity Gospel Pentecostalism teaches immigrants certain practices that make it easier to integrate into American culture. As a result, it gives them a better chance to thrive. As many of the immigrants I have highlighted in this book have said, their lives were changed for the better. Prosperity Gospel Pentecostalism led them out of drugs, gangs, and other destructive behaviors. It repaired their broken families and gave them hope when they were hopeless. They received real comfort and confidence when they needed it. In a world filled with fears, Prosperity Gospel Pentecostalism provided them with a real path toward autonomy and self-assurance. In these communities, I found immigrants who have taken a faith and made it their own. They have adapted it to suit their needs. They are happier, more confident, and living productive lives. Prosperity Gospel Pentecostalism provides a coping strategy for those who find themselves floating in an unfamiliar and antagonistic world. It is comforting to gather among those facing similar problems. There is a real psychological relief that comes with companionship. After all, the hostility one experiences from the world is aggravated when one feels alone. Prosperity Gospel Pentecostalism conceals their differences and softens their hardships. In a world full of agitation, any respite from the storm is welcome.

Prosperity Gospel Pentecostalism serves as a pathway to the life they desire. It keeps them wanting more while making them happy with what they have. It not only comforts but also inspires. It consoles those who are poor while condemning poverty. Like the sacred canopy, it provides an ordering of the universe that believers refuse to abandon. Much like Weber's analogy, Prosperity Gospel Pentecostalism is the railroad switchman that is putting these Latinx immigrants on track to successful lives in America.[2] Whether they will get to their destination is not as important as knowing that they are on their way. Prosperity Gospel Pentecostals are not passive Christians; they are not alienated in Marx's sense. They have not abandoned their decisions to God and accepted their fate. Instead, they firmly believe that their fate is in their hands and that their God is on their side.

These believers are convinced that they are masters of their own destiny. In sermons and in everyday conversations, many of these church members emphasize their power to determine their own futures. They say things such as the following:

GERARDO (from Iglesia Cristiana del Padre): God has already given me everything I need to prosper. It is up to me to succeed. I already have everything I need.

CRISTIANA (from Iglesia del Dios Victorioso): I have been anointed for victory. God has already anointed me. That anointing will keep me from harm and lead me to victory!

IGNACIO (from Iglesia Cristiana del Padre): My future depends on me. If I obey God, there is nothing that I cannot do.

Prosperity Gospel Pentecostalism as Empowerment

The many rules that Prosperity Gospel Pentecostals must observe can seem too big of a burden to place on anyone. The total responsibility of one's own future might not be something that the average person grapples with daily. The weight of that task is certainly not something that is constantly on an average person's mind. Prosperity Gospel Pentecostals believe that they have the power to determine their fate; their logic dictates that they have the power to bring about their own demise. The breaking of a single rule might result in destitution. But members of these churches do not perceive rules and authority as limitations and liabilities. Instead, these rules provide them with the framework by which to implement the prosperity formula. These are the rules that help them make sense of their world and justify their risky yet hopeful behaviors. Their positive-thinking faith leads them to interpret what would otherwise be oppressive rules as empowering guidelines that set them free. Their rules release them from what is culturally ingrained, such as being *machistas* for men. The rules and formula of Prosperity Gospel Pentecostalism help them break out of cycles that have entrapped them. Whether it is an addiction, an economic challenge, or a social stigma, Prosperity Gospel Pentecostalism gives them the rationale to step out of those traps. When Ignacio of Iglesia Pentecostal del Rey Divino talked about quitting smoking, he did not frame it as something he had to do in order for God to bless him (though he told me how embarrassed he was to engage in an activity that was morally unacceptable to the church). Instead he said, "I stopped smoking because I didn't have to anymore. I find pleasure in God now." Others talk about abstaining from certain behaviors, not as being forbidden from them but as being freed from them. The retelling of our stories is a way to Photoshop our lives. The truth is cleaned up to focus on the features we want to highlight. In the retelling of their testimonies, Prosperity Gospel Pentecostals are able to accentuate their agency. Prosperity Gospel Pentecostalism gives them the tools and the framework by which they can tell themselves a story about their own lives that has direction and purpose—most importantly, a story in which they are in control.

Unlike their prosperity, the power that these believers enjoy is not a state of mind alone. As they apply the Prosperity Gospel formula, their sense of empowerment leads them to real action with real-life consequences. In their churches, as they achieve holiness, invest their money, and work hard, they are rewarded with real responsibilities, like Paulina and Gustavo, both of whom became teachers of the church. They received these titles because of their devotion to the church and the prosperity they were able to achieve. Many in their positions eventually become pastors. In most cases, new leaders have little to no training or experience in any type of leadership role. Yet they master public speaking, group management, and project administration with ease. Lorena, the evangelist at Iglesia Cristiana del Padre, leads groups of ten to fifteen church members into trailer parks and apartment complexes and dispatches them to systematically knock on doors and hand out church pamphlets. She also does the training for every event, so that each person knows exactly what to say when confronted with a friendly or a hostile reception.

However, because all believers are tasked with the responsibility of sharing their faith, they all become "teachers" in their non-Christian social circles. An added incentive for evangelism lies in the fact that members who are the most courageous about sharing their faith and leading people to the church are rewarded with a higher status. The power they derive from this status is the assumption that, as those who know God and know his formula for success, they are superior to those who do not. A Prosperity Gospel Pentecostal is always better off than a nonbeliever. They live and act with a sense of real power and authority when they speak to nonbelievers. The practical purpose of evangelism is not only for ecclesiastical growth but also for the personal empowerment of all those who participate. Lorena says that she feels great pleasure after evangelizing, even when no converts were gained. Even if they face only rejection, Lorena and her team report success and delight at having done the work of God. Evangelism serves as a self-esteem booster. In their evangelistic missions, they encounter immigrants who are ignorant of the Prosperity Gospel formula. They hear of people's suffering and are reminded of their own sense of powerlessness before they came to faith. The exercise of evangelism reminds them that they are better off than those without hope for prosperity and better than their fellow immigrants.

The sense of privilege and entitlement that Prosperity Gospel Pentecostals have from God must be lived out in the real world, not restricted to their homes or churches. If the power they receive from God is real, then they must use that power everywhere. They believe there is nothing that cannot be achieved with the proper amount of faith and action. They share, with Puritans and fundamentalists, the notion of being a "light on a hill" for a nation. The only difference is that the prosperity they will bring to the nation will start, and hopefully remain, with them.

When Prosperity Fails

There are real risks in following the Prosperity Gospel formula. Media sources often focus on the rare tragedies of sick believers who died because they refused medical treatment or the poor giving their last penny to a televangelist. These stories are the rare exception, not the rule. All these churches are voluntary organizations, and those who do not believe simply leave. I never saw anyone being forced to do anything, and none of the church members ever expressed feeling pressure from church leaders to do or give anything. As I mentioned earlier, visitors came and left. Even as a researcher who was treated like one of them, I was never asked to give money or share anything about my life. Most of the financial risks taken by church members were taken for their own benefit—to start their own businesses or to buy their own houses and cars.

Simply put, Prosperity Gospel Pentecostals are not stupid or naive. The street smarts required to successfully immigrate to America and survive filters the type of people who make up these churches. These are immigrants with a large measure of wit and resolve. Many are forced to leave their homes and trek north, but few make it. Some return home before they reach the border. Some realize it's too hard once they arrive in the United States. The members of these churches are those who stayed and are working hard in the hopes of making it. These are individuals who are able to understand and apply extremely complicated postmodern Prosperity Gospel Pentecostal logic, which is often illogical and hard to follow. The doctrines and practices they believe in are sophisticated. It is precisely because they believe it that prosperity can never fail. Unlike prophecies with specific timelines, the prosperity they desire is always around the corner. In this way, their prosperity never fails to materialize; it is always just about to materialize.

The paradox of Prosperity Gospel Pentecostalism might keep believers from certain economic opportunities, but it is a paradox that they are willing to live with in exchange for confidence and comfort. Prosperity Gospel Pentecostalism offers more to its adherents than casinos could ever offer to a gambler. They might get the hope of striking it rich someday, but in the process of living in that hope, they are actively making a difference in their lives and in their communities, working and creating new opportunities. Through their faith, they gain the confidence necessary to face life in a new country.

The Dream of Meritocracy

Living with the paradox of Prosperity Gospel Pentecostalism might seem strange, but it is American at its core. Sociologist Matthew Desmond frames it perfectly: "Given the choice between modernity and barbarism, prosperity and poverty, lawfulness and cruelty, democracy and totalitarianism, America chose all of the above."[3] This is a nation built on the ideals of life, liberty, and the pursuit of happiness on the foundations of genocide against Native Americans, the enslavement of Africans, and the misery of its poor citizens. It is the paradox of a nation that enacted the Chinese Exclusion Act only to dedicate the Statue of Liberty four years later as a beacon of light to welcome all immigrants. Historically, the paradox of America is that the more earnest it seeks to reach her ideals, the further it gets away from it.

This paradox permeates America, and it is at the foundation of the economic and social inequalities that pervade this nation. It is found in capitalism, which requires capital in order to create capital. The pursuit of wealth for the sake of joy and stability often requires the sacrifice of the things one wishes to attain. It is the paradox of philanthropic billionaires dedicated to alleviating suffering while causing much of it in the accumulation of their wealth. As Yale University law professor Daniel Markovits has noted, "It is simply not possible to get rich off your own human capital without exploiting yourself and impoverishing your inner life, and meritocrats who hope to have their cake and eat it too deceive themselves."[4] In this sense, the paradox of Prosperity Gospel Pentecostalism is not unique to immigrants or to Pentecostals. It is an inherently American paradox because the meritocratic principles at the core of this nation are only a dream.

The logic of Prosperity Gospel Pentecostalism is the theodicy of America. It is the theodicy for rich and poor alike. Its miraculous meritocracy is a more advanced understanding of meritocracy because it acknowledges that hard work alone is not enough, a fact that evades many of the privileged. But the end goal is the same for the wealthy and the poor. It is therapeutic. Meritocracy helps the struggling feel better about their suffering by giving them hope for their future. It empowers them at the face of helplessness. It gives them a sense of freedom to choose their destiny even while they are entrapped in systemic oppression. As the Prosperity Gospel Pentecostals in this book have demonstrated, what is most important is not the destination but the journey. The comfort they get in pursuit of the American dream is the true reward they seek. For the rich and powerful, meritocracy serves the same purpose. It allows the prosperous to feel better about their wealth in the face of stark inequalities. The American dream must be earned, not gifted—so we are told. There is no honor in admitting that one's wealth and success resulted from chance or, worse, was unfairly attained. Thus, instead of miraculous meritocracy, the fortunate have patrimonial meritocracy—when success is the result of inheritances both tangible and intangible. There is entitled meritocracy for those born into cultures and institutions that privilege their success due to their class, race, ethnicity, or gender while depriving others of equal opportunities. These versions of meritocracy are therapeutic for the fortunate. As Max Weber noted, "The fortunate is seldom satisfied with the fact of being fortunate. Beyond this he needs to know that he has a right to his good fortune. He wants to be convinced that he "deserves" it, and above all, that he deserves it in comparison with others."[5] Meritocracy enables them to feel good about their status and provides an absolution for the suffering of others. It is powerful because it reproduces inequalities while simultaneously pacifying everyone on the full range of the socioeconomic ladder. It allows everyone to feel good without challenging the systems that produced their conditions. Those who have more will feel good about getting more and those who have less will feel good about giving it away.

The Limits of Prosperity Gospel Pentecostalism

The paradox of Prosperity Gospel Pentecostalism represents its best hope and its greatest limitation. It provides followers with great hope, but it limits their ability to prosper. The more faithful they are to the Prosperity Gospel formula, the more they have to sacrifice. Individuals with limited resources are constantly forced to choose where to place their time, talents, and treasures; they simply cannot do it all. They often have to choose between paying the rent in order to have a home or "paying the tithe" to receive their blessings. They must choose between working overtime and attending Bible study, saving their money or "planting a seed-faith" in the hope of a larger return. Every one of these decisions is calculated for the benefit of the believer. But it is a paradox believers cannot escape. They either lose out on real opportunities to prosper, or they are unfaithful to the Prosperity Gospel formula, which results in financial struggles.

Since they are taught self-reliant individualism, they do little in the way of political activism. Plus, their insistence on positive thinking creates a "be happy and don't complain" mentality. An outsider might see many reasons to complain, but their grievances are few because they might become negative thoughts, and focusing too much on the negative could sabotage the positivity they need to make the Prosperity Gospel formula work. This logic keeps them away from institutions of power and centers that can bring about change. Their adamant insistence on positive thinking and independence makes them unlikely to push for political change. In this respect, Prosperity Gospel Pentecostal Latinos are different from Catholic Latinos, who have had a long tradition of political protest and engagement. Since Prosperity Gospel Pentecostals believe that they have the power to change their reality, they have no need to seek out governmental help. This perspective on politics suits them, since many of them are undocumented and all of them are marginalized. Their distaste for politics is reinforced by their theology and their reality. Unlike traditional Pentecostals like Al Sharpton, who are extremely political, Prosperity Gospel Pentecostals are concerned with other things. It remains to be seen how a new generation of U.S.-born Prosperity Gospel Pentecostal Latinos will engage with politics.

The doctrines and practices of this church help immigrants integrate into mainstream American culture. They push them to desire the material comforts of American life, but they also instill and transform their values and beliefs. These churches encourage them to learn English and pursue further education. They give them the motivation to settle down and plant roots by buying homes and starting businesses. They make them relentlessly optimistic as they work tirelessly, hoping for the miraculous meritocratic system to pay off. In this way, this form of Prosperity Gospel Pentecostalism keeps these Latinx immigrants in the same position as the many nonwhite immigrants who came before them.

Since its inception, America has had an instrumental use of nonwhite bodies. Enslaved Africans were forced to work under inhumane conditions. Chinese workers built the Central Pacific Railroad, an unbelievably difficult and dangerous job. By the time the railroads were finished, the workers were almost exclusively Chinese. In 2017, roughly 70 percent of the farmworkers who pick fruits and vegetables in America were from Latin America, and over half were undocumented. There were white European immigrants who did similar work, but they and their descendants eventually got to live out the promises of the nation they helped to build. African Americans have consistently been excluded from the full rights of citizenship. Chinese workers were deported and banned through the Page Act of 1875, only five years after the completion of the railroads.[6] Latin American workers have faced similar predicaments since 2000. One out of every three dishwashers and one out of every five cooks are undocumented. They are the 25 percent of immigrants who make up the health and home-aid workers who care for the elderly and disabled. They do the hard, backbreaking, and dirty work out of the spotlight to support entire industries that the rest of us benefit from. The paradox of America is displayed in full in its own history, its present, and into the future. The millions of immigrants who are working to keep America prosperous are not allowed to be Americans.

The Best of Both Worlds

Soon after the inauguration of Donald Trump in 2017, I ran into Gustavo the painter at an immigration workshop held at the local Catholic church. I had not seen him since I concluded my field research. He looked the same, but now he had two children. His wife was filling out power-of-attorney forms. Over three hundred undocumented immigrants showed up at this workshop, where lawyers and volunteers from the community were helping immigrant families make plans in case they were deported. Gustavo was as upbeat as I remembered him. He was still an active member of Iglesia Christiana del Padre. The church had grown, but he told me that many of the people who were there when I did my research had moved. He invited me to visit his new house, which was about half an hour from the city. He and his wife had purchased the house two years before because they wanted more room for their children. He was still as busy as ever with work, which now included minor renovations. I mentioned how unfortunate it was that all the immigrants in that crowded room were there to make worst-case scenario plans. Gustavo shut me down right away: "No va a pasar nada, hermano!" (Nothing will happen, brother). "We've been living like this for all these years and we are still here, right? We are protected and blessed." His faith never wavered. The way he lived out his faith in the face of what many considered hopelessness was admirable. This event was only a few months after Trump's inauguration, and the desperation was palpable in that room—even for the U.S. citizens who had come to volunteer. But not Gustavo. "Ephesians says God *blessed* us with every spiritual blessing in the celestial places.[7] He already blessed us! It's in the past tense, Tony. It's past tense; we are already blessed! I was blessed with my house, my children, and I've already been blessed with my (legal residency) papers. I just have to have faith." Their number was called, and he had to go see the lawyer who would help them certify the documents that would give a friend the power of attorney to take care of his children and his property in case he was deported.

The irony of the situation was only obvious to me. Gustavo went through the process confident and happy. It must have been like taking his children to the doctor's office while fully confident that God would grant them good health. Or paying for homeowner's insurance while confident that no harm would come to his house. Filling out the power-of-attorney papers was part of the paradoxical logic that has helped him find meaning, comfort, and joy.

I began this book with the goal of describing a group of people for whom the doctrines and practices of Prosperity Gospel Pentecostalism are real and transformative. While my focus has been on the newest immigrants joining this American religious movement, many non-immigrants are joining, and many more are already part of the Prosperity Gospel movement. One of the largest black churches in America is the West Angeles Cathedral in Los Angeles, California. Its membership exceeds twenty-two thousand, and the lead pastor, Bishop Charles Blake, is on the board of directors for Oral Roberts University, the school founded by Prosperity Gospel teacher Oral Roberts. T. D. Jakes's Potter's House, Eddie L. Long's New Birth Missionary Baptist Church, and Creflo Dollar's World Changers Ministries Christian Center all claim membership of over thirty thousand people. In addition to media attention (both good and bad), Jakes, Long, and Dollar are the three most aggressive self-promoters. They stream their sermons through homes across America many times a week on more than one channel. In addition, they are among the best-selling African American religious authors.[8]

As Americans of all ethnicities, including lower-class white Americans, experience a decreasing sense of agency, they will seek out ways to feel empowered.[9] As long as there is inequality and oppression in this world, the yearning for autonomy and freedom will drive people to this form of faith—not because it will give them true liberation but because it will give them the tools to cope with it. These churches will continue to thrive by equipping believers to perform paradoxical thinking and hold contradictory thoughts in harmony. In this way, the poor can be rich, the sick can be healthy, and the weak can be powerful.

The immigrants in this book find their existence between two worlds. They have a home country but live in a country that is their home. They long for heavenly goods that manifest themselves in the here and now. They yearn for stability and inclusion in their new nation but refuse to completely give up their own culture. They desire comfortable lives but live with daily struggles. They live and move in communities where they are invisible, but their real presence is undeniable. They contribute, consume, and exist in real spaces, but they are legally, and sometimes socially, invisible. They are forced to inhabit two worlds, but they are not torn, discouraged, or confused. They have adopted a religion that promises them the best of both worlds. The paradox of Prosperity Gospel Pentecostalism gives them the best life "on earth as it is in heaven."

I tried to bring the reader into the world of Prosperity Gospel Pentecostals in order to offer a glimpse into the ways that this religion influences the daily lives of Latinx immigrants. How do they go on living, raising their children, and contributing to their communities under such uncertain and often fearful circumstances while facing blatant racism and discrimination? How do they remain hopeful in the face of despair? Different groups have found different sources of inspiration and strength. For the immigrants I encountered, the answer was their faith. Through Prosperity Gospel Pentecostalism, they are given the tools necessary to make sense of their hardship. They are able to reinterpret their identity from their countries of origin and synthesize it into their identity in America. Their new self-understanding as Prosperity Gospel Pentecostals motivates them to work hard, follow the rules, and dream big. Most importantly, they remain hopeful as they make their home in this nation.

The Future of Prosperity Gospel Pentecostalism

Joining a Prosperity Gospel Pentecostal church can be a complex decision that involves social, psychological, and spiritual factors. Individuals need to have the right personality to fit into these churches. Generally speaking, these churches are most attractive to those who have an entrepreneurial spirit and are willing to do anything to achieve their dreams. Immigrants who are willing to leave everything they have and risk their lives for the sake of a better future are likely to fit that profile. The charisma of the leaders and the practical teachings make this an attractive option for transplanted people searching for an ideology to guide their understanding of the world.

Even if believers feel discouraged, they stick with Prosperity Gospel Pentecostalism because there is no better social structure that encourages and comforts them. They know they do not want to go back to the past. Most of them had powerful conversions, and the life they have now, even if it is not filled with riches, is better than the one they had before. If nothing else, they have a community that supports them and dreams with them. They hope for the same dreams, face similar adversities, and fear the same challenges. In these churches, their beliefs are reaffirmed as they hear and see miraculous meritocracy at work. They encourage one another to stay relentlessly optimistic and see the rewards of those who stayed positive. The social cohesion they experience in these churches is the greatest blessing to a marginalized group of people living in the shadows of a society.

Although Prosperity Gospel Pentecostalism can turn into a paradox that traps believers in a cycle they cannot break out of, it also offers them an endless supply of comfort and hope. Their God will grant them salvation, but they are also confident that their God will grant them prosperity and abundance in this life. This God already knows the house they will live in, who they will marry, what job they will have, and how successful their children will be. They know that if they stay faithful to God's formula for prosperity, they will live in abundance. No matter what happens or what challenges they face, their God is in control, and they are in control of their God as long as they stick to the formula. A world filled with countless uncertainties and untold threats lures them to the faith that offers comfort. The sacred canopy that they have constructed offers them salvation from the pit of hopelessness and despair.

It is impossible to objectively decide if Prosperity Gospel Pentecostalism "works." For Gustavo, the painter described at the beginning of the book, and Paulina, described at the end, it worked. They followed the formula, they were faithful, they took action, and they got their desired results. Yet for Gerardo, the failed landscaper, it did not work at the time, but he still believes. A year after my research concluded, he sent me an email to tell me he was leaving for Colombia. He had fallen in love with a woman he met online. Her father was a pastor and wanted Gerardo to go plant churches there. Every now and then I get an email from him with pictures of his wife, his son, and the remote village church they have started. He is spreading the Prosperity Gospel he learned at Iglesia Cristiana del Padre.

The globalization of Prosperity Gospel Pentecostalism has been happening for many years. Today, the belief that God will grant prosperity and good health to those who have enough faith is common among Christians around the world.[10] In every country surveyed by the Pew Research Center's study on Pentecostals, the majority of all Christians believe that God will grant good health and relief from sickness to believers who show enough faith. There is something very intuitive about Prosperity Gospel Pentecostalism that resonates with people from all cultures and ethnicities. A 2014 survey of Latin American religions showed that a great majority of both Protestants and Catholics in Latin America believe that God will grant wealth and good health to believers who are faithful.[11] The largest network of Prosperity Gospel Pentecostal churches is not American but Brazilian. The Universal Church of the Kingdom of God is based in São Paolo, with millions of members in Brazil and millions more around the world. The largest church in the world is a Pentecostal church located in South Korea.[12] There is a phenomenon in China called "boss Christianity," in which laborers believe they can achieve their bosses' wealth through Christian faithfulness. They learn this because their bosses give credit to the Christian God for their success.[13] There have been many scholarly studies mapping the global movement of Pentecostalism, focusing on its political, historical, and theological significance.[14] But much is still unknown about the effects of this specific and ever-evolving branch of Pentecostalism known as Prosperity Gospel. At its core, it is an inherently American religion steeped in American ideals. As it is exported to other nations, the doctrines of Prosperity Gospel Pentecostalism intermingles with local religions and cultures. As Prosperity Gospel continues to spread globally, its dominant presence will overshadow native forms of Christianity. The cultural effects it will have on families, politics, and the economy can be substantial. Will global believers set aside the moral foundations that have sustained them as a people in order to adopt this modern American version of prosperity and psychological empowerment? Will Prosperity Gospel Pentecostals around the world set out to pursue their American dream without ever setting foot in America?

As long as the American dream maintains its allure, there will be immigrants who will risk everything to find a way to obtain it. Many roads may lead to the dream of material, emotional, and spiritual success. Some immigrants will go it alone and forge new paths, but history tells us that most sojourners do not travel alone. They follow the path well-traveled, the path that has worked for those who came before. For many, they will coast along the roads of privilege and cultural nepotism. For others, Prosperity Gospel Pentecostal churches will be ready to welcome them. Churches and Christians like the ones you have encountered here will be ready to receive them with open arms and proven tools to help them transform themselves. They will offer them a social structure in which fear is replaced by confidence, sadness with happiness, and despair with hope. Prosperity Gospel Pentecostalism will provide them a place where their struggles make sense and their future looks bright, a place where prosperity and success are only a prayer away.

Communities of dreamers like the ones in this book are thriving in every corner of the world. Like these immigrants, they are adapting and adopting the gospel of the American dream and making it their own, applying the same meritocratic formula to enjoy blessings on earth. Unbeknownst to them, they are changing themselves and their communities; they are redefining the American dream into a global dream.

Notes

Introduction

1. Cisneros, *Border Crossed Us.*

2. For a more thorough explanation, see Mora, *Making Hispanics.* The original document can be found in Statistical Policy Directive No. 15.

3. U.S. Census Bureau, "Facts for Features."

4. Patten, "Nation's Latino Population Is Defined by Its Youth."

5. For Latino growth, see Fry, "Latino Settlement in the New Century." For the number of first-generation immigrants, see "2004 National Survey of Latinos." For the future growth of Latinos, see Fry, "Latino Settlement in the New Century"; Passel and Cohn, "U.S. Population Projections: 2005–2050." For the Latino birth rate, see Dye, *Fertility of American Women.* For the latest census data on Latinos, see Humes, Jones, and Ramirez, "Overview of Race and Hispanic Origin."

6. See Selig Center for Economic Growth, "The Multicultural Economy: 1990–2009," 9. Llopis, "Advertisers Must Pay Attention."

7. Patten, "Nation's Latino Population Is Defined by Its Youth."

8. For Latinos as a political constituency, see "2004 National Survey of Latinos." See also Abrajano, *Campaigning to the New American Electorate,* 149.

9. Patten, "Nation's Latino Population Is Defined by Its Youth"; Krogstad et al., "Millennials Make Up Almost Half of Latino Eligible Voters in 2016."

10. See Cox, *Fire from Heaven*; Hollenweger, *Pentecostalism*; Synan, *Century of the Holy Spirit.* Though there is debate whether Charles F. Parham or William Seymour was the rightful founder of Pentecostalism (see Goff, *Fields White unto Harvest*), it is generally agreed that Seymour is responsible for the national and international growth of the movement.

11. Mulder, Ramos, and Marti, *Latino Protestants in America.*

12. Espinosa, *Latino Pentecostals in America.*

13. For the 1995 estimate, see Cox, *Fire from Heaven.* For the 2001 estimate, see Synan, *Century of the Holy Spirit.*

14. Christianity is currently the largest religion in the world, with over 31 percent of the world's population (see "The World Factbook"). The largest sect within Christianity is the Roman Catholic Church, with over one billion members. This predominance would seem to make sense, given that the Roman Catholic Church has the longest history, tracing its origins to the first disciples of Jesus. The second largest sect is the Eastern Orthodox Church, which was founded in 1054, with about two hundred million members. The Lutherans, founded by Martin Luther in the early 1500s, have slightly over seventy million adherents. The Anglican Church, founded around the same time by Henry VIII, was propagated around the world by the expansion of the

British Empire and today claims eighty million members. Baptists and Methodists, with their origins in the seventeenth and eighteenth centuries, respectively, account for a combined membership of less than fifty million worldwide. The growth of Pentecostalism, then, to its current estimate of over five hundred million in about one century, is remarkable.

15. Lopez and Cuddington, "Latinos' Changing Views of Same-Sex Marriage."

16. "Attitudes on Same-Sex Marriage."

17. Lopez et al., "Chapter 2: Latinos' View on Selected 2014 Ballot Measure Issues."

18. For the use of "neo-Pentecostal," see Anderson, *Introduction to Pentecostalism*; Harrison, *Righteous Riches*. For other names for Prosperity Gospel, see Hollinger, "Enjoying God Forever," 53. For Prosperity Gospel among African Americans, see Harrison, *Righteous Riches*. For the Assemblies of God resolution, see Assemblies of God, "Endtime Revival." For national and international opinions on the Prosperity Gospel, see "Spirit and Power."

19. For examples, see Jakes, *Reposition Yourself*; Osteen, *Your Best Life Now*; Meyer, *Power Thoughts*; Wilkinson, *Prayer of Jabez*.

20. For a comprehensive history of the Prosperity Gospel movement, see Bowler, *Blessed*.

21. D. W. Miller, *God at Work*.

22. These verses are traditionally interpreted as a typical salutation for the period. The wish for good health and prosperity was a personal greeting from the Apostle John to the members of the church. Unlike Robert's interpretation, it was not viewed as a promise from God.

23. For more on Roberts, see Hollinger, "Enjoying God Forever." Oral Roberts University was ranked in the top fifty colleges with master's degrees in the West by *U.S. News and World Report* and the *Princeton Review*. Some notable and influential Oral Roberts University alumni are Kenneth Copeland (of Kenneth Copeland Ministries), Ted Haggard (former president of the National Association of Evangelicals), John Osteen (father of Joel Osteen of Lakewood Church in Houston), Michele Bachmann (former congresswoman from Minnesota), Stephen Mansfield (author of *The Faith of George W. Bush*), Michael Graham (conservative Republican radio host), Kathy Lee Gifford (TV host), Creflo Dollar (World Changers International), Ross Parsley (OneChapel in Austin, Texas), and Marcos Witt (Grammy-winning musician). In a conversation with me, Pastor Gielis mentioned that he expected all his children to attend Oral Roberts University because he had learned so much from the man, including the blessings of the seed-faith offering.

24. Peale, *Power of Positive Thinking*.

25. Keith, "Trump Crowd Size Estimate."

26. Though this movement is known by many names, I refer to it as Prosperity Gospel because that is the most recognizable name for the movement. Some scholars have used "Word of Faith" and "Pentecostalism" interchangeably (Freston, "Transnationalisation of Brazilian Pentecostalism"), but I find reason not to do so. See also, Chesnut, *Born Again in Brazil*; Chesnut, *Competitive Spirits*. The Assemblies of God, the largest Pentecostal denomination in the world, has been critical of the Word of Faith movement from the start. Kenneth Hagin was forced out of the Assemblies of God

because of his teachings on prosperity (see Coleman, *Globalisation of Charismatic Christianity*). The Assemblies of God continues to reinforce its stance against Prosperity Gospel teachings and has issued an official resolution condemning the teachings of the Prosperity Gospel, with special censure against the use of this message for fund-raising purposes (see Assemblies of God, "Endtime Revival").

27. Graham Ambrose, "Joel Osteen Talks Hope, Wealth and Prayer Ahead of Denver Service," *Denver Post*, July 7, 2017, www.denverpost.com/2017/07/07/joel-osteen-talks-hope-wealth-prayer; Jakes, "What Is the Prosperity Gospel?"

28. Douthat, *Bad Religion*.

29. The cable channel Oxygen aired shows featuring Prosperity Gospel pastors called *Preachers of L.A.*, *Preachers of Detroit*, and *Preachers of Atlanta*.

30. See, for example, Coleman, *Globalization of Charismatic Christianity*; Harrison, *Righteous Riches*; Lee, *T. D. Jakes*; Lee and Sinitiere, *Holy Mavericks*; Marti, *Hollywood Faith*; Bowler, *Blessed*.

31. The Reverend Norman Vincent Peale (1898–1993), considered the father of positive thinking in American Christianity, was mentored by New Thought metaphysics pioneer Ernest S. Holmes. Peale's book, *The Power of Positive Thinking*, has been deeply influential for Christian leaders in the twentieth century. He was praised by evangelist Billy Graham and eulogized by President Bill Clinton. The self-esteem movement in America rose at the same time through the work of psychologists such as Abraham Maslow and Carl Rogers. For more on the self-esteem movement, see Snyder and Lopez, *Oxford Handbook of Positive Psychology*.

32. For these and the following statistics on Latinos, see "Changing Faiths."

33. "Changing Faiths," 29.

34. Durkheim, *Elementary Forms of Religious Life*.

35. Greenman and Yu, "Is Assimilation Theory Dead?" 109–137; Rumbaut, "Assimilation and Its Discontents," 923–960; Zhou, "Segmented Assimilation," 975–1008.

36. Thomas and Znaniecki, *Polish Peasant in Europe and America*; Park, "Human Migration and the Marginal Man," 881–893; Warner and Srole, *Social Systems of American Ethnic Groups*; Gordon, *Assimilation in American Life*; Portes and Zhou, "New Second Generation," 74–96; Zhou, "Segmented Assimilation," 825–858; Portes and Rumbaut, *Legacies*; Alba et al., "Immigrant Groups in the Suburbs," 446–460; S. K. Brown, "Delayed Spatial Assimilation," 193–209.

37. Gordon, *Assimilation in American Life*.

38. The United States Naturalization Law of March 26, 1790 (1 Stat. 103), stipulated that the right to citizenship was reserved for "white persons of good character."

39. Yang, *Chinese Christians in America*.

40. Portes and Zhou, "New Second Generation," 74–96.

41. Durkheim, *Elementary Forms of Religious Life*.

42. "Shifting Religious Identity of Latinos in the United States."

43. For detailed expositions of Latino Pentecostalism, see Ramirez, *Migrating Faith*; Espinosa, *Latino Pentecostals in America*; Espinosa, Elizondo, and Miranda, *Latino Religions and Civic Activism in the United States*; Sánchez-Walsh, *Latino Pentecostal Identity*.

44. Schieman et al., "Love Thy Self?," 293–318.

45. Marti and Ganiel, *Deconstructed Church*.
46. Warner, *Church of Our Own*; Yang, *Chinese Christians in America*.
47. Mulder, Ramos, and Marti, *Latino Protestants in America*.
48. Ammerman, *Bible Believers*.
49. Poloma, *Main Street Mystics*.
50. President Bill Clinton, speech to Democratic Leadership Council, 1993, quoted in Hochschild, *Facing Up to the American Dream*, 18.

Chapter One

1. Fundamentalist Christian churches that take the Bible literally believe that the return of the Jews to Israel and the establishment of the State of Israel is the fulfillment of biblical prophecy. These Christians are known as Christian Zionists, Zion being the Old Testament name for Jerusalem. They often use the existence of the State of Israel as evidence for the existence of God. They believe that the return of the Jewish people to Israel is a prerequisite for the Second Coming of Jesus, which, according to their beliefs, will take place on Mount Zion. The display of the flag of Israel in these churches is a symbolic identification with the chosen people of God.
2. Bowler, *Blessed*.
3. Coleman, *Globalisation of Charismatic Christianity*; Gbote and Kgatla, "Prosperity Gospel," 1–10; Yong and Attanasi, *Pentecostalism and Prosperity*.
4. "Spirit and Power."
5. Menjívar, *Fragmented Ties*.
6. Lee, *T. D. Jakes*; Lee and Sinitiere, *Holly Mavericks*.
7. Ammerman et al., *Studying Congregations*.
8. J. W. Williams, "Pentecostalization of Christian Zionism," 159–194; Newberg, *Pentecostal Mission in Palestine*; Baumann, "Political Engagement Meets the Prosperity Gospel," 359–385.
9. The average age in the church is an estimate, since not everyone returned their surveys. Dye, *Fertility of American Women*.
10. See Dye, *Fertility of American Women*.
11. National statistics in this paragraph are from "Changing Faiths."
12. "Gender Gap in Religion Around the World."
13. Tsang, "Integration of Immigrants," 1177–1198; Garcia, "Buscando Trabajo," 3–22.
14. The injunction to tithe is found in the Hebrew Bible as part of the Mosaic Laws. God requires the people to set aside a tenth of all they produce for the larger community (see Deuteronomy 14:22–27).
15. For research on American Christians' giving patterns, see Smith, Emerson, and Snell, *Passing the Plate*.
16. This verse is widely used by Prosperity Gospel preachers such as Creflo Dollar (www.creflodollarministries.org/Bible-Study/Study-Notes/Free%20to%20Tithe), Joel Osteen (www.joelosteen.com/Pages/Article.aspx?articleid=6473), and Kenneth Copeland (www.kcm.org/real-help/finances/learn/do-i-have-tithe).
17. Synan, "A Healer in the House?"; Hollenweger, *Pentecostalism*.

18. For the couple unable to conceive, Pastor Gielis claimed that God would "open up the womb" and they would have a baby within a year. Although that did not happen, the couple continued to be active members of the church.

19. In Spanish, "Pero los que esperan a Jehová tendrán nuevas fuerzas; levantarán alas como las águilas; correrán, y no se cansarán; caminarán, y no se fatigarán" (Reina-Valera, 1960).

20. Bergad, "Latino Population of New York City."

21. Berger, *The Sacred Canopy*.

Chapter Two

1. These two holidays are times when the Jewish people present themselves before God for judgment and amend their ways. These holidays usually fall in September, but Pastor Gielis was confident that October was the right month.

2. Weber, *Protestant Ethic and the Spirit of Capitalism*.

3. Freud, *Introductory Lectures on Psychoanalysis*.

4. Rieff, *Triumph of the Therapeutic*.

5. Scholars have argued that the basic tenets of the Prosperity Gospel movement did not originate from the famous Prosperity Gospel preachers of the twentieth century but rather from New England independent evangelist and Bible teacher Essek William Kenyon (1867–1948), a preacher who was heavily influenced by the New Thought movement. Most scholars, however, agree that Hagin and Roberts were the most important champions of this faith in the twentieth century. See, for example, Harrison, *Righteous Riches*; Anderson, *Introduction to Pentecostalism*; Perriman, *Faith, Health, and Prosperity*; Coleman, *Globalisation of Charismatic Christianity*.

6. McConnell, *A Different Gospel*.

7. What has been called the "Kenyon connection" is a controversial issue among critics and proponents of Prosperity Gospel Pentecostalism, with accusations of plagiarism and heresy launched between the two camps. For more, see Harrison, *Righteous Riches*; Coleman, *Globalisation of Charismatic Christianity*; Simmons, *E. W. Kenyon and the Postbellum Pursuit of Peace, Power, and Plenty*; Hollinger, "Enjoying God Forever"; McConnell, *A Different Gospel*.

8. "Positive Thinking: The Norman Vincent Peale Story."

9. As quoted in Peale, *Power of Positive Thinking*.

10. Berger, *The Sacred Canopy*.

11. Romero, "Que Seria de Mi." "Que seria de mi si no me hubieras alcanzado / Donde estaria hoy si no me hubieras perdonado / Tendria un vacio en mi corazon vagaria sin rumbo sin direccion / Si no fuera por tu gracia y por tu amor / Coro: Seria como un pajaro herido que se muere en el suelo / Seria como un ciervo que brama por agua en un desierto. Si no fuera por tu gracia y por tu amor."

Chapter Three

1. Crèvecoeur, *Letters from an American Farmer*.

2. Tocqueville, *Democracy in America*.

3. This was changed when Benjamin Franklin and Thomas Jefferson wanted to downplay the management of private property as a goal of government. See Franklin, *The Compleated Autobiography*.

4. Conversion to Pentecostalism is not a uniquely U.S. phenomenon. There is a global element to Pentecostalism that is transcending cultural and ethnic differences, as I highlight in the conclusion.

5. Cullen, *The American Dream*.

6. See Waters and Jiménez, "Assessing Immigrant Assimilation," 105–125.

7. Park and Burgess, *Introduction to the Science of Sociology*, 739–740.

8. See Thomas and Florian Znaniecki, *Polish Peasant in Europe and America*; Park, "Human Migration and the Marginal Man," 881–893; Warner and Srole, *Social Systems of American Ethnic Groups*; Gordon, *Assimilation in American Life*.

9. Blauner, *Still the Big News*; Acuña, *Occupied America*.

10. Portes and Zhou, "New Second Generation," 74–96; Zhou, "Segmented Assimilation," 825–858; Portes and Rumbaut, *Legacies*.

11. Jiménez and Fitzgerald, "Mexican Assimilation," 337–354.

12. Wright, Ellis, and Parks, "Re-placing Whiteness in Spatial Assimilation Research," 111–135; Alba and Nee, *Remaking the American Mainstream*; Gans, "Symbolic Ethnicity," 1–20.

13. Du Bois, *Souls of Black Folk*.

14. Du Bois, 1.

15. Gordon, *Assimilation in American Life*.

16. Glazer, "Is Assimilation Dead?" 122–136.

17. See Portes, "Immigration Theory for a New Century," 799–825; Portes and Rumbaut, *Immigrant America*; Portes and DeWind, *Rethinking Migration*; Rumbaut, "Paradoxes (and Orthodoxies) of Assimilation"; Alba and Nee, "Rethinking Assimilation Theory for a New Era of Immigration," 826–874; Barkan et al., "Race, Religion, and Nationality in American Society," 38–75; Kazal, "Revisiting Assimilation," 437–471; Morawska, "In Defense of the Assimilation Model," 76–87.

18. Alba and Nee, *Remaking the American Mainstream*.

19. Mexican Americans, along with Native Americans, are the only minority groups in the United States to be annexed by conquest and to have their rights protected by treaty (in the case of Mexican Americans, it was the Treaty of Guadalupe Hidalgo of 1848). Much like the Native American peace treaties, the enforcement of the Treaty of Guadalupe Hidalgo is also questionable.

20. Huntington, *Who Are We?*

21. Candelario, "'Black Behind the Ears,'" 55–72; Rodriguez, *Changing Race*; Ropp, "Secondary Migration and the Politics of Identity for Asian Latinos in Los Angeles," 19–29; Waters, *Black Identities*.

22. Waters and Pineau, *Integration of Immigrants into American Society*.

23. De Genova and Peuz, *Deportation Regime*; Dreby, *Everyday Illegal*.

24. Herberg, *Protestant, Catholic, Jew*; R. B. Williams, *Religions of Immigrants from India and Pakistan*; Warner and Witner, *Gathering in Diaspora*; Ebaugh and Chafetz, *Religion and the New Immigrants*.

25. On Fenggang Yang's "Sinicization," see Yang, "Chinese Gospel Church," 89–107; Yang, *Chinese Christians in America*. On Chinese immigrants in California, see Ng, "Seeking the Christian Tutelage," 195–214.

26. On religion as an agent of ethnic reaffirmation, see Herberg, *Protestant, Catholic, Jew*; Warner, "Work in Progress toward a New Paradigm for the Sociological Study of Religion in the United States," 1044–1093; R. B. Williams, *Religions of Immigrants from India and Pakistan*. On the persistence of native religion in the lives of immigrants, see Chong, "What It Means to Be Christian," 259–286; Bankston and Zhou, "Ethnic Church, Ethnic Identification, and the Social Adjustment of Vietnamese Adolescents," 18–37; F. Yang, *Chinese Christians in America*. On conversion fostering both ethnic reproduction and assimilation in a variety of minority groups, see Zhou, *Chinatown*; Yang and Ebaugh, "Transformations in New Immigrant Religions and Their Global Implications," 269–288; F. Yang, *Chinese Christians in America*; Fenton, *Transplanting Religious Traditions*; Haddad and Lummis, *Islamic Values in the United States*; Kashima, *Buddhism in America*; T. L. Smith, "Religion and Ethnicity in America," 1155–1185; Warner, "Place of the Congregation in the Contemporary American Religious Configuration," 54–99; Alexander, *Immigrant Church and Community*; Dolan, *Immigrant Church*; Mor, *Jewish Assimilation, Acculturation, and Accommodation*.

27. Villafañe, *Liberating Spirit*; Sánchez-Walsh, *Latino Pentecostal Identity*.

28. Wang, Yoshioka, and Ashcraft, "What Affects Hispanic Volunteering in the United States," 125–148.

29. The majority of the members at Iglesia Pentecostal del Rey Divino are fluent in English and often speak to one another in English rather than in Spanish. Pastors Gielis and Ramirez, along with their wives, speak English with only a trace accent, if any. Pastor Nolasco and his wife speak English with a heavier Spanish accent, but they are nevertheless comfortable speaking it and are often called upon to translate for members of the church.

30. For more on transnational migration, see Duany, *Blurred Borders*.

31. "Changing Faiths."

32. F. Yang, *Chinese Christians in America*.

33. Hurh and Kim, "Religious Participation of Korean Immigrants in the United States," 19–34.

34. In both Iglesia Cristiana del Padre in Virginia and Iglesia del Dios Victorioso in California, there were prayers against witches and "black magic." At Iglesia del Dios Victorioso, an exorcism was performed on a witch brought there by her family. The men held her arms as she screamed and cursed. The pastor and some of the men prayed with their hands on her head, which caused her to vomit on the stage. To my surprise, the following Sunday this former witch showed up at church with a Bible in hand, ready to join the church as a new person. She gave her testimony, identifying herself as a witch and a *curandera* (a folk healer). *Curanderos* and *curanderas* are not unusual in Latin American communities, and most are not considered witches. *Curanderos* traditionally employ holy water and other sacred items from the Roman Catholic Church tradition.

35. Iannaccone, "Why Strict Churches Are Strong," 1180–1211.

36. Lofland and Stark, "Becoming a World-Saver," 862–875.

37. Weber, *Protestant Ethic and the Spirit of Capitalism*.

38. Martin, *Tongues of Fire*; Martin, *Pentecostalism*; Stoll, *Is Latin America Turning Protestant?*

Chapter Four

1. Ammerman, *Bible Believers*.

2. See Ephesians 5:31–32: "'For this reason a man will leave his father and mother and be united to his wife, and the two will become one flesh.' This is a profound mystery—but I am talking about Christ and the church."

3. On this note, none of the church members ever spoke about same-sex marriage; that reality was simply too far from their worldview. For them, homosexuality was such an abominable sin that the possibility of marriage was not an option.

4. Bramlett and Mosher, *Cohabitation, Marriage, Divorce, and Remarriage*; Casper and Bianchi, *Continuity and Change in the American Family*; Wu and Wolfe, *Out of Wedlock*. For the number of single-mother households, see Suro, "Hispanic Family in Flux."

5. Skogrand et al., *Strong Marriages in the Latino Culture*.

6. Two years later, this couple is still childless but still very active in the church.

7. This is not unlike many charismatic and African American churches, where the pastor's wife is referred to as the "first lady" of the church and is often bestowed with a high level of authority.

8. Griswold del Castillo, *La Familia*; Vega, "Hispanic Families in the 1980s," 1015–1024.

9. Wilcox, *Soft Patriarchs, New Men*; Brusco, "Reformation of Machismo."

10. Torres, Solberg, and Carlstrom, "Myth of Sameness among Latino Men and Their Machismo," 164.

11. For domineering machismo, see Peñalosa, "Mexican Family Roles," 680–689. For more passive applications, see Hawkes and Taylor, "Power Structure in Mexican and Mexican-American Farm Labor Families," 807–811; Gutmann, "Introduction," 18.

12. Hurtado and Sinha, *Beyond Machismo*.

13. In Spanish, "Varon la Cabeza de Cristo." The title is recorded here from the label on the videotape, though it seems like it may be a misprint, as God is the head of Christ in the biblical reference.

14. Wilcox, "As the Family Goes."

Conclusion

1. Defoe, *Robinson Crusoe*.

2. Weber, *The Sociology of Religion*.

3. Matthew Desmond, "Capitalism," *New York Times Magazine*, August 18, 2019.

4. Markovits, "How Life Became an Endless, Terrible Competition."

5. Weber, *From Max Weber*, 271.

6. Forty-third Congress, sess. 1, chapter 141, 1875. "An act supplementary to the acts in relation to immigration" (https://www.loc.gov/law/help/statutes-at-large/43rd-congress/session-2/c43s2ch141.pdf).

7. Ephesians 1:3 "Praise be to the God and Father of our Lord Jesus Christ, who has blessed us in the heavenly realms with every spiritual blessing in Christ."

8. For an analysis of the Prosperity Gospel movement in black churches, see Harrison, *Righteous Riches*; Lee, *T. D. Jakes*.

9. Vance, *Hillbilly Elegy*.

10. "Spirit and Power."

11. "Religion in Latin America."

12. Anderson, *Introduction to Pentecostalism*.

13. Cao, *Constructing China's Jerusalem*.

14. Miller and Yamamori. *Global Pentecostalism*; Anderson, *Introduction to Pentecostalism*; Brown, *Global Pentecostal and Charismatic Healing*; Miller, Sargeant, and Flory, *Spirit and Power*.

Bibliography

Abrajano, Marisa A. *Campaigning to the New American Electorate: Advertising to Latino Voters*. Stanford, CA: Stanford University Press, 2010.

Acuña, Rodolfo. *Occupied America: The Chicano's Struggle toward Liberation*. New York: HarperCollins, 1972.

Alba, Richard D., and Victor Nee. *Remaking the American Mainstream: Assimilation and Contemporary Immigration*. Cambridge, Mass: Harvard University Press, 2003.

———. "Rethinking Assimilation Theory for a New Era of Immigration." *International Migration Review* 31, no. 4 (1997): 826–874.

Alba, Richard D., John R. Logan, Brian J. Stults, Gilbert Marzan, and Wenquan Zhang. "Immigrant Groups in the Suburbs: A Reexamination of Suburbanization and Spatial Assimilation." *American Sociological Review* 64, no. 3 (1999): 446–460.

Alexander, June Granatir. *The Immigrant Church and Community: Pittsburgh's Slovak Catholics and Lutherans, 1880–1915*. Pittsburgh, PA: University of Pittsburgh Press, 1987.

Ammerman, Nancy Tatom. *Bible Believers: Fundamentalists in the Modern World*. New Brunswick, NJ: Rutgers University Press, 1987.

Ammerman, Nancy Tatom, Jackson W. Carroll, Carl S. Dudley, and William McKinney, eds. *Studying Congregations: A New Handbook*. Nashville, TN: Abington Press, 1998.

Anderson, Allan. *An Introduction to Pentecostalism: Global Charismatic Christianity*. Cambridge: Cambridge University Press, 2004.

Assemblies of God. "Endtime Revival—Spirit-Led and Spirit-Controlled: A Response Paper to Resolution 16." Adopted by the General Presbytery of the Assemblies of God. August 11, 2000. https://static1.squarespace.com/static/57982559be6594e06f6f1dbd/t/57e06f8ee6f2e1f209ba906a/1474326416763/pp_endtime_revival.pdf.

"Attitudes on Same-Sex Marriage." Pew Research Center. May 14, 2019. www.pewforum.org/fact-sheet/changing-attitudes-on-gay-marriage.

Bankston, Carl L., III, and Min Zhou. "The Ethnic Church, Ethnic Identification, and the Social Adjustment of Vietnamese Adolescents." *Review of Religious Research* 38, no. 1 (1996): 18–37.

Barkan, Elliott R., Rudolph J. Vecoli, Richard D. Alba, and Olivier Zunz. "Race, Religion, and Nationality in American Society: A Model of Ethnicity: From Contact to Assimilation [with Comment, with Response]." *Journal of American Ethnic History* 14, no. 2 (1995): 38.

Baumann, Roger. "Political Engagement Meets the Prosperity Gospel: African American Christian Zionism and Black Church Politics." *Sociology of Religion* 77, no. 4 (2016): 359.

Bergad, Laird W. "The Latino Population of New York City, 1990–2015." Center for Latin American, Caribbean & Latino Studies, Graduate Center, City University of New York, December 2016.

Berger, Peter L. *The Sacred Canopy: Elements of a Sociological Theory of Religion*. New York: Anchor Books, 1990.

Blauner, Bob. *Still the Big News: Racial Oppression in America*. Philadelphia, PA: Temple University Press, 2001.

Bowler, Kate. *Blessed: A History of the American Prosperity Gospel*. New York: Oxford University Press, 2013.

Bramlett, Matthew D., and William D. Mosher. *Cohabitation, Marriage, Divorce, and Remarriage in the United States*. Vital and Health Statistics Series 23, no. 22. Hyattsville, MD: National Center for Health Statistics, 2002.

Brodie, Mollyann, Annie Steffenson, Jaime Valdez, Rebecca Levin, and Roberto Suro. *2002 National Survey of Latinos*. Menlo Park, CA: Kaiser Family Foundation; Washington, DC: Pew Hispanic Center, 2002. www.pewresearch.org/wp-content/uploads/sites/5/reports/15.pdf.

Brown, Candy Gunther, Ebook Central—Academic Complete and Oxford Scholarship Online Religion. *Global Pentecostal and Charismatic Healing*. Oxford: Oxford University Press, 2011.

Brown, Susan K. "Delayed Spatial Assimilation: Multigenerational Incorporation of the Mexican-Origin Population in Los Angeles." *City and Community* 6, no. 3 (2007): 193–209.

Brusco, Elizabeth. "The Reformation of Machismo: Asceticism and Masculinity among Colombian Evangelicals." In *Rethinking Protestantism in Latin America*, edited by Virginia Garrard-Burnett and David Stoll, 143–158. Philadelphia, PA: Temple University Press, 1993.

Candelario, Ginetta E. B. "'Black Behind the Ears'—and Up Front Too? Dominicans in the Black Mosaic." *Public Historian* 23, no. 4 (2001): 55.

Cao, Nanlai. *Constructing China's Jerusalem: Christians, Power, and Place in Contemporary Wenzhou*. Stanford, CA: Stanford University Press, 2011.

Casper, Lynne M., and Suzanne M. Bianchi. *Continuity and Change in the American Family*. Thousand Oaks, CA: Sage, 2002.

"Changing Faiths: Latinos and the Transformation of American Religion." Pew Research Center. April 25, 2007. www.pewforum.org/2007/04/25/changing-faiths-latinos-and-the-transformation-of-american-religion-2.

Chesnut, R. Andrew. *Born Again in Brazil: The Pentecostal Boom and the Pathogens of Poverty*. New Brunswick, NJ: Rutgers University Press, 1997.

———. *Competitive Spirits: Latin America's New Religious Economy*. New York: Oxford University Press, 2003.

Chong, Kelly H. "What It Means to Be Christian: The Role of Religion in the Construction of Ethnic Identity and Boundary among Second-Generation Korean Americans." *Sociology of Religion* 59, no. 3 (1998): 259–286.

Cisneros, Josue David. *The Border Crossed Us: Rhetorics of Borders, Citizenship, and Latina/o Identity*. Tuscaloosa: University of Alabama Press, 2014.

Coleman, Simon. *The Globalisation of Charismatic Christianity: Spreading the Gospel of Prosperity*. Cambridge: Cambridge University Press, 2000.
Cox, Harvey. *Fire from Heaven: The Rise of Pentecostal Spirituality and the Reshaping of Religion in the Twenty-First Century*. Reading, MA: Addison-Wesley, 1995.
Crèvecoeur, J. Hector St. John de. *Letters from an American Farmer; And, Sketches of Eighteenth-Century America*. New York: Penguin Books, 1981.
Cullen, Jim. *The American Dream: A Short History of an Idea That Shaped a Nation*. New York: Oxford University Press, 2003.
De Genova, Nicholas, and Nathalie Peutz, eds. *The Deportation Regime: Sovereignty, Space, and the Freedom of Movement*. Durham, NC: Duke University Press, 2010.
Defoe, Daniel. *Robinson Crusoe*. Edited by Thomas Keymer and James William Kelly. New ed. Oxford: Oxford University Press, 2007.
Dolan, Jay P. *The Immigrant Church: New York's Irish and German Catholics, 1815–1865*. Baltimore: Johns Hopkins University Press, 1975.
Douthat, Ross Gregory. *Bad Religion: How We Became a Nation of Heretics*. New York: Free Press, 2012.
Dreby, Joanna. *Everyday Illegal: When Policies Undermine Immigrant Families*. Oakland: University of California Press, 2015.
Du Bois, W. E. B. *The Souls of Black Folk*. Edited by Brent Hayes Edwards. Oxford: Oxford University Press, 2007.
Duany, Jorge. *Blurred Borders: Transnational Migration Between the Hispanic Caribbean and the United States*. Chapel Hill: University of North Carolina Press, 2011.
Durkheim, Émile. *The Elementary Forms of Religious Life*. Translated by Karen E. Fields. New York: Free Press, 1995.
Dye, Jane Lawler. *Fertility of American Women: June 2008*. Washington, DC: U.S. Census Bureau, 2010. https://www.census.gov/prod/2010pubs/p20-563.pdf.
Ebaugh, Helen Rose. "Religion and the New Immigrants." In *Handbook of the Sociology of Religion*, edited by Michelle Dillon, 225–239. Cambridge: Cambridge University Press, 2003.
Ebaugh, Helen Rose, and Janet Saltzman Chafetz. *Religion and the New Immigrants: Continuities and Adaptations in Immigrant Congregations*. Walnut Creek, CA: Altamira Press, 2000.
Espinosa, Gastón. *Latino Pentecostals in America: Faith and Politics in Action*. Cambridge, MA: Harvard University Press, 2014.
Espinosa, Gastón, Virgilio P. Elizondo, and Jesse Miranda. *Latino Religions and Civic Activism in the United States*. New York: Oxford University Press, 2005.
Fenton, John Y. *Transplanting Religious Traditions: Asian Indians in America*. New York: Praeger, 1988.
Franklin, Benjamin. *The Compleated Autobiography*. Edited by Mark Skousen. Washington, DC: Regnery History, 2005.
Freston, Paul. "The Transnationalisation of Brazilian Pentecostalism." In *Between Babel and Pentecost: Transnational Pentecostalism in Africa and Latin America*, edited by André Corten and Ruth Marshall-Fratani, 1196–215. London: C. Hurst, 2001.

Freud, Sigmund. *Introductory Lectures on Psychoanalysis*. Translated by James Strachey. New York: Norton, 1977.
Fry, Richard. "Latino Settlement in the New Century." Pew Hispanic Center. October 2008.
Gans, Herbert J. "Symbolic Ethnicity: The Future of Ethnic Groups and Cultures in America." *Ethnic and Racial Studies* 2, no. 1 (1979): 1–20.
Garcia, Carlos. "Buscando Trabajo: Social Networking among Immigrants from Mexico to the United States." *Hispanic Journal of Behavioral Sciences* 27, no. 1 (2005): 3–22.
Gbote, Eric Z. M., and Selaelo Thias Kgatla. "Prosperity Gospel: A Missiological Assessment." *Hervormde Teologiese Studies* 70, no. 1 (2014): 1.
"The Gender Gap in Religion around the World: Women Are Generally More Religious Than Men, Particularly among Christians." Pew Research Center. March 22, 2016. www.pewforum.org/2016/03/22/the-gender-gap-in-religion-around-the-world.
Glazer, Nathan. "Is Assimilation Dead?" *Annals of the American Academy of Political and Social Science* 530 (1993): 122–136.
Goff, James R., Jr. *Fields White unto Harvest: Charles F. Parham and the Missionary Origins of Pentecostalism*. Fayetteville: University of Arkansas Press, 1988.
Gonzales, Felisa. "2006, Hispanics in the United States Statistical Portrait." Pew Research Center. January 23, 2008. www.pewresearch.org/hispanic/2008/01/23/2006-statistical-information-on-hispanics-in-united-states.
Gordon, Milton M. *Assimilation in American Life: The Role of Race, Religion, and National Origins*. New York: Oxford University Press, 1964.
Greenman, Emily, and Yu Xie. "Is Assimilation Theory Dead? The Effect of Assimilation on Adolescent Well-Being." *Social Science Research* 37, no. 1 (2008): 109–137.
Griswold del Castillo, Richard. *La Familia: Chicano Families in the Urban Southwest, 1848 to the Present*. Notre Dame, IN: University of Notre Dame Press, 1984.
Gutmann, Matthew C. "Introduction" in Gutmann ed. *Changing Men and Masculinities in Latin America*. Durham, NC: Duke University Press, 2003.
Haddad, Yvonne Yazbeck, and Adair T. Lummis. *Islamic Values in the United States: A Comparative Study*. New York: Oxford University Press, 1987.
Harrison, Milmon F. *Righteous Riches: The Word of Faith Movement in Contemporary African American Religion*. New York: Oxford University Press, 2005.
Hawkes, Glenn R., and Minna Taylor. "Power Structure in Mexican and Mexican-American Farm Labor Families." *Journal of Marriage and Family* 37, no. 4 (1975): 807–811.
Herberg, Will. *Protestant, Catholic, Jew: An Essay in American Religious Sociology*. Completely rev. ed. Garden City, NY: Doubleday, 1960.
Hochschild, Jennifer L. *Facing Up to the American Dream: Race, Class, and the Soul of the Nation*. Princeton, NJ: Princeton University Press, 1995.
Hollenweger, Walter J. *Pentecostalism: Origins and Developments Worldwide*. Peabody, MA: Hendrickson, 1997.
Hollinger, Dennis P. "Enjoying God Forever: An Historical / Sociological Profile of the Health and Wealth Gospel." *Trinity Journal* 9, no. 2 (1988): 131.

Humes, Karen R., Nicholas A. Jones, and Roberto R. Ramirez. *Overview of Race and Hispanic Origin: 2010*. Washington, DC: U.S. Census Bureau, 2011.
Huntington, Samuel P. *Who Are We? The Challenges to America's National Identity*. New York: Simon & Schuster, 2004.
Hurh, Won Moo, and Kwang Chung Kim. "Religious Participation of Korean Immigrants in the United States." *Journal for the Scientific Study of Religion* 29, no. 1 (1990): 19.
Hurtado, Aída, and Mrinal Sinha. *Beyond Machismo: Intersectional Latino Masculinities*. Austin: University of Texas Press, 2016.
Iannaccone, Laurence R. "Why Strict Churches Are Strong." *American Journal of Sociology* 99, no. 5 (1994): 1180–1211.
Jakes, T. D. *Reposition Yourself: Living Life without Limits*. New York: Atria Books, 2007.
———. "What Is the Prosperity Gospel?" Accessed November 18, 2019. www.tdjakes.com/posts/what-is-the-prosperity-gospel.
Jiménez, Tomás, and David Fitzgerald. "Mexican Assimilation: A Temporal and Spatial Reorientation." *Du Bois Review: Social Science Research on Race* 4, no. 2 (2007): 337.
Kashima, Tetsuden. *Buddhism in America: The Social Organization of an Ethnic Religious Institution*. Westport, CT: Greenwood Press, 1977.
Kazal, Russell A. "Revisiting Assimilation: The Rise, Fall, and Reappraisal of a Concept in American Ethnic History." *American Historical Review* 100, no. 2 (1995): 437–471.
Keith, Tamara. "Trump Crowd Size Estimate May Involve 'The Power of Positive Thinking.'" National Public Radio. Washington, DC. January 22, 2017. www.npr.org/2017/01/22/510655254/trump-crowd-size-estimate-may-involve-the-power-of-positive-thinking.
Krogstad, Jens Manuel, Mark Hugo Lopez, Gustavo López, Jeffrey S. Passel, and Eileen Patten. "Millennials Make Up Almost Half of Latino Eligible Voters in 2016." Pew Research Center. January 19, 2016. www.pewhispanic.org/2016/01/19/millennials-make-up-almost-half-of-latino-eligible-voters-in-2016.
Lee, Shayne. *T. D. Jakes: America's New Preacher*. New York: New York University Press, 2005.
Lee, Shayne, and Phillip Luke Sinitiere. *Holy Mavericks: Evangelical Innovators and the Spiritual Marketplace*. New York: New York University Press, 2009.
Llopis, Glenn. "Advertisers Must Pay Attention to Hispanic Consumers as Rising Trendsetters in 2013." *Forbes*, January 9, 2013.
Lofland, John, and Rodney Stark. "Becoming a World-Saver: A Theory of Conversion to a Deviant Perspective." *American Sociological Review* 30, no. 6 (1965): 862–875.
Lopez, Mark Hugo, and Danielle Cuddington. "Latinos' Changing Views of Same-Sex Marriage." Pew Research Center. June 19, 2013. www.pewresearch.org/fact-tank/2013/06/19/latinos-changing-views-of-same-sex-marriage.
Lopez, Mark Hugo, Jen Manuel Krogstad, Eileen Patten, and Ana Gonzalez-Barrera. "Chapter 2: Latinos' View on Selected 2014 Ballot Measure Issues." October 16, 2014. www.pewhispanic.org/2014/10/16/chapter-2-latinos-views-on-selected-2014-ballot-measure-issues.

Markovits, Daniel. "How Life Became an Endless, Terrible Competition," *Atlantic*, September 2019.
Marti, Gerardo. *Hollywood Faith: Holiness, Prosperity, and Ambition in a Los Angeles Church*. New Brunswick, NJ: Rutgers University Press, 2008.
Marti, Gerardo, and Gladys Ganiel. *The Deconstructed Church: Understanding Emerging Christianity*. New York: Oxford University Press, 2014.
Martin, David. *Pentecostalism: The World Their Parish*. Oxford: Blackwell, 2002.
———. *Tongues of Fire: The Explosion of Protestantism in Latin America*. Oxford: Blackwell, 1990.
McConnell, Dan. *A Different Gospel*. Peabody, MA: Hendrickson, 1994.
Menjívar, Cecilia. *Fragmented Ties: Salvadoran Immigrant Networks in America*. Berkeley: University of California Press, 2000.
Meyer, Joyce. *Power Thoughts: 12 Strategies to Win the Battle of the Mind*. New York: Hachette, 2010.
Miller, David W. *God at Work: The History and Promise of the Faith at Work Movement*. Oxford: Oxford University Press, 2007.
Miller, Donald E., Kimon Howland Sargeant, and Richard W. Flory. *Spirit and Power: The Growth and Global Impact of Pentecostalism*. Oxford: Oxford University Press, 2013.
Miller, Donald E., and Tetsunao Yamamori. *Global Pentecostalism: The New Face of Christian Social Engagement*. Berkeley: University of California Press, 2007.
Mor, Menahem, ed. *Jewish Assimilation, Acculturation, and Accommodation: Past Traditions, Current Issues, and Future Prospects.* Lanham, MD: University Press of America, 1992.
Mora, G. Cristina. *Making Hispanics: How Activists, Bureaucrats, and Media Constructed a New American*. Chicago: University of Chicago Press, 2014.
Morawska, Ewa. "In Defense of the Assimilation Model." *Journal of American Ethnic History* 13, no. 2 (1994): 76.
Mulder, Mark T., Aida Ramos, and Gerardo Marti. *Latino Protestants in America: Growing and Diverse*. Lanham, MD: Rowman & Littlefield, 2017.
Newberg, Eric Nelson. *The Pentecostal Mission in Palestine: The Legacy of Pentecostal Zionism*. Eugene, OR: Pickwick, 2012.
Ng, Kwai Hang. "Seeking the Christian Tutelage: Agency and Culture in Chinese Immigrants' Conversion to Christianity." *Sociology of Religion* 63, no. 2 (2002): 195.
Osteen, Joel. *Your Best Life Now: 7 Steps to Living at Your Full Potential*. New York: Hachette, 2004.
Park, Robert E. "Human Migration and the Marginal Man." *American Journal of Sociology* 33, no. 6 (1928): 881–893.
Park, Robert E., and E. W. Burgess. *Introduction to the Science of Sociology*. Chicago: University of Chicago Press, 1921.
Passel, Jeffrey S., and D'vera Cohn. "U.S. Population Projections: 2005–2050." Pew Research Center. February 11, 2008.
Patten, Eileen. "The Nation's Latino Population Is Defined by Its Youth." Pew Hispanic Center. April 20, 2016. www.pewhispanic.org/2016/04/20/the-nations-latino-population-is-defined-by-its-youth.

Peale, Norman Vincent. *The Power of Positive Thinking*. New York: Ishi Press, 2011. First published 1952 by Prentice Hall (New York).
Peñalosa, Fernando. "Mexican Family Roles." *Journal of Marriage and Family* 30, no. 4 (1968): 680–689.
Perriman, Andrew. *Faith, Health, and Prosperity: A Report on Word of Faith and Positive Confession Theologies*. Carlisle, UK: Paternoster, 2003.
Poloma, Margaret M. *Main Street Mystics: The Toronto Blessing and Reviving Pentecostalism*. Walnut Creek, CA: AltaMira Press, 2003.
Portes, Alejandro. "Immigration Theory for a New Century: Some Problems and Opportunities." *International Migration Review* 31, no. 4 (1997): 799–825.
Portes, Alejandro, and Josh DeWind. *Rethinking Migration: New Theoretical and Empirical Perspectives*. New York: Berghahn Books, 2007.
Portes, Alejandro, and Rubén G. Rumbaut. *Immigrant America: A Portrait*. 2nd ed. Berkeley: University of California Press, 1996.
———. *Legacies: The Story of the Immigrant Second Generation*. Berkeley: University of California Press, 2001.
Portes, Alejandro, and Min Zhou. "The New Second Generation: Segmented Assimilation and Its Variants." *Annals of the American Academy of Political and Social Science* 530 (November 1993): 74–96.
"Positive Thinking: The Norman Vincent Peale Story." Crouse Entertainment. Video File. February 13, 2012. http://www.crouseentertainment.com/crouse-entertainment-productions/positive-thinking-the-norman-vincent-peale-story.
Ramirez, Daniel. *Migrating Faith: Pentecostalism in the United States and Mexico in the Twentieth Century*. Chapel Hill: University of North Carolina Press, 2015.
"Religion in Latin America: Widespread Change in a Historically Catholic Region." Pew Research Center. November 13, 2014. www.pewforum.org/2014/11/13/religion-in-latin-america.
Rieff, Philip. *The Triumph of the Therapeutic: Uses of Faith after Freud*. New York: Harper & Row, 1968.
Rodriguez, Clara E. *Changing Race: Latinos, the Census, and the History of Ethnicity in the United States*. New York: New York University Press, 2000.
Romero, Jesús Adrián. "Que Seria de Mi." Track 7 on *Cerca De Ti*. Vastago Producciones, 1998.
Ropp, Steven Masami. "Secondary Migration and the Politics of Identity for Asian Latinos in Los Angeles." *Journal of Asian American Studies* 3, no. 2 (2000): 219–229.
Rumbaut, Rubén G. "Assimilation and Its Discontents: Between Rhetoric and Reality." *International Migration Review* 31, no. 4 (1997): 923–960.
———. "Paradoxes (and Orthodoxies) of Assimilation." *Sociological Perspectives* 40, no. 3 (1997): 483–511.
Sánchez-Walsh, Arlene M. *Latino Pentecostal Identity: Evangelical Faith, Self, and Society*. New York: Columbia University Press, 2003.
Schieman, Scott, Alex Bierman, Laura Upenieks, and Christopher G. Ellison. "Love Thy Self? How Belief in a Supportive God Shapes Self-Esteem." *Review of Religious Research* 59, no. 3 (2017): 293.

Selig Center for Economic Growth. "The Multicultural Economy: 1990–2009." Terry College of Business, University of Georgia. May 2004.
Shaull, Richard, and Waldo A. Cesar. *Pentecostalism and the Future of the Christian Churches: Promises, Limitations, Challenges*. Grand Rapids, MI: W.B. Eerdmans, 2000.
"The Shifting Religious Identity of Latinos in the United States." Pew Research Center. May 7, 2014. www.pewforum.org/2014/05/07/the-shifting-religious-identity-of-latinos-in-the-united-states.
Simmons, Dale H. *E. W. Kenyon and the Postbellum Pursuit of Peace, Power and Plenty*. Lanham, MD: Scarecrow Press, 1997.
Skogrand, L., Daniel Hatch, Archana Singh, and Reva Rosenband. "Strong Marriages in the Latino Culture." Unpublished manuscript. Logan: Utah State University, 2004.
Smith, Christian, Michael O. Emerson, and Patricia Snell. *Passing the Plate: Why American Christians Don't Give Away More Money*. Oxford: Oxford University Press, 2008.
Smith, Timothy L. "Religion and Ethnicity in America." *American Historical Review* 83, no. 5 (1978): 1155–1185.
Snyder, C. R., and Shane J. Lopez. *Oxford Handbook of Positive Psychology*. Oxford: Oxford University Press, 2009.
"Spirit and Power: A 10-Country Survey of Pentecostals." Pew Research Center. October 5, 2006. www.pewforum.org/2006/10/05/spirit-and-power.
Statistical Policy Directive No. 15. "Race and Ethnic Standards for Federal Statistics and Administrative Reporting." Office of Management and Budget, 1977.
Stoll, David. *Is Latin America Turning Protestant?: The Politics of Evangelical Growth*. Berkeley: University of California Press, 1990.
Suro, Roberto. "The Hispanic Family in Flux." Brookings Institute. November 15, 2007. www.brookings.edu/research/the-hispanic-family-in-flux.
Synan, Vinson. *The Century of the Holy Spirit: 100 Years of Pentecostal and Charismatic Renewal, 1901–2001*. Nashville, TN: Thomas Nelson, 2001.
———. "A Healer in the House? A Historical Perspective on Healing in the Pentecostal/Charismatic Tradition." *Asian Journal of Pentecostal Studies* 3, no. 2 (2000): 189.
Thomas, William Isaac, and Florian Znaniecki. *The Polish Peasant in Europe and America: Monograph of an Immigrant Group*. Boston: Richard G. Badger, Gorham Press, 1918.
Tocqueville, Alexis de. *Democracy in America*. Translated and edited by Harvey C. Mansfield Jr. and Delba Winthrop. University of Chicago Press, 2000.
Torres, José B., V. Scott, H. Solberg, and Aaron H. Carlstrom. "The Myth of Sameness among Latino Men and Their Machismo." *American Journal of Orthopsychiatry* 72, no. 2 (2002): 163–181.
Tsang, Wing. "Integration of Immigrants: The Role of Ethnic Churches." *Journal of International Migration and Integration* 16, no. 4 (2015): 1177–1193.
"The 2004 National Survey of Latinos: Politics and Civic Participation." Pew Hispanic Center and Kaiser Family Foundation. July 22, 2004. www.pewresearch.org

/hispanic/2004/07/22/pew-hispanic-centerkaiser-family-foundation-2004-national-survey-of-latinos.
"2002 National Survey of Latinos." Pew Hispanic Center and Kaiser Family Foundation. December 2002. www.pewresearch.org/wp-content/uploads/sites/5/reports/15.pdf.
U.S. Census Bureau. "Facts for Features: Hispanic Heritage Month 2016." October 12, 2016. www.census.gov/newsroom/facts-for-features/2016/cb16-ff16.html.
Vance, J. D. *Hillbilly Elegy: A Memoir of a Family and Culture in Crisis.* New York: Harper, 2016.
Vega, William A. "Hispanic Families in the 1980s: A Decade of Research." *Journal of Marriage and Family* 52, no. 4 (1990): 1015–1024.
Villafañe, Edin. *The Liberating Spirit: Toward an Hispanic American Pentecostal Social Ethic.* Grand Rapids, MI: Eerdmans, 1993.
Wang, Lili, Carlton F. Yoshioka, and Robert F. Ashcraft. "What Affects Hispanic Volunteering in the United States: Comparing the Current Population Survey, Panel Study of Income Dynamics, and the AIM Giving and Volunteering Survey." *Voluntas: International Journal of Voluntary and Nonprofit Organizations* 24, no. 1 (2013): 125.
Warner, R. Stephen. *A Church of Our Own: Disestablishment and Diversity in American Religion.* New Brunswick, NJ: Rutgers University Press, 2005.
———. "Immigration and Religious Communities in the United States." In *Gatherings in Diaspora: Religious Communities and the New Immigration,* edited by R. Stephen Warner and Judith G. Wittner, 3–36. Philadelphia, PA: Temple University Press, 1998.
———. "The Place of the Congregation in the Contemporary American Religious Configuration." In *American Congregations, Volume 2: New Perspectives in the Study of Congregations,* edited by James P. Wind and James W. Lewis, 54–99. Chicago: University of Chicago Press, 1994.
———. "Work in Progress toward a New Paradigm for the Sociological Study of Religion in the United States." *American Journal of Sociology* 98 (March 1993): 1044–1093.
Warner, R. Stephen, and Judith G. Wittner. *Gatherings in Diaspora: Religious Communities and the New Immigration.* Philadelphia, PA: Temple University Press, 1998.
Warner, W. Lloyd, and Leo Srole. *The Social Systems of American Ethnic Groups.* New Haven, CT: Yale University Press, 1945.
Waters, Mary C. *Black Identities: West Indian Immigrant Dreams and American Realities.* New York: Russell Sage Foundation, 1999.
Waters, Mary C., and Tomás R. Jiménez. "Assessing Immigrant Assimilation: New Empirical and Theoretical Challenges." *Annual Review of Sociology* 31 (2005): 105–125.
Waters, Mary C., and Marisa Gerstein Pineau, eds. *The Integration of Immigrants into American Society.* Washington, DC: National Academies Press, 2015. https://doi.org/10.17226/21746.
Weber, Max. "Basic Sociological Terms." In *Economy and Society,* edited by Guenther Roth and Claus Wittich. Berkeley: University of California Press, 1968.

———. *From Max Weber: Essays in Sociology*. Translated and edited by H. H. Gerth and C. Wright Mills. Abingdon, Oxon: Routledge, 1991.
———. *The Protestant Ethic and the Spirit of Capitalism*. London: Routledge, 2001.
———. *The Sociology of Religion*. Boston: Beacon Press, 1993.
Wilcox, William Bradford. "As the Family Goes." *First Things*. May 2007. www.firstthings.com/article/2007/05/as-the-family-goes.
———. *Soft Patriarchs, New Men: How Christianity Shapes Fathers and Husbands*. Chicago: University of Chicago Press, 2004.
Wilkinson, Bruce. *The Prayer of Jabez: Breaking Through to the Blessed Life*. Colorado Springs, CO: Multnomah Books, 2000.
Williams, Joseph W. "The Pentecostalization of Christian Zionism." *Church History* 84, no. 1 (2015): 159.
Williams, Raymond Brady. *Religions of Immigrants from India and Pakistan: New Threads in the American Tapestry*. Cambridge: Cambridge University Press, 1988.
"The World Factbook." Central Intelligence Agency. Accessed November 18, 2019. https://www.cia.gov/library/publications/the-world-factbook/geos/xx.html.
Wright, Richard, Mark Ellis, and Virginia Parks. "Re-Placing Whiteness in Spatial Assimilation Research." *City and Community* 4, no. 2 (2005): 111–135.
Wu, Lawrence, and Barbara L Wolfe. *Out of Wedlock: Causes and Consequences of Nonmarital Fertility*. New York: Russell Sage Foundation, 2001.
Yang, Fenggang. *Chinese Christians in America: Conversion, Assimilation, and Adhesive Identities*. University Park: Pennsylvania State University Press, 1999.
———. "Chinese Gospel Church: The Sinicization of Christianity." In *Religion and the New Immigrants: Continuities and Adaptations in Immigrant Congregations*, edited by Helen Rose Ebaugh and Janet Saltzman Chafetz, 89–107. Walnut Creek, CA: AltaMira Press, 2000.
Yang, Philip Q. *Post-1965 Immigration to the United States: Structural Determinants*. Westport, CT: Praeger, 1995.
Yong, Amos, and Katy Attanasi. *Pentecostalism and Prosperity: The Socio-Economics of the Global Charismatic Movement*. New York: Palgrave Macmillan, 2012.
Zhou, Min. *Chinatown: The Socioeconomic Potential of an Urban Enclave*. Philadelphia, PA: Temple University Press, 1992.
———. "Segmented Assimilation: Issues, Controversies, and Recent Research on the New Second Generation." *International Migration Review* 31, no. 4 (1997): 975–1008.

Index

1 Corinthians 11:3, 138
1 Kings 17, 44–45
3 John 1:2, 9

abortion, 7
Abraham (biblical), 70, 133
abundant life. *See* prosperity and wealth
acculturation, 107
action, 72–73, 77–81, 90
Acts 2, 5
addiction. *See* drugs; alcohol use
adhesive identity, 110–111
adhesive integration, 15
adultery, 123
Africa, 31–32
African Americans, 3, 5, 6, 106–107, 109, 123; enslavement of, 102, 163, 165; New York population, 57, 58; Pentecostal churches, 7; Prosperity Gospel movement and, 167
alcohol use, 40, 46, 98, 120, 121, 123, 148, 158–159
Alejandro, 40, 45, 130, 140
alienation, 20
"altar call," 47–50
American dream: assimilation theory and, 14–17, 105–12; components of, 153–158; as divine destiny, 103; globalization of, 170; gospel of, 17–20, 24, 51, 90, 91, 105, 110–112, 154, 158–161, 163; 165–166, 170; ideals of, 163; inequalities and, 163–164; Latinx faith in, 3, 17, 29, 51, 90; 91, 98–120, 153–154, 165–166; middle-class lifestyle as, 114; post 1960s, 105; realities of, 102–103, 163–164; risk-taking and, 114
American Exceptionalism, 103
American identity: "adhesive," 110–111; adoption of, 165–166 (*see also* assimilation); anti-immigrant sentiment and, 4, 102, 109; citizenship and, 15, 41–42, 94, 120, 152–153, 158, 165, 173n38; culture wars and, 157; definitions of, 101–103, 108; founding ideals and, 107; immigration law and, 102, 107, 158, 165, 173n38; integration and, 112–115; as "light on a hill," 161; middle-class aspirations and, 15, 16–17, 24, 106, 114; paradoxes of, 102–103, 163–164, 166; plurality of cultures and, 15; process of, 15, 19, 20; racial categorizations and, 3; romanticized definition of, 101–102; skin color and, 3, 15, 17, 24, 102, 106–107, 165, 173n38; societal integration vs., 112–115; westward expansion and, 103, 105
Ana, 46, 77–78, 124
Analia, 126, 157
Anglican Church, 171–172n14
Anglo-Saxons, 106, 107
anointing, 37, 47
April (month), 67, 70–71
Argentina, 25
Asia, 31–32
Assemblies of God, 31, 172–173n26
assertiveness, 114
assimilation, 105–115; alternative theory of, 106–107, 114–115; barriers to, 106, 108; classical theory of, 14–17, 105–106, 198; diversity and, 107, 158, 5; "double consciousness" and, 107, 109; integration vs., 112–115; internal, 24; linear, 15, 107, 108, 112; paradox of, 14–17; Prosperity

assimilation (cont.)
Pentecostalism as vehicle of, 24, 110–112, 158–159; segmented, 106, 108; structural, 117
Assimilation in American Life (Gordon), 107
Azusa Street Revival, 5–6

baptism, 118
Baptists, 172n14
Berger, Peter, 64, 88
Bible, 5, 32, 46, 69, 158, 175n1; anointing, 47; calendar, 68; covenants with God, 70; family unit, 122, 129, 134; offering miracles, 44–45; parables, 81, 133; quotations from, 32; tithing, 174n14; truth of, 82–83
black Americans. *See* African Americans
Blake, Charles (bishop), 167
blessings, 6–9, 16, 18, 32, 68–69, 75, 78, 81–82, 83. *See also* health; prosperity and wealth
blue-collar workers, 39
Brazil, 104, 169–170
Buenos Aires, 25
Burgess, Ernest, 105–106
Bush, George H. W., 74
Bush, George W., 4
business ownership, 17, 76–77, 114, 120, 151, 152, 165

calendar, human vs. divine, 66–72, 95, 172n1
California, 25, 26, 51, 94. *See also specific cities*
Calveti, Daniel, 63
capitalism, 16, 163
Carla, 146
Carter, Jimmy, 74
Catholic Church, 3, 7, 13, 15, 165; Prosperity Pentecostal converts from, 14, 115, 169; size of, 171n14; Spanish-language Mass, 16, 35, 116
celebrities, 4, 12
Census, U.S., 3
Central Pacific Railroad, 165
certitudo salutis, 118–119, 120
Cerullo, Morris, 37, 71; World Evangelism Institute, 41
charismatic Christianity, 7, 13, 23, 27, 31
Charlottesville (Va.), 1, 21, 22, 30, 33. *See also* Iglesia Christiana del Padre
children, 40, 52, 131–134, 157
Chinese Exclusion Act of 1882, 102
Chinese immigrants, 15, 102, 110–111, 165
Christ. *See* Jesus Christ
Christian Church of the Father. *See* Iglesia Cristiana del Padre
Christianity, 6–17, 100, 110, 111, 115–120, 158, 171–172n14; charismatic, 7, 13, 23, 27, 31; divine calendar, 67–72; early, 32, 68; evangelical, 11, 13–14, 74, 163, 173n31; as family model, 19–20, 122–129, 140–142; fundamentalist, 24, 96, 154, 157, 161, 174n1; good behavior rewards, 31, 32; ideal hierarchy, 128–129; mainstream, 11; *petitio principii*, 82; positive thinking movement, 9–10, 74, 78, 173n31; salvation, 32, 117–120, 169; self-help, 9; tithing, 44. *See also* Catholic Church; Pentecostalism; Prosperity Gospel Pentecostalism; Protestantism
Christian Science, 74
Christian Zionists, 60, 174n1
Christmas, 68, 69
Church of the Victorious God. *See* Iglesia del Dios Victorioso
citizenship, 15, 41–42, 94, 158; limitations, 120, 165, 173n38. *See also* undocumented immigrants
Citizenship and Immigration Services, U.S., 152–153
class. *See* social class
clergy. *See* pastors
Clinton, Bill, 29, 74, 173n31
cohabiting couples, 136
collection. *See* offering
Colombia, 57, 112, 115, 149–150, 151, 169

Columbus, Christopher, 103
confession, positive, 10, 74
Constantine the Great, Emperor of Rome, 68
conversion, 14, 98–101, 111, 114, 115–118
Crèvecoeur, J. Hector St. John, 101, 102, 103, 107, 114
Cristina, 54, 121–122, 123, 148, 159
Cruz, Ted, 4
Crystal Cathedral (Calif.), 25
Cuban Americans, 4, 109
culture wars, 157

Daniela, 55, 86–87, 90
David (biblical), 70
Day of Atonement, 67, 68, 175n1
December, 69
democracy, 103
demons, 73, 116, 177n34
deportation, 88, 114, 165–167; threat of, 19, 26, 93–94, 109, 166–167
depression, emotional, 63, 73
Desmond, Matthew, 163
Diego, 54, 121–122, 123
diversity, 107, 158, 165
divine rewards. *See* God
divorce, 123, 145–146
Dollar, Creflo, 12, 167, 174n16
domestic abuse, 123, 138–139
Dominican Republic, 57, 58–59, 88, 91, 109, 115, 139
donations. *See* offering; tithing
"double consciousness," 107, 109
drugs, 40, 46, 54, 55, 58, 98, 118, 120, 121, 123, 148, 158–159
Durkheim, Émile, 14, 16

Ecuador, 57
Eddy, Mary Baker, 74
Eduardo, 88–89, 90
education level, 39, 41, 165
elderly congregants, 61–64
Elizabeth, 61
Emerson School of Oratory, 74
emotions, 62–63, 64, 72; outburts of, 24, 27, 49, 77
empowerment, 65, 79, 160–161
English language, 17, 35, 41, 42, 110, 112, 113–114; fluency, 16, 55, 149, 151, 177n29; immigrant learning, 165
Enlace (Spanish-language TV channel), 14
entrepreneurship, 17, 76–77, 114, 120, 151, 152, 165
Ephesians 5, 22–23, 129
equality, 102–103
ethnicity, 17, 23, 102, 109, 111–114; U.S. largest growing group, 4
European immigrants, 108, 136, 165
evangelicals, 7, 11, 13–14, 26, 74, 118, 131, 161–63, 173n31
exorcism, 177n34

faith, 8–11, 47–48, 57, 168, 169; as action basis, 72–73, 77–83, 90; entitlements of, 31, 80, 148; hopelessness vs., 166; imperfect, 83; miracles and, 154; monetary offering as act of, 78; physical manifestation of, 119; practical, 79–80; prosperity linked with, 10, 13, 41, 74–77, 82, 85, 151–152, 154, 157–158, 168; psychological underpinnings of, 73. *See also* positive thinking
faithful waiting, 77–81
faith healer, 63
falling backwards to ground, 27, 49, 116, 132–133, 150
family, 122–144; centrality of, 122–125; Christian model of, 19–20, 122–130, 140–142; exemplary, 134–135; extended, 136; gender roles, 129–131, 144, 148 (*see also* machismo); hierarchy, 130–131, 140–142; ideal, 20, 40, 122–125, 128–131, 135, 140–142; ideal vs. reality, 136–137, 142–144, 147–148; nontraditional, 136; nuclear, 40, 122–123, 125, 136; as sacred institution, 128. *See also* parenting

farmworkers, 54, 165
fathers, 123, 129, 132, 139; machismo and, 141–142
Favor-Day Church (Anaheim, Calif.), 25
fear, 63, 77, 85, 94–95
Feliciano, 49–50, 75–76
Fernandez, Carlos, 60–61
financial donations. *See* offering; tithing
financial prosperity. *See* prosperity and wealth
flags, 30, 37, 59, 174n1
Ford, Gerald, 74
Francisco, 54, 142, 145
Franklin, Benjamin, 176n3
Freidzon, Claudio, 25
Freud, Sigmund, 73–74
fundamentalist Christians, 154, 161, 174n1; Prosperity Pentecostals vs., 24, 96, 157

Gabriela, 150
gangs, 158
gay marriage, 7
Gebel, Dante, 25
gender, 13, 14, 33, 52, 150–152; donations to church, 155–156; family roles, 129–131, 140–142, 144, 146; hierarchy, 23, 41, 133–134, 139–140; marital roles, 128–134, 135, 140–142, 145, 147, 148; occupations and, 39, 131–132, 143; parenting and, 132, 143; patriarchy and, 137, 141. *See also* machismo; women
Genesis, 129
genocide, 163
gentrification, 58, 59–60, 64
George Lopez (TV program), 4
Gerardo, 47, 76–77, 79, 83–84, 91, 120, 126, 135, 159, 169
Gielis, Federico (Charlottesville pastor), 25, 26–27, 30–31, 34, 35–36, 38–48, 55, 80, 150, 151, 154–155, 175n18; background of, 40–41, 46, 55, 112, 115; congregant offerings and, 43–44; English language and, 177n29; family and, 124, 129–130, 132, 134–135, 137, 146, 148; *gran cosecha, la* (the Great Harvest) sermon, 66–72, 95, 175n1; infertility advice, 175n18; "Man, the Head of Christ" sermon, 138; marital roles and, 128, 130; meritocracy and, 149; personal wealth of, 38, 42, 46; Sunday service and, 50–51; wife's spiritual role and, 135
Gielis, Veronica ("la pastora"), 35, 41, 42, 43–44, 124, 128, 130, 131; workshops and retreats, 135, 151, 153
giving. *See* offering; tithes
globalization, 6–7, 15–16, 20, 58, 111, 115, 169–170, 172n14
Gloria, 88–89, 89
glossolalia. *See* speaking in tongues
God, 4, 9, 10, 16, 18, 44–50, 57, 63, 78, 81–85, 90, 91, 103–104, 115, 120, 148, 151, 157; action and, 77; American destiny and, 103; bias of, 96; calendar of, 66–72, 95, 175n1; covenants with, 70; encounters with, 6–7, 48–50, 63, 161; endorsement by, 47, 90, 114, 161–162; entitlement and, 90; everyday signs of, 6–7; family structure and, 131, 133; fear of, 96; grace of, 119; healing by, 77; marriage and, 122, 126; merit-based favors of, 80; personal plan from, 33, 64; prosperity calendar, 66–72, 95; prosperity formula, 169; reciprocity with, 80; requests to, 85; rewards from, 3, 31, 38. 46, 47, 68, 77, 80; "testing" by, 44, timing of, 67–68, 69; universal plan of, 101; will of, 96
Gordon, Milton, 15
grace, 119; meritocracy vs., 80
Graham, Billy, 74, 173n31
gran cosecha, la (the great harvest), 66–72
Gustavo, 16, 18, 154, 158, 160–161; background of, 1–3, 4; machismo and,

140, 141–142; success of, 169; undocumented status of, 166
Gutmann, Matthew, 138

Hagin, Kenneth Erwin, 37, 59, 74–75, 172–173n26; teachings, 8–9, 175n5
healing: faithful waiting, 77–81; medical, 77; miraculous, 63, 86–88, 116, 118; physical, 62–64, 86–88; psychological and emotional, 62–64; senior congregants and, 62–64; space for (*see* prayer and healing area); spiritual, 6, 7, 31, 73, 74–75, 88–89, 116
health, 3, 9, 10, 13, 90, 120, 169; medication use, 92; Prosperity Pentecostal promises of, 31
Hebrew Bible. *See* Bible
Hispanics. *See* Latin America; Latinx immigrants
Holmes, Ernest S., 173n31
Holy Spirit, 5, 6, 129, 130; conversion and, 118; physical reception of, 48–50, 71, 119; presence of, 7, 115. *See also* speaking in tongues
home ownership, 17, 105, 114, 153, 165, 166
homosexuality, 7, 123, 132
hope. *See* optimism
humanitarianism, 28–29
Huntington, Samuel, 108
husbands. *See* marriage

Iglesia Christiana del Padre (Charlottesville, Va.), 16, 21, 22, 33–51, 90, 91, 132, 166, 169, 177n34; audio-visuals, 154–155; Catholic churches and, 116; daily involvement of congregants, 42, 46; demographics, 30, 38–42, 51, 54, 112, 113; faith of congregants, 76–77, 90, 149; families and, 124, 125, 131, 134, 136–137, 143; founding of, 34, 35, 41; interior layout, 37–38, 39, 47–50, 53; leadership structure, 40, 41, 45, 52, 161; marriage and, 126, 130, 140, 142, 143, 144, 146; meeting places, 30, 35–38, 149; pastor and wife (*see* Gielis, Federico; Gielis, Veronica); as representative of all Latinx Prosperity Pentecostal churches, 34; Spanish language service, 113; status of congregants, 33, 93; testimony by congregants, 4, 121–122, 123, 143, 149–53, 159, 160–161; worship services, 34, 42–51
Iglesia del Dios Victorioso (Oceanside, Calif.), 21, 22, 26, 51–57, 90, 95–96, 113, 123, 132, 157, 177n34; attendance, 54–55; Catholic churches and, 116; challenges faced by congregants, 56–57; conversion stories, 98–101; demographics, 112; electronic equipment, 54; faith of congregants, 54, 57, 75–78, 90; families and, 125, 131, 136, 145; gender roles and, 144; history of, 52–53; interior layout, 53–54; leadership structure, 52, 55–56; machismo and, 138, 142; meeting place, 53–54; miraculous healing, 86–88; pastor (*see* Nolasco, Pedro); Spanish language service, 113; status of congregants, 33–34, 54–55, 93, 94; structure of, 52–53; witchcraft belief, 116, 177n34; worship services, 34, 52–53, 113, 144
Iglesia Pentecostal del Rey Divino (New York City), 21, 22, 57–64, 88–89, 123, 139; Catholic churches and, 116; charismatic leadership, 134; demographics, 34, 61–62, 112; elderly congregants, 61–64, 155; faith of congregants, 90, 160; gender role negotiation, 144; history of, 57–59; importance of family, 124, 125, 131, 134, 136, 254; interior layout, 60–61; machismo and, 139; meeting place, 59–61; pastor (*see* Ramirez, David); Spanish language service, 113

Ignacio, 159, 160
illegal immigrants. *See* undocumented immigrants
immigration: application approval, 152–153; challenges, 18, 47; church affiliation, 115–116; first generation, 111; identity, 4, 15, 18, 24, 81, 101, 107, 109–115, 165–166; networking among communities, 36; New York City demographics, 57, 105; opponents of, 4, 102, 109; reasons for, 114–115; paradoxes of, 163; relationship with home countries, 112; stages of, 33–36; U.S. law, 102, 107, 158, 165, 173n38. *See also* American dream; assimilation; citizenship; Latinx immigrants; undocumented immigrants
Immigration and Naturalization Act of 1965, 107
individualism, 16, 79, 164
infertility, 133, 175n18
Isaac (biblical), 70, 133
Isaiah 40:31, 50
Israel, State of, 69, 157 Christian Zionists and, 60, 174n1; flag of, 30, 37, 174n1

Jacob (biblical), 70
Jakes, T. D., 11, 12, 37, 167
Jefferson, Thomas, 176n3
Jesus Christ, 55–56, 57, 125, 129, 171n14, 178n1; acceptance of, 47–48; calendar and, 67–68, 69
Jewish people, 58, 60; calendar, of, 67–68, 69, 175n1; religious symbols, 30, 32, 60; State of Israel and, 30, 37, 69, 157, 174n1
Joshua (biblical), 134
Juan Pablo, 98–101, 110–112, 115, 118

Kennedy, John F., 103
Kenyon, E. W., 74, 175n5
"Kenyon Connection," 175n7
Korean immigrants, 115–116
Kuhlman, Katherine, 63

Lakewood Church (Houston, Tex.), 12
language. *See* English language; Spanish language
Latin America: Catholicism, 15, 16, 116, 165; family model, 122, 140–141; machismo, 137–142, 150, 160; Pentecostalism, 5–6, 12–13, 15–16, 31, 37, 50–51, 58, 111, 115, 119, 169–170
Latinx immigrants, 3–7, 30; ambiguous status of, 167–168; American celebrities, 4; American citizenship and, 41–42; American dream and, 3, 29, 51, 90, 91, 118–120, 151–154; 165–166; Americanization of, 17–18, 24, 110–115, 158–159, 165–166; Americanization stages, 21–22, 33–36;as America's fastest growing ethnic group, 4; assimilation paradox, 14š–147, 108–110; demographics, 38–39, 57, 165; deportation threat, 19, 26, 88, 114, 166–167; education level, 39, 41, 165; empowerment of, 65; family structure of, 123, 136–137; first generation, 34; heritage of, 108; homelands of, 3, 115; median age, 39; New York City population, 57; obstacles faced by, 165–166; Prosperity Pentecostal converts, 5–6, 7, 13–14, 16–17, 20–25, 30, 34, 51, 65, 78, 91, 92, 111–112, 116, 117–118, 146, 150, 154, 156–159, 168; racial diversity, 3, 108–109; seasonal workers, 54–55; single-mother households, 123; skin color, 17; socialization of, 65; uncertainty and, 88–89; undocumented, 19, 26, 30, 93–94, 165; youth of, 5
learned optimism, 114
liberation theology, 7
life coaches, 12
linear assimilation, 15, 107, 108, 112
Long, Eddie L., 167
Lopez, George, 4
Lorena, 35, 41, 42, 126–127, 147, 161
Los Angeles, 5, 167

Lower East Side (New York City), 57, 59–60
lynchings, 5

machismo, 137–142, 150, 160; classic, 141; definitions of, 138; etymology of term, 138; repudiation of, 138–142, 147; softer form of, 139–140
Malachi 3:10, 44
Manifest Destiny, 103
Marble Collegiate Church (New York City), 9–10
Mario, 43, 47
Markovits, Daniel, 163
marriage, 7, 40, 54, 218n16; conflict negotiation, 144–146; decision making, 141; divorce, 123, 145–146; domestic abuse, 123, 138–139; as God's will, 122, 126; ideal, 125–130; machismo and, 138–139, 150; male dominance, 128–134, 135, 139–142, 145, 47, 148; mate selection, 126; monogamy, 125; role of wife, 129, 147; as single women's goal, 41, 126–127. *See also* family
Marta, 40, 130
Martines, Rafael, 61–62
Maslow, Abraham, 173n31
material blessings. *See* prosperity and wealth
Matthew 13, 81
Matthew 25:14–30, 96–97
means as ends, paradox of, 11, 77, 82, 83–84
media, 6–7, 12, 14, 25, 91
medical healing, 77, 92
men. *See* gender; machismo
meritocracy, 20, 80–82, 149–153, 163–165. *See also* miraculous meritocracy
Methodists, 172n14
Mexican Americans, 4, 5–6, 57, 176n19
Mexico, 52, 55, 98, 112; territories, 3, 108
Meyer, Joyce, 37
middle-class Americans, 15, 16–17, 24, 106, 114
militarian Christianity, 8
ministry. *See* pastors
miracles, 6–7, 11, 38, 48, 50, 68, 71; acts of faith and, 154; church space for, 150; financial, 44–45, 91–92; healing, 63, 86–88, 116, 118; intervention and, 154; physical, 62–64, 85, 86–88
miraculous meritocracy, 10–11, 80–82, 168; definition of, 82; paradox of, 11, 163–164
modern Pentecostalism. *See* neo-Pentecostalism
monasticism, 32
money, 32, 78, 91, 92, 119, 120. *See also* offering; prosperity and wealth; tithing
Monica, 61
Moody, D. L., 8
moral values, 7, 19
Mosaic law, 174n14
mothers, 132, 136, 144; ideal, 147; stay-at-home, 131, 143; working, 143. *See also* single mothers
motivational speakers, 12
Mount Zion, 157n1
music, 13, 31, 37, 52, 62, 63, 72, 154

national identity, 112, 113–115
Native Americans, 103, 163, 176n19
Naturalization Act of 1790, 102, 173n38
negative thoughts, 10, 83, 165
neo-Pentecostalism, 7–8, 10, 11, 31, 116. *See also* Prosperity Gospel Pentecostalism
New Birth Movement, 167
New Thought, 8, 10, 74, 173n31
New York City, 9–10, 21, 22, 25, 34, 55, 88; immigrant demographics, 57; immigrant uncertainty, 94; Lower East Side, 59–60. *See also* Iglesia Pentecostal del Rey Divino

Nixon, Richard, 3, 74
Noah (biblical), 70
Nolasco, Cecilia, 52, 56, 137
Nolasco, Pedro (Oceanside pastor): background and conversion of, 118; English language and, 177n29; family values, 129, 137, 146, 148; gender roles and, 132, 133–134; parable from Matthew, 96–97; physical healing, 86–87; sermon themes, 112–113, 138

Obama, Barack, 103
Oceanside (Calif.), 21, 22, 26, 33–34. *See also* Iglesia del Dios Victorioso
October, 67–72, 175n1
offering, 11, 43–45, 63, 71–72, 78–80; motivation for, 44–45; of time and service, 63, 155
optimism, 7, 13, 14, 63, 64–65, 74, 83, 146, 147; positive psychology and, 114; Prosperity Pentecostal, 75–76, 77, 168–169
Oración y Los Milagros, La, 47–50
Oral Roberts University, 9, 167
Orange County (Calif.), 25
Osteen, Joel, 11, 12, 75

Pablo, 98–99
Page Act of 1872, 102, 165
Palin, Sarah, 8, 116
parables, 81, 96, 133
paradox: of identities and beliefs, 111–115; of means derailing ends, 11, 77, 82, 83–84; of Prosperity Pentecostalism, 11–12, 17, 19–20, 77, 81–85, 97, 102, 103–105, 115, 120, 123, 126, 127–128, 147–148, 158, 162, 163–165, 167–169
parenting, 131–134, 175n18. *See also* fathers; mothers
Parham, Charles F., 171n10
Park, Robert, 105–106
Passover, 67
pastors: anointing by, 47; authority of, 32–33; celebrity, 12–13; charisma of, 8, 23, 168, 47, 134–135 (*see also* televangelists); family ideal and, 135; healing time and, 49–50; mischaracterization of, 91; Pentecostal function of, 48, 155, 167; positive thinking and, 74–75; preaching by, 8, 45–46, 138; prosperity doctrine and, 32–33, 116; research study examples, 25–28, 37–42 (*See also* Gielis, Federico; Nolasco, Pedro; Ramirez, David); sermons, 46–47, 59, 154, 155; speaking in tongues and, 50. *See also* televangelists
patriarchy, 137, 141
Paulina, 126, 149, 155, 160–161; success formula, 169; testimony, 147, 149–153, 157–158
Peale, Norman Vincent, 9–10, 74, 78
Pentecostalism: beliefs and practices, 5–7, 13, 23, 26, 27, 42–43, 47, 48–51; characterization of, 24; global spread of, 6–7, 15–6, 20, 58, 111, 115, 169–170, 172n14; Latin American conversion rate, 5–6, 12–13, 15–16, 31, 37, 58, 111, 115, 119, 169–170; liberation theology vs., 7; origins of, 5–8, 174n10; political activism, 165; promises of, 34; Prosperity Gospel belief vs., 8, 10, 50–51 (*see also* Prosperity Gospel Pentecostalism); worldwide growth of, 6–7
petitio principii, 82
Pew Research Center, 169
politics, 4–5, 152, 164, 165
Porter's House, 167
Portes, Alejandro, 15, 108
positive confession, 10, 74
positive psychology, 51, 74–75, 81–82, 85, 104–105, 114, 148, 157–158, 164–165; healing and, 11, 62–64
positive thinking, 8, 9, 12, 13, 74–75, 77–82, 85, 90, 147; doubt and, 83; drawbacks of, 164; movements, 75, 78, 173n1; as Prosperity Gospel formula, 81, 82, 90, 148, 157–158, 160
Potter's House (Dallas, Tex.), 12, 167

poverty, 70, 95
Power of Positive Thinking, The (Peale), 173n31
praise team, 52
prayer, 11; efficacy of, 48–50, 89; of elderly congregants, 63–64; objects of, 92; physical signs of potency of, 49–50; spontaneous, 43
prayer and healing area, 37–38, 39, 47–50, 52, 53, 55, 60, 144, 150–51
Prayer and the Miracles, The, 47–50
preachers. *See* pastors; *specific names*
predestination, 70
presidential election of 2016, 4
"primitive" religion, 16
private property, 176n3
prophecy, 7
prosperity and wealth, 3, 6–10, 12–13, 27, 51, 65, 116, 120; achievement of, 42; blueprint for, 72–73; definitions of, 90–93, 154; as divine reward, 44, 68, 95; doctrine of, 32–33; dream of, 18; emotional well-being as, 64; faith linked with, 10, 13, 41, 56, 74–77, 82, 85, 151–52, 154, 157–158, 168; forms of, 116; formula for, 46–47, 82–84, 90–93, 95, 126, 151, 154, 155, 169; investment in promise of, 30–33, 43–45; limits to, 164; material goods and, 75–76, 83–84, 105; meaning for elderly people of, 62–64; as mental state, 154; nuclear family and, 125; offering and, 43–45; paradox of, 163–164; planting seeds of, 120; positive thinking and, 160; promises of, 10, 31, 38, 43–45, 56, 69–70, 158; pursuit of, 163; rarity of, 90; risks and, 162; "softer" connotation of, 11; spiritual significance of, 80; upward mobility and, 110
Prosperity Gospel Pentecostalism, 8–29, 172–173n26; action and, 77–81; as American dream Gospel, 17–20, 24, 51, 90, 91, 105, 110–112, 154, 158–161, 163, 165–166, 170; appeal of, 169; aspiration vs. reality of, 102; assessment of efficacy of, 27–29, 64–65, 158–161, 169–170; attractions of, 13, 17–19, 56, 64–65, 85–88, 91, 110, 111–112, 115, 116–117, 168–170; basic tenets of, 9–10, 16, 31–33, 44–45, 55, 56, 64–65, 72–81, 118, 148, 151–152, 154, 175nn5, 7; benefits of, 18–19, 160–161, 162; case study of, 21–29, 31, 33, 64–65; Catholic converts to, 14, 115, 169; central paradox of, 11; charismatic pastors, 23, 134–135; Christian orthodoxy vs., 158; community created by, 17–18, 168; contradictions of, 65; conversion stories, 14, 98–101, 111, 114, 115–118; as coping strategy, 159; critics of, 31, 78; cross-cultural appeal of, 169–170; distinguishing features, 8; divine endorsement of, 47, 90, 114, 161–162; doctrinal roots of, 9–10, 44, 57; early champions of, 74–75; emotionalism and, 24, 27, 49, 77; empowerment from, 160–161; evangelizing emphasis of, 13–14; faith concept of, 74, 75, 157–158, 168; formula of, 16, 55, 68–69, 73, 77, 81–88, 92–93, 128, 139, 154, 165; future of, 168–170; gender and, 13, 23, 33, 39–40, 52, 135, 144, 147–148, 150–152; globalization of, 20, 169–170; goals of, 104–105, 111–112; growth post-1960s of, 12–13; historical precedents for, 32; hope and, 146, 154 (*see also* optimism); humanitarianism of, 28–29; immigrant adjustments to, 16–17 (*see also* Latinx immigrants); as individualistic, 79; influence of, 3, 8. 11, 20, 31, 56, 64–65, 84–85, 154–155; intangible rewards of, 155; language and, 113–114, 177n29; Latin American Pentecostalism vs., 50–51; marginalization of, 116; marketing of, 12, 13–14; media view of, 25, 91; as meritocracy, 80; mischaracterization of, 91–92; most important practice of,

Prosperity Gospel Pentecostalism (cont.) 37–38; multiple names for, 172–73n26; negative connotations of, 11; optimistic message of, 7, 13, 14, 63, 64–65, 75–76, 77, 83, 168–169; paradoxical logic of, 11–12, 17, 19–20, 77, 81–85, 97, 102, 103–105, 115, 120, 123, 126, 127–128, 147–148, 158, 162, 163–165, 167–169; pastors, 9, 12, 23, 26 (*see also specific congregations and names*); positive psychology and, 51, 74–75, 81–82, 85, 104–105, 148, 157–158, 164–165; positive thinking movement vs., 78; practices of, 27, 28, 43–45, 68–69, 79–80, 147, 148, 155, 158–161, 168; promises of, 12, 34; reinforcement of, 154; relativism and, 81, 135; salvation evidence of, 119–120; self-empowerment message of, 33, 72–82, 85–86; "softer" form of, 11; stages of, 33; Sunday service components, 13, 34, 47–51; ultimate goal of, 104; unintended consequences of, 24; worldview of, 10, 16, 31, 154–157; worldwide influence of, 8, 20, 64–65
Protestant ethic, 119, 120
Protestantism, 7, 13, 15, 24, 103; Latin American converts, 25, 115, 169; predestination belief, 70; salvation certainty, 118; sects, 171–172n14. *See also* evangelicals; Pentecostalism
psychology, 9, 73. *See also* positive psychology
psychosis, 73
psychotherapy, 73–74
Puerto Ricans, 4, 57, 58, 59, 94
Puritans, 161

Quimby, Phineas, 74

Rachel (biblical), 133
racial identity, 15; American exclusions, 10, 102, 103, 137n38; "double consciousness," 107, 109; Latinx diversity, 3, 108–110; New York City demographics, 57. *See also* African Americans; skin color
racism, 4, 6, 106, 107, 168
radio programs, 8, 12
Ramirez, David (New York City pastor), 25, 58–59, 61, 115, 122; family and, 62, 122, 124–125, 131, 134, 136; on machismo, 139
Ramirez, Diana (pastor's wife), 62
rationalization, 33, 154
Reagan, Ronald, 74, 103
religion, 14, 21, 118. *See also specific religions*
Remaking the American Mainstream (Alba and Nee), 108
repressed memories, 73
Republican Party, 4
Rhema Bible Training Center (Tulsa, Okla.), 8
riches. *See* prosperity and wealth
risk, 10, 77, 79, 151–152, 162
River Church (Anaheim, Calif.), 25
Roberts, Oral, 8, 9, 59, 74–75, 167, 175n5
Robinson Crusoe (Defoe), 153
Rogers, Carl, 173n31
role models, 23, 46, 113–114
Roman Catholic Church. *See* Catholic Church
Roman Empire, 32, 68
Rosh Hashanah, 67, 175n1
Rubio, Marco, 4
Rumbaut, Ruben G., 108

Sacred Canopy, The (Berger), 21
sacrifice, 44, 63, 77, 78–79, 120, 164
salvation, 32, 117–120, 169
San Diego (Calif.), 33, 51, 90, 98, 121
Sandro, 44, 126, 142, 143
Sarah (biblical), 133
seasonal workers, 54–55
"second baptism," 118
"Seed Faith" concept, 9
segmented assimilation theory, 106, 108

selective integration, 15, 110
self-actualization, 11, 16, 74
self-confidence, 85, 114
self-empowerment, 33, 72–82, 85–86
self-esteem, 12, 173n31
self-help Christianity, 9
self-reliance, 119, 164
Seligman, Martin, 114
sermons, 46–47, 59, 154; function of, 155
Seymour, William Joseph, 5, 6, 174n10
Sharpton, Al, 8, 165
sin, 70, 95
single mothers, 39–40, 46, 77–78, 123, 124–25, 126, 136, 143, 145, 150–151
single women, 41, 126–127
skin color, 15, 17, 24, 102, 106–107, 165, 173n38; assimilation and, 107; black/white dichotomy, 3, 163; Latinx ambiguity, 17, 108–109. *See also* African Americans; white Americans
"slain in the spirit," 40
slavery, 102, 163, 165
soccer, 155
social class: inequalities, 20; middle-class Protestant norms, 15, 16–17, 24, 106, 114; upward mobility, 14–16, 105, 110
socialization, 22
Solomon (biblical), 70
sons, 133–134
Sotomayor, Sonia, 4
Souls of Black Folk, The (Du Bois), 106–107
Spanish language, 5, 25, 119, 177n29; Catholic Mass, 16, 35, 116; Pentecostal church services, 16, 22, 34, 35, 37, 58, 113, 149; television, 14
speaking in tongues (glossolalia), 5, 6, 7, 13, 27, 31, 50, 72, 77, 116–119, 132
Spirit. *See* Holy Spirit
spiritual healing, 6, 7, 31, 73–75, 88–89, 116
spiritual renewal, 111
Star of David, 60
Statue of Liberty, 163
"straight line" assimilation, 15
Suave Machismo, 137–140
success, 83, 90, 105; correlates of, 114; external factors, 158; formula for, 55, 80, 125, 127. *See also* prosperity and wealth
Success-N-Life (TV program), 44
suffering, 70, 118
Sunday, Billy, 8
supernatural beliefs, 16, 55–56
synagogue, 58, 60

talents, parable of the, 96
Teen Challenge, 58
Telemundo, 14
televangelists, 12–14, 44, 75, 78, 120, 167
telenovela, 155–156
testimony, 43, 149–153
"This is your time," 50–51
Tilton, Robert, 44
tithing, 77, 126, 151, 164, 174n14; offering vs., 44
Tocqueville, Alexis de, 103
Tompkins Square Park riot of 1988, 58
tongue speaking. *See* speaking in tongues
Toronto Blessing (revival), 25
traditional family. *See* family
Trinity Broadcasting Network, 14
Trump, Donald, 4, 9–10, 74, 166

undocumented immigrants, 19, 26, 30, 93–94, 109–110, 157; application approval, 152, 165; assimilation of, 114–115. *See also* deportation
United States. *See* American dream; American identity
Universal Church of the Kingdom of God (Brazil), 104, 169–170
Univision, 14
upward mobility, 14–16, 105, 110

videos, 52–53, 154
Virginia. *See* Charlottesville

wealth. *See* prosperity and wealth
Weber, Max, 70, 118–119, 120, 159, 164
West Angeles Cathedral (Los Angeles), 167
westward expansion, 103, 105
white Americans, 3, 7, 24, 102, 110–111, 118, 173n38; classical immigration theory and, 106, 110; core values, 107; as immigrants, 15, 165; middle-class Protestant norms, 15, 16–17, 24, 114
wife. *See* marriage
Wilcox, W. Bradford, 137
Winfrey, Oprah, 12
witchcraft, 116, 177n34
women: gender hierarchy and, 23, 41, 133–134, 139–140; marital submission of, 128–134, 135, 140–141, 148; motherhood as vocation, 144; Prosperity Pentecostal lay leaders, 13, 135, 151; single, 41, 126–127 (*see also* single mothers); traditional gendered jobs, 39, 131–132
Word of Faith (magazine), 8
Word of Faith movement, 8–9, 172–173n26. *See also* Prosperity Gospel Pentecostalism
work, 10–11, 84–85; gendered, 39, 139–132; prayer for, 92
work ethic, 80
working families, 143–144
World Changers Ministries Christian Center, 167
World Evangelism Institute, 41
worldly rewards. *See* prosperity and wealth
World of Faith movement, 74
World Changers Church International, 12

Yang, Fenggang, 15, 110–111
Yolanda, 135, 141, 143, 153
Yom Kippur, 67, 68, 175n1
youth pastor, 52

Zhou, Min, 15
Zion, 157n1, 178n1
Zionism, Christian, 60, 174

Where Religion Lives

JODI EICHLER-LEVINE, *Painted Pomegranates and Needlepoint Rabbis: How Jews Craft Resilience and Create Community* (2020).

TONY TIAN-REN LIN, *Prosperity Gospel Latinos and Their American Dream* (2020).

LAUREN R. KERBY, *Saving History: How White Evangelicals Tour the Nation's Capital and Redeem a Christian America* (2020).

Printed in the USA
CPSIA information can be obtained
at www.ICGtesting.com
LVHW091428010224
770631LV00004B/529

9 781469 658957